WHAT OTHERS ARE SAYING

"*Thinking God* provides a wealth of biblical insight to help new and experienced believers know the joy of living the risen life and serves as a great resource for discipleship and personal bible study."

—Dr. Anthony W. Allen,
President of Hannibal-LaGrange University

"Life through the lens of godliness is exactly what you will see in *Thinking God*. It is an unparalleled privilege to sit under Pastor Phil Hunter's teaching and now everyone has the opportunity to share in this blessing by reading this powerful book. As a psychologist I see people try and fail everyday to change their behavior and then wonder why they still live a compromised and wasted life. They are missing the critical ingredient of changing their thinking that underlies their behavior. Pastor Phil Hunter gets it and reveals exactly how to do this daily in our lives by learning to 'Think God!'"

—Dr. Holly Brand,
Professor of Psychology, Conference Speaker

"Dr. Phil Hunter is one of the most gifted writers and speakers I have ever met. In *Thinking God*, he brings us to a clear understanding of how we can develop and maintain a meaningful relationship with God. This book is a must-read for every Christian who has a desire to grow spiritually!"

—Woodrow (Woodie) Burt, PhD,
President Emeritus, Hannibal-LaGrange University

"I have listened to my pastor, Phil Hunter, teach the scriptural principles in *Thinking God* for sixteen years. In these pages you will find wisdom for experiencing the life changing power of allowing God to rule your thoughts. Phil has learned, lived, and faithfully taught these truths for many years, and I am so glad he has finally found time to put them in writing. I encourage fellow professors, pastors, church leaders, and all Christ followers to read this book carefully."

—Andy Chambers,
Senior Vice President for Student Development and
Professor of Bible, Missouri Baptist University, St. Louis

"I have the greatest family in the world. I have a beautiful wife of twenty years. We have five great children from the ages nine to seventeen. I also have a privilege to be a pastor at a church with some of the most wonderful Christ followers anywhere on the planet. These people mean so much to me. As a result, I am so excited about this book. It is a must read for every pastor! I believe all of us have a deep passion to guide our family in a God honoring way, so we can watch them grow into who God intends them to be. We also, have this same deep desire for our church. In order for us to see God accomplish these things, we must first be the person God created us to be. This book will not only teach us as pastors, but will give us tangible tools to pass on to those we love. This book will encourage and equip us as pastors to live in the abundance and victory in Christ, so we can then encourage our people to do the same. It will allow us to live and equip in the areas of marriage, parenting, sharing our faith, living in humility, forgiveness, and suffering, just to name a few. How I thank God for this incredible resource for pastors of all ages. Go Reach the World!"

—Bob Caldwell,
Pastor of Outreach, First Baptist Church,
Arnold, Missouri

"Phil is creative, living on the edge, a path-finder ever finding and doing whatever it takes to please Jesus, leading the way for others to follow, willing to do whatever it takes to advance the Kingdom of God, sharing Jesus everywhere and in every way, loving and encouraging others, bold, courageous, enthusiastic, confrontational when required in doing what is right, 'at the top' as one of the most witnessing, evangelistic pastors whom I have ever known. Phil Hunter simply loves Jesus, people, righteousness, the Word of God…and faithfully lives and loves it all out as a lifestyle, running the course of life with vigor, passion, and in the will of God…ever desiring to please God. *Thinking God* can be a wonderful help in your walking with God!"

—Harold Hendrick,
Public Affairs Director, KSIV, St. Louis

"I've known Phil Hunter for over thirty years and have never known a man more committed to sharing the faith and developing others in their faith and witness. Here, in this excellent book, he brings us to embrace godliness and holiness as a mindset and lifestyle. I recommend it to every disciple of the Lord Jesus. You will be blessed and enriched by the reading."

—Dr. Larry Lewis,
Former President of Hannibal-LaGrange University and
North American Mission Board

"As a young pastor, a couple of times a year I would leave my church office and drive to St. Louis to spend time with Dr. Phil Hunter. No matter where we would go, in a very natural 'this is my second nature' way, Phil would share Jesus…always! I needed that constant encouragement to be faithful and I always received it. I've known Phil over twenty-five years and his zeal for Jesus has touched countless lives. He has faithfully modeled his 'Jesus is Enough' mantra throughout our years of friendship. In *Thinking God*, you'll experience honest, earthy reflection, confessions of shortcomings, and biblically based cries for spiritual renewal that can turn a cold heart warm or make a warm heart glow. It's a great memoir of how Jesus blesses the person who honors him."

—Dr. Ken Parker,
Senior Pastor, First Baptist Church, Kearney, Missouri

"As pastors, we know Jesus has won the victory. His victory is a truth in our heads, but is it a passionate force in our hearts? Like you, I want it to be. For His Name sake, I desire to walk in the victory of Jesus in my marriage, as a parent and in the church I pastor. *Thinking God* by Dr. Phil Hunter is biblical practical truth that will equip us and encourage us as pastors to daily experience the abundance of our Lord's victory."

—Kenny Qualls,
Senior Pastor, First Baptist Church, Arnold, Missouri

"When considering all the people that have crossed my path, few have impacted my life like Phil Hunter. His newest book, *Thinking God*, provides insight into a Spirit-filled life and what it takes to walk with God for a lifetime. With many living as though the Christian life is a playground, Phil challenges that notion clearly and convincingly with the appropriate scriptures. The Christian life is a battleground and impossible to live without Christ. *Thinking God* takes us on a journey to live for Christ and what to do when faced with the alternative. The alternative is unbiblical. Phil calls for us to live a life with an observable difference. Growing spiritually, being evangelistic and reproducing our lives in discipling relationships through mentoring is the expected outcome. Thus, *Thinking God* brings forth lessons in a simple yet practical way all the while challenging us to be radically different in our manner and disposition as God's people."

—William Taylor,
Leadership Team & Missions Pastor,
Houston's First Baptist Church

"I have known Dr. Phil Hunter for more than thirty years as a colleague and close friend in ministry. In *Thinking God*, Dr. Hunter gives us an overview of how to walk in victory in the Christian life in some very vital areas of our lives. This book is not the writing of a theoretician but the time-tested writing of a practitioner of the Christian faith. Dr. Hunter shares with us the truth and the hope of the Gospel and gives us the road to the victorious life. Don't read this book unless you want to see your life transformed and changed. Read *Thinking God* and your life will never be the same again!"

—Jim Wells,
Strategic Partners Team Leader,
Missouri Baptist Convention

"Phil Hunter's book, *Thinking God*, is as unique and outstanding as the man who wrote it! Phil Hunter is one-of-a-kind in all of the world. His engaging personality and his absolutely sold out heart to the gospel comes through in every page. From professional athletes to high visibility entrepreneurs to the homeless, to the 'down and out' and even to common men like me; everybody who encounters this man FEELS the love of God. Every word that comes out of this man's mouth points the reader or the listener to the heart of Jesus."

—Dr. Joe White,
President, Kanakuk Kamps

"Dr. Phil Hunter is one of the most godly pastors and men whom I have ever met. He reminds me of Daniel. He is uncompromising in his faith and belief in our Lord and Savior Jesus Christ. He also is like Paul. He is infectious as a witness. He loves people. He proves this every day when he shares the gospel with anyone who will hear. His book, *Thinking God*, is not only for pastors and seminary students, but it is also for church members and non-Christians. It is a pastoral guidebook that gives great insights on how to put on the helmet of salvation and the armor of God to win the spiritual battles we face. If we don't 'think God' and put on the helmet, we will compromise and fall. We will not have peace with God. We will fail in our relationships with our families and friends. We will wallow in our sins and remain in darkness. We will build our 'Golden Calves' and idols. We will walk away from the Great I Am and from all his blessings and protection. *Thinking God* can help change an individual's life. It is filled with scripture, wisdom and a love of a pastor. Dr. Hunter provides valuable godly counsel to help us on the narrow road, so we will have victory in this difficult life. I heard Billy Graham once say, 'Whatever you think about the most during your day, this is your god.' I pray that Christians and non-Christians will read this book and be transformed by God's Word Made Flesh, our Lord Jesus Christ."

—Keith W. Young,
CEO of Secure Wisdom and Principal of
Tampa Bay Financial Group

THINKING
GOD

THINKING GOD

When God Rules Your Thoughts

PHILLIP R. HUNTER

TATE PUBLISHING
AND ENTERPRISES, LLC

Published by Tate Publishing & Enterprises, LLC
127 E. Trade Center Terrace | Mustang, Oklahoma 73064 USA
1.888.361.9473 | www.tatepublishing.com

Tate Publishing is committed to excellence in the publishing industry. The company reflects the philosophy established by the founders, based on Psalm 68:11,
"The Lord gave the word and great was the company of those who published it."

Book design copyright © 2015 by Tate Publishing, LLC. All rights reserved.
Cover design by Allen Jomoc
Interior design by Jomar Ouano

Published in the United States of America
ISBN: 978-1-63268-749-4
Religion / Christian Life / General
14.11.07

DEDICATION

Because of the pressures and challenges pastors have, I dedicate this book to encourage them. God wants you to experience, live, model, and communicate Christ's abundance and victory in your life, marriage, parenting, and ministry!

Because of the pressures and challenges Christian university and seminary professors have, I dedicate this book to encourage them. God wants you to experience, live, model, and communicate Christ's abundance and victory in your life, marriage, parenting, and ministry!

Because of my love for my family and desire for each of them to experience God's grace, goodness, and greatness in their lives, I dedicate this book to encourage my wife, Roni; my children, Phillip, Shelly, Josh, Julie, Matt, and Lauren; and my precious grandchildren, Atley, Avery, Canon, Champ, Britton, Briley, Ollie, Raylee, and Suhre. God wants you to experience, live, model, and communicate Christ's abundance and victory in each of your lives!

ACKNOWLEDGMENTS

I have been blessed, blessed, blessed, and will forever be grateful to:

My parents, who so perseveringly loved me, prayed for me, taught me, encouraged me, disciplined me, modeled before me, and challenged me to live a life of thinking God. Praise the Lord for everything God has continued to teach me from the many seeds of God's Word and ways they planted and watered in my life.

My pastors and professors, who so faithfully loved me, prayed for me, taught me, encouraged me, modeled before me, and challenged me to live a life of thinking God. Praise the Lord for these godly men who have made more of a difference in my life than they will ever know.

The people in every church I have been privileged to serve on staff since 1970, and certainly those in West County Community Church, who have so graciously loved me, prayed for me, taught me, and encouraged me to live a life of thinking God. Praise the Lord for the indescribable blessing of being encouraged and equipped by being a covenant member of a local church.

The pastors, church staff, denominational staff, and professors, who have loved me, prayed for me, and served with me the last forty-four years. Praise the Lord for these hundreds of godly men and women who have encouraged and equipped me to live a life of thinking God.

Stacy Newton, my secretary, who has taught me how to use a computer and has assisted me greatly throughout this project in preparing the text. Praise the Lord for this faithful servant and co-laborer in the Lord, who has been there to rescue me countless times when my computer and I were not getting along.

The staffs of West County Community Church, Living Water Academy, and ZOE Ministries, who love me, pray for me, and daily serve the Lord and others with me. Praise the Lord for these committed, loving, praying, faithful, encouraging, and gifted persons, who serve with me to accomplish the work of the ministry.

Dr. Andy Chambers, senior vice president for student development and professor of Bible at Missouri Baptist University, who provided great insight for the apologetics study in Part I and Dr. Holly Brand, associate professor of psychology at Missouri Baptist University, who provided the incredible list for raising godly children in Part II. They, along with Dr. Gretchen Fleming, Curriculum Dean of Living Water Academy, have been a constant source of encouragement throughout this project. Each of them has also assisted me in the proof-reading of the text. Praise the Lord for each of these special persons who faithfully serve as a "Barnabas" in our church family and to me.

Dr. Joe and Babs Brooks, Brad and Diane Gilbert, Scott and Carey McNair, and Gary and Claudine Nielson, who have partnered with me in their excitement to deliver the message of this book to pastors and professors in our Christian universities and seminaries. Praise the Lord for these longtime friends and special brothers and sisters in Christ, who have such love for God and vision to make a difference to the glory of God in this way.

Keith Young, a longtime friend and passionate witness for Christ, who connected me with Tate Publishing, and has continued to walk with me in this adventure of having this book published to encourage and equip others in their walk with God. Praise the Lord for supplying every need I have had in this process by giving me this special friend, prayer warrior, and co-laborer in the Lord.

Mary Ozor, my project manager; Charles Dominic Sanchez, my editing reviewer; Julie Christie Guangko, my editor; and Alana Duffle, my acquisitions editor at Tate—praise the Lord for each of these gifted persons, who serve the Lord with diligence and excellence by assisting authors, like me, to deliver our message to others in building the kingdom of God.

My loving and servant-hearted wife, Roni, who is my best friend, accountability partner, greatest cheerleader, prayer partner, and co-laborer in the Lord in all of the challenges of life. Praise the Lord for everything we have learned and continue to learn in all the seasons of life by thinking God.

My children and grandchildren, who faithfully love me, pray for me, encourage me, and teach me in the journey of thinking God in more ways than I could ever write. Praise the

Lord for the joyous and endless blessings of a family who love Jesus and one another.

God, "who is able to do far more abundantly than all that we ask or think, according to the power at work within us, to him be glory in the church and in Christ Jesus throughout all generations, forever and ever. Amen" (Ephesians 3:20-21). Praise the Lord for what he is going to do in and through your life as you are encouraged and equipped to increasingly live your life, thinking God.

CONTENTS

Part III
Because God Is the One Lord God

FOREWORD

Have you ever been on a mission trip?

Remember how you were repeatedly told, "As we prepare to go on this trip, this is all about God. This is not about us. This trip is about sharing Christ and serving others." And everyone wholeheartedly agreed.

Remember the praying you did everyday yourself, and then with your mission team, family members, and friends humbling yourselves to be God's servants. You totally depended on God to meet all of your needs according to his promises. You trusted God to empower you, direct you, prepare you, provide for you, protect you, and work in and through you to accomplish his will in your life. You were purposed in your heart to walk by faith according to the authority of God's Word rather than walk by sight and be distracted and discouraged by your feelings or circumstances. You lived with the conviction, "If God is for us, who can be against us" (Romans 8:31)?

Remember the weeks, months, or even years of preparation needed for you and your team to get ready for the mission you knew God had called you to accomplish.

Remember the day you left home anticipating everything God was going to do because you and your team had spent so much time in prayer and preparation. You went with the confidence, "For God gave us a spirit not of fear but of power and love and self-control" (2 Timothy 1:7).

Remember upon arriving at your destination for your mission, you had one priority of proclaiming Jesus to as many as possible by your words of grace and truth and your acts of service. You lived with the courage they saw in Peter and John in the book of Acts. The persons you ministered to "recognized that you had been with Jesus" (Acts 4:13).

Remember at the end of your mission trip how your team came together just like the apostles did with Jesus after "he sent them out two by two, and gave them authority over the unclean spirits" (Mark 6:7, 30). You and your team members excitedly shared with each other the mighty things each of you had seen God do the past week. You said, "I will never be the same." You were resolved to go home and live with the same priority, purpose, and passion to know God, please God, honor God, serve God, and share God with everyone possible.

Going on a mission trip is thinking God. Thinking God, we are set free from the bondage of being self-absorbed and thinking me. Thinking God, we give ourselves away to God and to his glory (1 Corinthians 10:31). Thinking God, we "walk by the Spirit, and do not gratify the desires of the flesh" (Galatians 5:16). Thinking God, we enjoy being faithful, fruitful, and fulfilled in our walk with the Lord. And we love every moment of it!

Yet, far too many have been on mission trips thinking God, only to return to their home, place of work, and church to find themselves thinking again, "life is all about me." In the challenges, pressures, and problems of daily living, they find themselves distracted, discouraged, and defeated.

Reading this book, you will see I have had more disappointments, failures, frustrations, hurts, sickness, sorrow, suffering, sin, trouble, and discouragement in my life than you could ever imagine. Yet, you will also see how by God's grace (Romans 12:3), and by thinking God, I have been able to "overcome the evil one" (1 John 2:14), and be "more than a conqueror through Christ" (Romans 8:37). God desires that abundance and victory for each of us.

Reflecting on the greatness, goodness, and grace of God in my life following a week of seeing God's mighty acts including many commit their lives to Christ on a mission trip to Costa Rica in June of 2012, God convicted me, "You are not getting any younger. You need to write what I have been teaching you throughout your life about having the priority, perspective, purpose, power, passion, and peace of God's Word rule your life.

Experiencing the abundance and victory of Christ's love, joy, peace, and power should not be limited to mission trips. Having the priority of seeking the kingdom of God first (Matthew 6:33), daily sharing Jesus Christ with others (Mark 1:17), and daily serving and loving others (John 13) should not be limited to mission trips.

Following Jesus Christ as the Lord and Savior of your life should not be just for a certain part of your life. Following Jesus Christ is to be your life (Colossians 3:1-17). You will see how I learned this as a child by thinking God. *Thinking God* is for all children. You will see how I learned this as a teenager by thinking God. *Thinking God* is for all teenagers. You will see how I learned this as a college student by thinking God.

Thinking God is for all college students. You will see how I have continued to learn this as an adult by increasingly thinking God. *Thinking God* is for all adults.

Thinking God, instead of thinking me, is a never ending journey of learning to delight in the Word of God, to meditate day and night on the Word of God, and to be careful to obey the Word of God regardless of our trials, tests, temptations, and triumphs.

Reading this book, I believe you will come to the same conviction I have come to believe: thinking me, instead of thinking God, is Satan's greatest scheme against us as God's people. It is certainly Satan's greatest scheme against us as pastors and church leaders. My purpose in writing this book is that many would be encouraged and equipped to live their lives thinking God and thereby, stop being "outwitted by Satan and ignorant of his designs" (2 Corinthians 2:11).

Thank you for being a person who wants to experience everything God has for you by thinking God every day for the rest of your life!

In Christ's love and service,
Phillip R. Hunter

PREFACE

Thinking God is what Jesus modeled in his earthly ministry. Thinking God, Jesus faced and overcame every temptation, pressure, problem, and need by the power of being under the authority of God's Word (Matthew 4:4, 6, 10). Thinking God, Jesus began every day in prayer with the priority of being submitted to the will of the Father (Mark 1:35). Thinking God, Jesus came down from heaven not to do his will but to do the will of the Father who sent him (John 6:38). Thinking God, Jesus came not to be served but to give his life as a ransom for many (Matthew 20:28). Thinking God, Jesus came to seek and save those who are lost (Luke 19:10). Thinking God, Jesus knew he could do nothing by himself (John 5:19). Thinking God, Jesus was able to accomplish everything the Father had sent him to be and do (John 19:30). Thinking God, Jesus modeled everything he taught (Matthew 5:3–16).

The passage in 1 John 2:6 tells us: "Whoever claims to live in him must walk (think) as Jesus did." Forty-four of my sixty-three years have been spent serving on staff in churches as a minister of music and youth, a pastor, and working with pastors, denomination leaders, and college and seminary professors as an associate and director of evangelism of Missouri Baptist Convention. It breaks my heart how many have not learned how to humbly live this victorious life modeled by our Lord in his earthly ministry. We have preached hard and sung heartily "victory in Jesus," but often have not modeled Thinking God in our marriages, our parenting, and to each other in our churches. Rather than Thinking God and being defined by God's Word, so many Christian leaders and those they lead struggle daily in confusion instead of being "more than a conqueror" in Christ (Romans 8:37).

Webster's Collegiate Dictionary (Tenth Edition) defines *confused* as one "being perplexed or disconcerted; disordered or mixed up." *The American Heritage Dictionary of the English Language(New College Edition)* defines *confused* as one "perplexed, bewildered, or befuddled." Confused, many Christian leaders live much of their lives distracted, discouraged, and defeated. Thinking God, we can live in the abundance and victory of Christ's conviction, confidence, and courage, being submitted to the authority of God's Word and surrendered to the presence of the Holy Spirit (2 Corinthians 2:14).

Confused, we often fall to the lie that "there is rest in quitting"—quitting on God, quitting in our marriage, quitting in ministry, quitting on one another, quitting on ourselves.

The Bible profoundly promises: "Therefore, if anyone is in Christ, he is a new creation; the old has gone, the new has come. All this is from God, who reconciled us to himself through Christ and gave us the ministry of reconciliation: that God was reconciling the world to himself in Christ, not counting men's sins against them. And he has committed to us the message of reconciliation" (2 Corinthians 5:17–19).

Look again at this passage of Scripture that is very familiar to many but is lived out by far too few: "All this is from God, who reconciled us." The word reconciled is *katallasso*, which means "to change or exchange." Everything God did in Christ to redeem us was for the purpose of changing us and exchanging our old life of lies, condemnation, darkness, rebellion, independence, shame, and an empty and wasted life to have a new life in Christ. This "change" and "exchange" demands a new way of thinking: Thinking God according to the Word of God. Since you will never change your behavior until you change your thinking, God saved you to change your thinking. Otherwise, you would never experience what God has saved you for—himself (Colossians 1:16–22; 2:6–12; 3:1–17).

God saved us to bring glory to himself (Matthew 5:16). God saved us to love him first with all our hearts and with all our souls and with all our minds (Deuteronomy 6:5; Matthew 22:37). God saved us to love one another (John 13:34). God saved us to live by the Spirit and not gratify the desires of the sinful nature (Galatians 5:16). God saved us to be givers (Acts 20:35). God saved us to be kind and compassionate to one another and to forgive each other (Ephesians 4:32). God saved us to be humble before him and one another (1 Peter 5: 5–6). God saved us to set our hearts on things above (Colossians 3:1–2). God saved us to die and have our lives hidden with Christ in God (Colossians 3:3). There are thousands of other biblical statements that could be made here, but hopefully you get the point—God saved us so we could live supernatural and radically different lives than most professing Christians are living.

Thinking God, we learn to think humility and choose to be:

- Submitted to the authority of God's Word (John 8:31–32);

- Surrendered to the presence of the Holy Spirit (Ephesians 5:17–18);

- Settled to whose we are (1 Corinthians 6:19–20);

- Surrounded by other Christians for encouragement and accountability (Hebrews 10:23–25); and

- Sharing Jesus every day, everywhere, all the time with others (Acts 5:42).

God has promised us, "We have been given everything we need for life and godliness through our knowledge of him" (2 Peter 1:3). The more we "grow in the grace and knowledge of our Lord and Savior Jesus Christ" (2 Peter 3:18) in Thinking God, the more we will move from living in a crisis of compromise, conflict, confusion, and living as a victim to being victorious in Christ and living with his preeminence, perspective, purpose, power, passion, provision, and peace (Philippians 3:7–16).

Growing up, I remember hearing my mom say when I was being self-absorbed (rebellious, lazy, irritable, or selfish), "Honey, as you think in your heart, so you will be" (Proverbs 23:7, KJV). At different times, following my foolish or irresponsible behavior, my dad would ask me, "Son, what were you thinking?" My reply often was "I guess I wasn't thinking too well." Looking at the Christian community, I think most of us would agree that many are not thinking too well.

Participating in Sword Drill, a children and youth Bible memory program in our church from the third through ninth grade, I was highly blessed and favored by God's grace and goodness to memorize over three hundred verses from the Bible during those years. I will be forever grateful to my mom for having a heart for God's Word and the perseverance to encouragingly lead me to continue to "hide God's Word in my heart" that I might learn the value of Thinking God (Psalm 119:11).

Thinking God in those early years enabled me to go through middle school, high school, and college being "more than a conqueror" in Christ most of the time (Romans 8:37). Thinking God, I was able to enjoy a faithful walk with God and honor my parents' desires instead of being compromising and in conflict with God and godly authority (Ephesians 6:1–3). Thinking God, I was able to live according to the Word of God instead of being confused in the lost culture of Washington state where my family moved when I was fourteen (Romans 12:1–2).

During my college years and into my young adult years, my mom began to memorize chapters of God's Word, and she challenged me to do likewise. Already having a hunger and a thirst for God's Word and having experienced the overcoming power of Thinking God in my life, I began to memorize chapters of the Bible with her. The first chapter we memorized together was Psalm 103. Thinking God by quoting this passage of Scripture and praising the LORD with "all my inmost being and not forgetting all his benefits" (Psalm 103:2) was and is a great and godly way to start and spend the day. Thinking God equipped me to attend Eastern Washington State College, serve on church staff, lead many to Christ, and graduate by God's grace and truth without becoming rebellious and confused in what was a very rebellious and confusing time (1969–1973) for students on state college campuses.

Until we memorize the Word of God, we cannot meditate on it day and night, so we may be able to do everything written in it (Joshua 1:8). Not Thinking God, we will never know God's success as he promised Joshua (Joshua 24:15).

Until we learn to listen and obey God's authority in our lives, we are destined for destruction (Proverbs 14:12). Not Thinking God, we do not live in God's protection and provision of obeying his Word (Proverbs 1–9).

Until we learn to keep our minds stayed on God, we will not know the power of God's perfect peace (Isaiah 26:3). Not Thinking God, we live in anxiousness rather than guarded by God's peace (Philippians 4:6–7).

Until we build our lives on the perfect Word of God, the foundation of our lives will fail, and our lives will fall apart with a great crash (Matthew 7:24–27). Not Thinking God, we build nothing that lasts instead of living a life that brings honor and glory to God forever and ever (1 Timothy 1:17).

Until we know the discipline of holding on to our Lord's teaching, we will stay in bondage instead of being set free in God's truth (John 8:31–32). Not Thinking God, we live in the frustration of being deceived and living in lies instead of living in Christ's freedom (Galatians 5:1).

Until we are transformed by the renewing of our minds, we will live confused and will easily fall to the temptation of being conformed to the patterns of this world (Romans 12:2). Not Thinking God, we miss God's purpose of shining like stars in the universe, holding out the word of life (Philippians 2:15–16).

Until we think about those things that are true, noble, right, pure, lovely, and admirable, we will not know the indescribable joy of experiencing godly excellence and what is truly praiseworthy (Philippians 4:8). Not Thinking God, we miss God's best that he has prepared for our lives (1 Corinthians 2:9).

Today could be the first day of a new and victorious life for you. Resolve in your heart that you are going to learn to make Thinking God a priority in your life. Thinking God, you will have a new rejoicing in the Lord, a greater awareness of the presence and power of the Lord, and a new attitude of gratitude in the Lord (1 Thessalonians 5:16–18).

Because of God's kindness, mercy, grace, and truth in my life, I was saved fifty-six years ago, and I have never gotten over his greatness, grace, and goodness for me. Shouldn't that be normal for every person who receives the person of the Holy Spirit in their lives at salvation (2 Corinthians 4:16)? I was called by God forty-nine years ago to commit my life to Christian vocational ministry to love and reach the lost with the gospel of Jesus Christ and to love and "prepare God's people for works of service, so that the body of Christ may be built up until we all reach unity in the faith and in the knowledge of the Son of God and become mature, attaining to the whole measure of the fullness of Christ. Then we will no longer be infants, tossed back and forth by the waves, and blown here and there by every wind of teaching and by the cunning and craftiness of men in their deceitful scheming. Instead, speaking the truth in love, we will in all things grow up into him who is the Head, that is, Christ. From him the whole body, joined and held together by every supporting ligament, grows and builds itself up in love, as each part does its work" (Ephesians 4:12–16). It's called "making disciples of all nations, baptizing them in the name of the Father and of the Son and of the Holy Spirit, teaching them to observe all that I have commanded you. And behold, I am with you always, to the end of the age" (Matthew 28:19–20).

Once we trust Jesus Christ to be our Lord and Savior, God wants to lead us to "always walk in Christ's triumphal procession and spread everywhere the fragrance of the knowledge of him" (2 Corinthians 2:14). I pray you will allow God to use the truths of this book to transform your life to think as Jesus thought, so you will know the reality of "Christ in you, the hope of glory" (Colossians 1:27), the Spirit-filled life (Ephesians 5:17–18), his abundant life (John 10:10), his fruitful life (John 15:5), his victorious life (2 Corinthians 2:14), and a life "immeasurably more than you could ask or imagine according to his power that is at work within you" (Ephesians 3:20).

At the beginning of each of the following chapters, I have listed several verses which God has used throughout my life to encourage and equip me to live in Christ's victory that relates to the topic of that chapter. Memorize as many of these verses as you can, and you will see how in Thinking God, you will "be transformed by the renewal of your mind" (Romans 12:2) to live the abundant, affirmed, beloved, contented, comforted, delivered, disciplined, encouraged, forgiven, faithful, fulfilled, good, gracious, humble, hopeful, justified, kind, loving, merciful, near to God, overcoming, patient, persevering, prudent, prepared, redeemed, reconciled, restored, significant, secure, sufficient, thankful, trustworthy, understanding, and wise life God has promised you and intended for you to live for your joy and the glory of God (John 15:11; 1 Corinthians 10:31)!

Let God rule your thoughts!

Thinking God—I will never change my behavior until I allow God to change my thinking. If you are not already doing so, begin to memorize one or more verses of Scripture each week, so God can rule your thoughts (2 Corinthians 5:17-18).

Truth to Remember—The more I "grow in the grace and knowledge of my Lord and Savior Jesus Christ" (2 Peter 3:18) in Thinking God, the more I will move from living in a crisis of compromise, conflict, confusion and living as a victim to being victorious in Christ and living with his preeminence, perspective, purpose, power, passion, provision and peace (Philippians 3:7-16).

Thinking God in Reflecting—I want this to be the first day of the rest of my life in resolving to make Thinking God a priority in my life. Thinking God, I will have a new rejoicing in the Lord, a greater awareness of the presence and power of the Lord, and a new attitude of gratitude in the Lord (1 Thessalonians 5:16-18).

PART I

BECAUSE I ONLY HAVE ONE LIFE

Thinking God: What Are God's Intentions for You?

Memorize God's Word!

"Blessed is the man who walks not in the counsel of the wicked, nor stands in the way of sinners, nor sits in the seat of scoffers; but his delight is in the law of the LORD, and on his law he meditates day and night. He is like a tree planted by streams of water that yields its fruit in its season, and its leaf does not wither. In all that he does, he prospers. The wicked are not so, but are like chaff that the wind drives away. Therefore the wicked will not stand in the judgment, nor sinners in the congregation of the righteous; for the LORD knows the way of the righteous, but the way of the wicked will perish" (Psalm 1:1–6).

"As a deer pants for flowing streams, so pants my soul for you, O God" (Psalm 42:1).

"Be still, and know that I am God. I will be exalted among the nations, I will be exalted in the earth!" (Psalm 46:10).

"Have mercy on me, O God, according to your steadfast love; according to your abundant mercy blot out my transgressions. Wash me thoroughly from my iniquity, and cleanse me from my sin" (Psalm 51:1–2)!

"Bless the LORD, O my soul, and all that is within me, bless his holy name! Bless the LORD, O my soul, and forget not all his benefits, who forgives all your iniquity, who heals all your diseases, who redeems your life from the pit, who crowns you with steadfast love and mercy, who satisfies you with good so that your youth is renewed like the eagle's" (Psalm 103:1–5).

"For my thoughts are not your thoughts, neither are your ways my ways, declares the LORD. For as the heavens are higher than the earth, so are my ways higher than your ways and my thoughts than your thoughts" (Isaiah 55:8–9).

"But seek first the kingdom of God and his righteousness, and all these things will be added to you" (Matthew 6:33).

"Not everyone who says to me, 'Lord, Lord,' will enter the kingdom of heaven, but the one who does the will of my Father who is in heaven" (Matthew 7:21).

"Everyone then who hears these words of mine and does them will be like a wise man who built his house on the rock. And the rain fell, and the floods came, and the winds blew and beat on that house, but it did not fall, because it had been founded on the rock. And everyone who hears these words of mine and does not do them will be like a foolish man who built his house on the sand. And the rain fell, and the floods came, and the winds blew and beat against that house, and it fell, and great was the fall of it" (Matthew 7:24–27).

"For the law was given through Moses; grace and truth came through Jesus Christ" (John 1:17).

"A new commandment I give to you, that you love one another: just as I have loved you, you also are to love one another. By this all people will know that you are my disciples, if you have love for one another" (John 13:34–35).

"But thanks be to God, who in Christ always leads us in triumphal procession, and through us spreads the fragrance of the knowledge of him everywhere" (2 Corinthians 2:14).

"For godly grief produces a repentance that leads to salvation without regret, whereas worldly grief produces death" (2 Corinthians 7:10).

"Blessed be the God and Father of our Lord Jesus Christ, who has blessed us in Christ with every spiritual blessing in the heavenly places" (Ephesians 1:3).

"For by him all things were created, in heaven and on earth, visible and invisible, whether thrones or dominions or rulers or authorities—all things were created through him and for him. And he is before all things, and in him all things hold together. And he is the head of the body, the church. He is the beginning, the firstborn from the dead, that in everything he might be preeminent" (Colossians 1:16–18).

"Therefore, as you received Christ Jesus the Lord, so walk in him, rooted and built up in him and established in the faith, just as you were taught, abounding in thanksgiving" (Colossians 2:6–7).

"If then you have been raised with Christ, seek the things that are above, where Christ is, seated at the right hand of God. Set your minds on things that are above, not on things that are on earth. For you have died, and your life is hidden with Christ in God. When

Christ who is your life appears, then you also will appear with him in glory" (Colossians 3:1–4).

"But be doers of the word, and not hearers only, deceiving yourselves" (James 1:22).

"For this is the love of God, that we keep his commandments. And his commandments are not burdensome. For everyone who has been born of God overcomes the world. And this is the victory that has overcome the world—our faith" (1 John 5:3–4).

∞⁃∞

I loved the Lord with all my heart and had been wholeheartedly preaching, teaching, and sharing his perfect Word to everyone I could, but I found myself greatly discouraged and defeated at the age of thirty-three. It was a miserable existence, and I knew it was totally contrary to what God had promised me as his child (Romans 8:37). I had become distracted in all of the demands of life and ministry. I had become careless in the midst of all of God's blessings in my life. Distracted and careless, I had forgotten a very important truth of Thinking God: God is always more interested in what he does in me than through me (2 Corinthians 4:16).

I had resigned as pastor of a loving and growing church in Redmond, Oregon to become the associate director of evangelism of the Missouri Baptist Convention. Moving 1,860 miles in June to Jefferson City, Missouri, we experienced a humidity we were not accustomed to, and it made us sick whenever we went outdoors. This made it difficult for us to look for a home to purchase and settle our family. Not able to find a home before all our things arrived in the moving truck, we rented an apartment, where the tenant below us enjoyed loud country music and the tenant above us liked rock and roll, especially late at night. Leaving our parents and all our brothers and their families and extended family, my wife and I both struggled with homesickness. My wife was two months pregnant with our third son and struggled with morning sickness morning, noon, and night. Two weeks after arriving in Missouri, I was rear ended in a serious car accident and was in bed for several weeks with back injuries and a whiplash to my neck. Struggling with migraine headaches and an upset stomach from the medication for my pain, my life was certainly not as I had planned. After about a month of suffering in a condition that was not improving, I began to sink into a depression, "thinking me" rather than Thinking God and leaving me in tears much of the time.

Frustrated and depressed over my situation, I declared to my wife one day, "I wish we would have never come to this horrible place. This is the worst decision I have ever made." Like Elijah when he was not Thinking God and saying stupid things (1 Kings 19:3–4), I was not Thinking God and was saying stupid things. Little did I know that the greatest days and years of experiencing God in my life and through my life were ahead of me in Missouri. I am grateful that my wife spoke the hard truth to me by responding, "Why don't you go back to bed and listen to some of those great messages you have preached on how we always have victory in Jesus Christ? You sure are not acting like you have much victory."

I responded, "I will do just that." I went back to bed, pulled the covers over my head, and cried like a baby who acts (thinks) like life is totally out of control because he is not in control. Finally (you can only cry for so long and having a pity party accomplishes nothing good or beneficial) broken before God and desperate for God to move in my life, I prayed, "Father, I desperately need you to deliver me from this pit." God always meets us at the level of our need and desire.

Here's the glorious good news of God's greatness, goodness and grace: When we call to God with all our hearts, God meets us where we are and leads us to where we need to be and to go. God is always there to take us back to Thinking God. God has given us his Word to return us to Thinking God. I began to read through the Proverbs. When I got to Proverbs 3:26, "For the LORD shall be thy confidence, and shall keep thy foot from being taken," the LORD spoke to me powerfully and said, "You do not know me as your confidence. You have made my blessings your confidence. *I am* the LORD (Exodus 3:14). I must be your confidence or you will always be shaken when things are not going as you would like."

Seeking the LORD with all my heart (Psalm 42:1–3) and being still before the LORD (Psalm 46:10) for the next several days in bed, God "restored me" (Psalm 23:3; 51:2) and began to teach me a new understanding of Thinking God and being properly related to him as my confidence.

Properly related to God as our confidence, we will think humility and choose to be:

- Submitted to the authority of his Word and godly authority—John 8:31–32;

- Surrendered to his presence—Ephesians 5:17–18;

- Settled to whose we are—1 Corinthians 6:19–20;

- Surrounded by Christians for encouragement and accountability—Hebrews 10:23–25; and

- Sharing Christ every day, everywhere, all the time—Acts 5:42.

Isn't it amazing what we can forget in our discouragement: We were created by God and for God to live in the preeminence of Christ (Colossians 1:16–22)! God wants us to know him better than anyone or anything else and to make him known to others more than anything or anyone else (Colossians 2:6–12; 3:1–17). Knowing God in this way and sharing God in this way is accomplished by Thinking God—thinking and obeying his Word (James 1:22; 1 John 5:3).

Otherwise, we may be redeemed or "born again" (John 3:1–8), but we live by the "flesh" (1 Corinthians 3:1–4) and with a self-centered attitude of "Get all you can, can all you get, sit on the can, and shoot anyone who comes near the can." Remember the writer of Ecclesiastes who had everything in his "can" the world could offer but was still searching for what was missing in his life. He wrote:

> "I thought in my heart, 'Come now, I will test you with pleasure to find out what is good.' But that also proved to be meaningless. 'Laughter,' I said, 'is foolish. And what does pleasure accomplish?' I tried cheering myself with wine, and embracing folly—my mind still guiding me with wisdom. I wanted to see what was worthwhile for men to do under heaven during the few days of their lives. I undertook great projects: I built houses for myself and planted vineyards. I made gardens and parks and planted all kinds of fruit trees in them. I made reservoirs to water groves of flourishing trees. I bought male and female slaves and had other slaves who were born in my house. I also owned more herds and flocks than anyone in Jerusalem before me. I amassed silver and gold for myself, and the treasure of kings and provinces. I acquired men and women singers

and a harem as well—the delights of the heart of man. I became greater by far than anyone in Jerusalem before me. In all this my wisdom stayed with me. I denied myself nothing my eyes desired; I refused my heart no pleasure. My heart took delight in all my work, and this was the reward for all my labor. Yet when I surveyed all that my hands had done and what I had toiled to achieve, everything was meaningless, a chasing after the wind; nothing was gained under the sun."

(Ecclesiastes 2:1–11, NIV)

If you are "chasing after the wind," stop wasting your life living and working with all your heart for what the world cannot give you: significance (your life counts), security (you are deeply loved and respected by those you deeply love and respect), and sufficiency (you know your needs are met). When the disciples were anxious about these things, Jesus said to them: "But seek first his kingdom and his righteousness, and all these things will be given to you as well" (Matthew 6:33). Jesus spent his ministry teaching the disciples about the reign of God's rule in their lives—living under the authority of God's Word, Thinking God. But they were spiritually slow, just like we are (Matthew 17:14–17).

The good news is "if (when) we are faithless, he will remain faithful, for he cannot disown himself" (2 Timothy 2:13). Thinking God, Jesus persevered and spent forty more days following his suffering by showing himself to his disciples and giving them many convincing proofs that he was alive as he spoke about the kingdom of God (Acts 1:3). The fact you are reading this book should be an encouragement to you of God's faithful work in creating a desire in your life to increasingly learn to have the mind of Christ in all your thinking (Philippians 2:5). Do not ever lose heart in your journey of learning God's ways by Thinking God (2 Corinthians 4:16–18).

Isn't it amazing what we can forget in our discouragement: We were created for loving and lasting relationships with God and others (John 13:34–35)! Not Thinking God and not obeying his Word, we will fail in our temptations, we will stay discouraged in our insecurities, we will be defeated in our failures, we will be overwhelmed in our challenges, we will become resentful in our disappointments, we will be bitter in our hurts, and we will live condemned by our sin. Add to all that baggage is fearfulness and unresolved anger which are common side effects from not Thinking God and not obeying his Word. It should not surprise you that in these conditions it is impossible for us to be able to properly relate to others.

Until we are properly related to ourselves by Thinking God and living obedient to his Word—that is, being affirmed, beloved, contented, comforted, delivered, disciplined, encouraged, faithful, forgiven, gracious, hopeful, humble, kind, loving, merciful, overcoming, patient, persevering, prudent, reconciled, restored, secure, thankful, trustworthy, understanding, and wise (just to name some characteristics of Thinking God)—we will continue to find ourselves living in the frustration of a crisis of compromising to trust and obey God's Word as the authority for our lives. Where does this crisis of compromising leave us? Living in a storm of conflict and going down the road of resentment, bitterness, unresolved anger, and blame leaves us confused as to why life cannot be better than it is.

In conflict, we withdraw from God and keep our distance from those who can help us in a spirit of "grace and truth"

(John 1:17). In that conflict, we live in a state of confusion whereby we justify our sin, deny our sin, disguise our sin, and compare our sin with others. Confused, it gives us a sense of relief in our misery to be critical of those who are in God-ordained authority who could help us the most. Not Thinking God, we live in the misery of an unending string of broken relationships, being upset, feeling alienated, revengeful, and alone.

Many in the church think being properly related to God means: "being a good person," "being baptized as a baby," "praying the sinner's prayer," "believing in God," "being a church member," or even "being an active church member who serves and gives." Yet, look at the "fruit" of many in the church (Matthew 7:16–20). Many pray little except in a time of great need. Because of pride and unresolved anger, few pray together as husband and wife on a daily basis. (The exception of this possibly is at mealtime, especially when the pastor is a guest for dinner.) Many do not have a hunger for God's Word (Matthew 5:6). There is a growing trend in many churches to not even bring the Bible to church because most would feel uncomfortable being asked to look up a passage of scripture. Many pastors are fearful about persons feeling uncomfortable and not returning to their church, so they are careful in their preaching not to say anything to upset the people (2 Timothy 3:1–5; 4:3–4). "Deny yourself and take up your cross and follow me" (Luke 9:23) seems out of date to many. Many do not have the power to forgive (Matthew 6:14–15) or the passion of God and the confidence in God's promises to give (Acts 20:35). Many spend their lives attempting to hide the pain in their marriages and the conflict in their dysfunctional families.

Not properly related to God, many in the church struggle with all kinds of addictions just like those in the world. Because of not Thinking God, the divorce rate in marriage in the church is tragically about the same of those outside the church. It is becoming more and more common for couples, who consider themselves Christians, to live together unmarried and see nothing wrong in their arrangement.

Even many who truly have had "godly sorrow leading them to repentance" (2 Corinthians 7:10) and who have trusted God's promise: "For it is by grace we are saved through faith" in the perfect and complete work of Christ (Ephesians 2:1–10) still live their lives miserable often having pity parties and panic attacks instead of "always being led in triumphal procession in Christ and spreading everywhere the fragrance of the knowledge of him" (2 Corinthians 2:14). It is tragic how the majority of professing Christians, including many church leadership, live their lives in "survival mode"—that is, happy if they are getting what they want and discouraged and defeated if they are not experiencing life as they desired because they have never learned to "walk by the Spirit and not gratify the desires of the flesh" (Galatians 5:16).

According to Bibleinfo.com, there are three thousand five hundred and seventy-three promises in the Bible. According to www.swartzentrover.com, there are six hundred and thirteen commands in the Old Testament and one thousand and fifty commands in the New Testament. God's commandments are really God's promises because God never gives us a command without promising to be our power and provision to do the command.

Just imagine what would happen in your life if you lived moment by moment, Thinking God's five thousand and two hundred and thirty six promises and commands and being properly related to him. Thinking God and living in the preeminence of Christ, you would be properly related to God, yourself, and others. Being "more than a conqueror" in Christ (Romans 8:37), you would enjoy loving and lasting relationships with others because in Christ's victory you would be "spreading everywhere the fragrance of the knowledge of him" (2 Corinthians 2: 14).

Thinking God—God is always there to take me back to Thinking God. God has given me his Word to rule my thoughts (Proverbs 3:26).

Truth to Remember—God's commandments are really God's promises to me because God never gives me a command he has not promised to be my power and provision to do the command (John 15:5).

Thinking God in Reflecting—Imagine what would happen in my life if I lived moment by moment, Thinking God's 5,236 promises and commands in being properly related to him, myself and others (2 Corinthians 2:14)?

THINKING GOD: WHAT IS TRUSTWORTHY TO BE YOUR AUTHORITY?

Memorize God's Word!

"Is anything too hard for the Lord? At the appointed time I will return to you, about this time next year, and Sarah shall have a son" (Genesis 18:14).

"And Sarah conceived and bore Abraham a son in his old age at the time of which God had spoken to him" (Genesis 21:2).

"As for you, you meant evil against me, but God meant it for good, to bring it about that many people should be kept alive, as they are today" (Genesis 50:20).

"Hear, O Israel: The Lord our God, the Lord is one. You shall love the Lord your God with all your heart and with all your soul and with all your might" (Deuteronomy 6:4-5).

"The law of the Lord is perfect, reviving the soul; the testimony of the Lord is sure, making wise the simple; the precepts of the Lord are right, rejoicing the heart; the commandment of the Lord is pure, enlightening the eyes; the fear of the Lord is clean, enduring forever; the rules of the Lord are true, and righteous altogether. More to be desired are they than gold, even much fine gold; sweeter also than honey and drippings of the honeycomb. Moreover, by them is your servant warned; in keeping them there is great reward" (Psalm 19:7–11).

"There is a way that seems right to a man but its end is the way to death" (Proverbs 14:12).

"Every word of God proves true; he is a shield to those who take refuge in him" (Proverbs 30:5).

"The steadfast love of the LORD never ceases; his mercies never come to an end; they are new every morning; great is your faithfulness. 'The LORD is my portion,' says my soul, 'therefore I will hope in him'" (Lamentations 3:22–24).

"Enter by the narrow gate. For the gate is wide and the way is easy that leads to destruction, and those who enter by it are many. For the gate is narrow and the way is hard that leads to life, and those who find it are few" (Matthew 7:13–14).

"If you love me, you will keep my commandments" (John 14:15).

"For though we walk in the flesh, we are not waging war according to the flesh. For the weapons of our warfare are not of the flesh but have divine power to destroy strongholds. We destroy arguments and every lofty opinion raised against the knowledge of God, and take every thought captive to obey Christ" (2 Corinthians 10:3–5).

"All Scripture is breathed out by God and profitable for teaching, for reproof, for correction, and for training in righteousness, that the man of God may be complete, equipped for every good work" (2 Timothy 3:16–17).

"But he gives more grace. Therefore it says, 'God opposes the proud, but gives grace to the humble'" (James 4:6).

"At the end of your life you will groan, when your flesh and body are spent. You will say, 'How I hated discipline! How my heart spurned correction! I would not obey my teachers or listen to my instructors. I have come to the brink of utter ruin in the midst of the whole assembly'" (Proverbs 5:11–14).

"For a man's ways are in full view of the Lord, and he examines all his paths. The evil deeds of a wicked man ensnare him; the cords of his sin hold him fast. He will die for lack of discipline, led astray by his own great folly" (Proverbs 5:21–23).

₨⌓

You can live any way you want. You can sin as much as you want, but you cannot choose your consequences. Always know: sin will take you further than you want to go, keep you longer than you want to stay, and cost you more than you want to pay. That's one of the reasons why, if I had one hundred zillion lives to live, I would live every one of them under the perfect and protective authority of God's Word.

Born in 1951 and growing up in Warren, Arkansas, I was raised in a community with strong Christian values, and the Bible was accepted by most as God's perfect Word. One of the most popular hymns to sing at that time was "Trust and Obey."

> When we walk with the Lord in the light of His Word,
> What a glory He sheds on our way!

While we do His good will;
He abides with us still,
And with all who will trust and obey.
Trust and obey,
for there's no other way
to be happy in Jesus,
but to trust and obey.

(Words by Daniel Brink Towner & John Henry Sammis—Public Domain)

Weekly church attendance was the norm for the majority of people in Warren. All businesses were closed on Sundays. There were no organized sports practiced or played on Sunday. Most families went to church. Children were expected to honor and obey their parents and schoolteachers with responses of "Yes, sir," and "Yes, ma'am." Students started each day with the pledge to the American flag and reciting the 23rd Psalm and the Lord's Prayer with their teachers in public schools. Parents and teachers were expected to discipline children of all ages up to high school with the "board of higher learning" because it was common sense to discipline your children by what the Bible taught (Proverbs 3:11–12; 22:15). Disrespect to a person of recognized authority (parent or schoolteacher) was unthinkable and severe consequences usually followed.

Then the sixties came. My dad was a horticulturist and had been employed by the University of Arkansas as a county extension agent in southeast Arkansas following World War II. He led Bradley County to be a national leader in the tomato industry. With such success, my dad was invited by Washington State University to lead the horticultural work in what is known as the Columbia Basin Project.

We moved to Ephrata, Washington in June of 1964. My new "Northwest" friends thought it was very strange and humorous for me to say: "Yes, sir," and "Yes, ma'am" to my parents and even more "weird" for me to respond with such respect to all my public schoolteachers. My new neighbor friends told me they had never had friends who obeyed their parents on the "first call" to come home like they observed in my brothers and me. However, "bad company corrupts good character" (1 Corinthians 15:33). After a year of living in Washington, my brothers and I began to say at times "Yeah" rather than: "Yes, sir," and "Yes, ma'am" in responding to adults. We increasingly found ourselves not being as sensitive to hear our parents call to "Come home" until the second, third, or fourth call.

Good Christian values and environment are wonderful, and I am so grateful to God and my parents for my upbringing, but our rather quick change in behavior is a good example of what God says about all of us regardless of where or how we were raised:

"The heart is deceitful above all things and beyond cure. Who can understand it" (Jeremiah 17:9)?

"We all, like sheep, have gone astray, each of us has turned to his own way; and the Lord has laid on him the iniquity of us all" (Isaiah 53:6).

"As it is written: 'There is no one righteous, not even one; there is no one who understands, no one who seeks God'" (Romans 3:10–11).

"As for you, you were dead in your transgressions and sins, in which you used to live when you followed the ways of this world and of the ruler of the kingdom of the air, the spirit who is now at work in those who are disobedient. All of us also lived among them at one time, gratifying the cravings of our sinful nature and following its desires and thoughts. Like the rest, we were by nature objects of wrath" (Ephesians 2:1–3).

Because of this sinful nature, we all have an attitude of rebellion toward authority that leaves us confused. We think, *I don't care what God or anyone else says, I am going to do it my way.* This is the attitude of sin. In that attitude of not Thinking God, "we all have fallen short of the glory of God" and of what God intended for us (Romans 3:23). Apart from God reconciling our thinking by his grace and truth revealed to us in Jesus Christ so we choose to repent and change our minds about our rebelliousness toward God (Mark 1:15, 2 Corinthians 7:10), we live our entire lives in the crisis of compromise, conflict, and confusion, thinking we do not need God. To experience abundant life as God redeemed us to have (John 10:10), we must resolve this foundational question of life—Who is trustworthy to be the authority for our lives?

In the seventies and eighties, there was a growing conflict over the authority of the Bible within many major Christian denominations, universities, and seminaries across America. Many professors in conservative Christian universities, and seminaries, as well as pastors in conservative churches began to question whether the Scriptures in their entirety were the inspired Word of God, free from error in their original written form.

Over the past fifty years, we have continued to see one of the saddest verses in the Bible become a growing attitude of so many professing Christians: "Every man did that which was right in his own eyes" (Judges 21:25). I have continued to learn—whatever the challenge or need—there is no hope for a new beginning in Christ, a lasting change for God, reconciliation or, growth, until we learn in Thinking God to submit our lives to the authority of God's Word.

This is one of the greatest discoveries I have ever made: Thinking humility and being submitted to the authority of God's Word and one another is life-giving (Philippians 2:1–8). Since we were created by God and for God to live in him, only in him can all things hold together when Christ is preeminent in our lives (Colossians 1:16-18). We cannot enjoy life as God intended unless we choose to live under the authority of God's Word. We must understand: we cannot be over (be more than a conqueror in Christ) until we are under the authority of God's Word!

God never has and never will bless rebels. It is against God's holiness (Leviticus 19:1–2; Deuteronomy 5:6–9; 1 Peter 1:13–16). God has promised us, "Do not be deceived: God cannot be mocked. A man reaps what he sows. The one who sows to please his sinful nature, from that nature will reap destruction; the one who sows to please the Spirit, from the Spirit will reap eternal life. Let us not become weary in doing good for at the proper time we will reap a harvest if we do not give up" (Galatians 6:7–9). "Doing good" is living under the authority of God's Word.

If you have never done this, take a week and spend one hour each day listing the blessings of God's power, provision, and protection promised to you in Psalm 119:1–176 when you choose to live under the authority of God's Word. You will be overwhelmed with thanksgiving of the privileges of living under the authority of God's perfect Word (Psalm 19:7–11), flawless Word (Proverbs 30:5–6), and God-breathed Word (2 Timothy 3:16–17).

So you ask, "How do I know God's Word is trustworthy to be my authority?" If you are thinking that, I know how you feel. This may surprise you because of everything I have already said, but I found myself asking my new pastor at college that very question in the confusion I was experiencing in the fall of 1969. Two months before graduating from high school, I had painfully watched my dad, pastor, and other men I loved and had greatly respected for years begin to choose sides and fight until one side "won" and one side "lost." It's called a "church fight" resulting in a "church split." It always leaves many in the church confused, frustrated, and hurting. Outside the church, it always leaves many more confused, cynical, and even more distant in considering the saving gospel of Jesus for their lives.

What made this experience additionally painful to my family was that our family had started this church in our home when we had moved to Washington. Five months after this great conflict and confusion in my life occurred, some of my friends attended Woodstock in Bethel, New York on August 15 to18, where five hundred thousand young and rebellious concertgoers gathered for a weekend concert that included thirty-two acts. They declared by their immorality, use of drugs, and riotous living that "there is no absolute authority for us!"

Confused greatly by what was happening in my family, church, and world, I will forever be grateful for my new college pastor's response to my question, "How do we really know the Bible is God's Word and is trustworthy to trust and obey with all our hearts?" He replied, "You must do apologetics and resolve that question for yourself." I had never heard of apologetics.

Apologetics means "a defense; a vindication." My pastor encouraged me to, "Do your due diligence and come to your own personal conviction about the Bible being God's perfect Word and being trustworthy to be the authority for your life." Because most Christians have never done their due diligence concerning the Bible, they live their lives in a crisis of compromise, conflict, and confusion when it comes to wholeheartedly obeying God's Word in their entire lives.

Through much study, prayer, and discussion with my pastor and his wife, I came to a deep conviction that I desire for you as well. If you are struggling with the authority of God's Word in your life, I invite you to scrutinize the Bible with me as I share with you some unbelievable miracles about the Bible. As I have shared these truths with many through the years and continue to do so, I have seen God bring them to their own personal conviction that the Bible is trustworthy to be the authority for their lives and to trust Jesus Christ to be their personal Lord and Savior. I pray this will be your joy as well!

Be the jury concerning these four miracles about the Bible and consider:

The Miracle of the Prophecies in the Old Testament Perfectly Fulfilled in Jesus Christ

As you look at the prophecies in the left hand column that show the details about Christ's birth, life, ministry, death, resurrection, and return, you can see in the middle column the Old Testament reference giving the prophecy and the approximate date the prophecy was given. The far right column provides the New Testament reference where the prophecy is fulfilled.

Prophecies of Christ Fulfilled		
Prophecy	Old Testament Prophecy	New Testament Fulfillment
Messiah to be the seed of the woman	Genesis 3:15 (before 4000 BC)	Matthew 1:21; Galatians 4:4
Messiah to be the seed of Abraham	Genesis 12:3 (2050), 18:18 (2036)	Matthew 1:2; Luke 3:34; Acts 3:25; Galatians 3:16
Messiah to be of the seed of Isaac	Genesis 17:19 (2050)	Matthew 1:2; Luke 3:34
Messiah to be of the tribe of Judah	Genesis 49:10 (1900)	Matthew 1:2; Luke 3:33
Messiah to be of the seed of Jacob	Numbers 24:17, 19 (1424)	Matthew 1:2; Luke 3:34
Messiah to be of the seed of David	Psalm 132:11 (960); Jeremiah 23:5 (610); 33:15 (587); Isaiah 11:10 (735)	Matthew 1:6; Luke 1:32-33; Romans 1:3; Acts 2:30
Messiah to be born of a virgin	Isaiah 7:14 (735)	Matthew 1:18-25; Luke 1:26-35
Bethlehem to be the place of Messiah's birth	Micah 5:2 (740)	Matthew 2:1; Luke 2:4-6
Messiah to be the Son of God	Psalm 2:7 (1000); Proverbs 30:4 (950); Isaiah 9:6 (740)	Luke 1:32; Matthew 3:17
Messiah's birth during the slaughter of children	Jeremiah 31:15 (587)	Matthew 2:16-18
Homage and tribute paid to Messiah by great kings	Psalm 72:10-11 (970)	Matthew 2:1-11
Messiah to be brought out of Egypt	Hosea 11:1 (750)	Matthew 2:14-15
The way prepared for the Messiah	Isaiah 40:3-5 (700); Malachi 3:1 (420)	Mark 1:2-3; Luke 3:4-6
Messiah preceded by Elijah	Malachi 4:5 (420)	Matthew 11:13
Galilee to be the first area of Messiah's ministry	Isaiah 9:1-8 (735)	Matthew 4:12-16
Messiah will perform miracles	Isaiah 35:5-6 (710)	John 11:47; Matthew 11:3-6
Messiah will be meek and mild	Isaiah 42:2-3; Isaiah 53:7 (700)	Matthew 12:18-20; Matthew 26:62-63
Messiah will minister to the Gentiles	Isaiah 42:1; Isaiah 49:1-8 (700)	Matthew 12:21
Messiah to be a prophet like Moses	Deuteronomy 18:15, 19 (1425)	Matthew 21:11; John 6:14; John 1:45; Acts 3:22-23
Messiah would speak in parables	Psalm 78:2-4 (1000)	Matthew 13:34-35
Messiah would be rejected by his own people, the Jews	Isaiah 53:3 (700)	John 1:11; Luke 23:18
Messiah would be adored by infants	Psalm 8:2 (1000)	Matthew 21:15-16
Messiah was not believed by many	Isaiah 53:3 (700)	John 12:37-38
Messiah will enter the Temple with authority	Malachi 3:1 (420)	Matthew 21:12
Messiah will enter Jerusalem on a donkey	Zechariah 9:9 (500)	Matthew 21:1-10
Messiah, the stone the builders rejected, to become the head cornerstone	Psalm 118:22-23 (970-700?); Isaiah 8:14-15(735); Isaiah 28:16 (700)	Matthew 21:42-43; Acts 4:11; Romans 1:32-33; Ephesians 2:20; 1 Peter 2:6-8

Prophecy	Old Testament Prophecy	New Testament Fulfillment
Messiah would be betrayed by a close friend	Psalm 41:9 (1000)	Luke 22:47-48
Messiah would be betrayed for 30 pieces of silver	Zechariah 11:12 (500)	Matthew 26:15
Messiah forsaken by His disciples	Zechariah 13:7 (500)	Matthew 26:31, 56
The crucifixion experience	Psalm 22 (1000); Psalm 69:21 (980)	Matthew 27:34-50; John 19:28-30
Messiah would be sneered and mocked	Psalm 22:7-8 (1000)	Luke 23:35
Messiah would be reproached	Psalm 69:9 (980)	Romans 15:3
Messiah would be accused by false witnesses	Psalm 35:11 (700)	Mark 14:57-58
Messiah was silent to accusations	Isaiah 53:7 (700)	Mark 15:4-5
Messiah was spat on and struck	Isaiah 50:6 (700)	Matthew 26:67
Messiah was hated without reason	Psalm 35:19 (980)	John 15:24-25
Messiah was our vicarious sacrifice	Isaiah 53:5 (700)	Romans 5:6, 8
Messiah was crucified with transgressors	Isaiah 53:12 (700)	Mark 15:27-28
Messiah would pray for his enemies	Psalm 109:4 (980)	Luke 23:34
Messiah would be pierced	Zechariah 12:10 (500); Psalm 22:16 (1000)	John 19:34, 37
Messiah was buried with the rich	Isaiah 53:9 (700)	Matthew 27:57-60
Messiah to be raised from the dead	Psalm 16:10 (1000)	Acts 13:35-37
Messiah would ascend to heaven	Psalm 68:18 (1000)	Luke 24:51; Acts 1:9
Messiah to be a priest like Melchizedek	Psalm 110:4 (1000)	Hebrews 5:5-6
Messiah to be at the right hand of God	Psalm 110:1 (1000)	Matthew 27:64; Hebrews 1:3
The gospel according to Isaiah (The suffering Messiah brings salvation)	Isaiah 52:13-53:12 (700)	The four gospels
The New and Everlasting Covenant	Isaiah 55:3-4; (700) Jeremiah 31:31-33 (587)	Matthew 26:28; Mark 14:24; Luke 22:20; Hebrews 8:6-13
Messiah, the Right Arm of God	Isaiah 59:16; Isaiah 53:1 (700)	John 12:38
Messiah as Intercessor	Isaiah 59:16 (700)	Hebrews 9:15
Twofold mission of the Messiah	Isaiah 61:1-11 (700)	Luke 4:16-21
Messiah is called "The Lord"	Jeremiah 23:5-6 (610)	Acts 2:36
The time of Messiah's coming prophesied	Daniel 9:24-26 (538)	Galatians 4:4; Ephesians 1:10
The coming of the Holy Spirit in the days of the Messiah	Joel 2:28 (586)	Acts 2:16-18
Opposition of the nations	Psalm 2:2 (1010)	Revelation 19:19
Messiah's final victory over death	Isaiah 25:8 (700)	1 Corinthians 15:54; Revelation 7:17; 21:4
The glorious Messiah	Isaiah 63:1 (700)	Revelation 19:11-16
Messiah as King	Psalm 2:6-9 (1010)	Revelation 19:15-16
Submission of all nations to Messiah's rule	Isaiah 2:4; Micah 4:1-4 (740)	Revelation 12:5
The Gentiles shall seek the Messiah of Israel	Isaiah 11:10 (735)	Revelation 11:25

(This listing of prophecies was adapted from the Ryrie Study Bible, Charles Caldwell Ryrie, 1976 and the Open Bible, 2001.)

Think about it. What is the possibility of someone telling you hundreds or even thousands of years from now who the president of a particular nation would be, his birthplace, his genealogy that goes back two thousand years, the circumstances surrounding his birth, and then details about his life, work, death, burial, and after his death. Of course, "With man this is impossible, but with God all things are possible" (Matthew 19:26).

The Miracle of the Resurrection of Jesus Christ and How That Changed History

Remember what happened when Jesus was crucified. His disciples were paralyzed in fear (John 20:19–20). Even a week after the resurrected Jesus had appeared before them, the disciples were still locked behind closed doors (John 20:26-28). Without the Lord's resurrection, their fear factor and feeling of hopelessness would have brought an end to Christianity in a short period of time (1 Corinthians 15:17–18).

But Jesus is a resurrected Lord. He appeared to more than five hundred brothers at one time after his crucifixion (1 Corinthians 15:6). Jesus then showed himself to his disciples and gave many convincing proofs that he was alive. He appeared to them over a period of forty days and spoke about the kingdom of God (Acts 1:3). And they finally got it. Because Jesus Christ is the resurrected Lord—there was no more doubt that he was the Christ, the Son of the living God, the Messiah. The proof was in their obedience. They stopped arguing and started obeying no matter what he asked them to do (Acts 1:12–14). They were willing to suffer, and they even died along with many in the early church. With such a confident faith, "the world was turned upside down" (Acts 17:6).

Read Roman history and you will see the Roman emperors did not take it lightly for anyone to be called "Lord" other than themselves. The early Christians were persecuted, imprisoned, and martyred for confessing "Christ is Lord" (Romans 10:9). Yet, because of the resurrected Christ, they could not be silenced or intimidated. They continued to live for Christ, share Christ, and die for Christ, confessing victoriously "Christ is the risen Lord!" Two hundred and eighty years following Christ's resurrection in 313, a Roman emperor, Constantine, believed there was such power in Christ's cross, he put a cross on the shield of each of his men before going into a battle where the odds were greatly against them. After amazingly winning that battle, he professed Christ and legalized Christianity as the official religion of the Roman Empire. If there was no resurrection of Jesus Christ, Christianity would have died hundreds of years earlier (1 Corinthians 15:14), and Constantine would have never known anything about the power of the cross of Christ (1 Corinthians 1:18).

The Miracle of the Bible

The Bible is God's written revelation to man. The Bible is made up of sixty-six books, thirty-nine in the Old Testament and twenty-seven in the New Testament. The Old Testament was written for the most part in Hebrew with a few Aramaic passages. The New Testament was written in Greek. It was written over a period of one thousand five hundred years by about forty men who came from varying backgrounds, including shepherds, professors, doctors, fishermen, and a tax collector. Some were well educated while others had little exposure to the academic disciplines of their day. In spite of both the long span of time involved and the diversity of human authorship and three languages, the Bible has one central unifying theme—Jesus Christ, the Redeemer of man. There is no book like it. It is a supernatural book that tells you how you can have a supernatural birth so you can have a supernatural life. It has been the number one best seller for more than seventy years. Keep scrutinizing.

Since the printing press was not invented by Guttenberg until 1440, for over two thousand eight hundred years, the only way there was another copy of the Scriptures was to be hand copied. What are the chances the Bible as we have it today could be authentic after two thousand eight hundred years of different men copying it one letter, one word, one sentence, one book, one copy at a time? That's right, zero. And that's what many began to say in the 1500s as well. With this ability to print, all knowledge and information were distributed to the masses like never before. This time period in history was called the Great Enlightenment. A philosophy began to grow, which I heard several of my professors at Eastern say in the early seventies and which is prevalent in higher education today: "Science is what can be trusted and faith is foolishness." The word *atheist* was born during this era. They sarcastically said, "Hand copied for over two thousand eight hundred years, it is impossible for the Bible to be authentic."

And then the greatest archaeological discovery in history was made—the Dead Sea Scrolls. Discovered in 1947 in Qumran near the Dead Sea, the Dead Sea Scrolls included some five hundred manuscripts that were written or copied between 250 BC and AD 68. These manuscripts are fragments of every Old Testament book except Esther (and they are still looking for Esther in archaeological digs) including all of Isaiah and large portions of the Psalms, demonstrating the reliability of the Old Testament. Before this, the oldest copy of Isaiah was from the eleventh century AD. The Isaiah scroll discovered at Qumran is dated at around 150 BC. The two scrolls demonstrated how, copied by man through the centuries, God protected and preserved his Word. Nearly twelve centuries separate the two copies of Isaiah. Yet, when skeptics compare them, they find the two manuscripts to be nearly identical. If you ever have the opportunity to see the Dead Sea Scrolls, do it and you will be amazed!

In high school and college, the three great philosophers that our teachers and professors had us study were Aristotle, Socrates, and Plato. Whereas there are over five thousand six hundred Greek manuscripts of the New Testament, we possess only a handful of manuscripts of Plato and Aristotle's works. The Bible has no equal among ancient books even though it has had the greatest number of enemies attempting to destroy it.

Furthermore, no archaeological discovery has ever undermined any fact reported in the Bible. Rather, archaeological discoveries have supported the Bible's history and the peoples and places involved, even down to the words used to describe local customs and names.

The Miracle of Transformed Lives

The Bible is a supernatural book (Psalm 19:7–11; Psalm 119:1–176; 2 Timothy 3:16–17). It takes a supernatural book to bring a supernatural birth (John 3:1-8; Ephesians 2:1–10) that leads to a supernatural life (2 Corinthians 5:17–21). The Bible promises those who are "in Christ" will be secure in his love (1 John 4:18), guarded by his peace (Philippians 4:7), abounding in hope (Romans 15:13), and fulfilled in living out his purpose in their lives (Colossians 1:27). Nothing in your past—your sin, your suffering, or your sorrow—can prevent this supernatural birth and supernatural life from happening but you (2 Peter 3:9). Do not live beneath your privilege without Jesus Christ or even beneath your privilege in Jesus Christ. You are living beneath your privilege if you are not daily and humbly submitting your life to the authority of God's Word and surrendering your life to the presence and power of the Holy Spirit (1 Peter 5:5–7).

So what do you think? Isn't it time for you to give a verdict based on the evidence you have just read regarding this most important question: Is the Bible trustworthy to be your authority? I trust that you said yes. If you have already said yes to that question, I trust that the Holy Spirit used this study to encourage and equip you to have greater conviction, confidence, and courage to live every day in humble submission to the authority of God's Word—Thinking God.

Thinking God—Thinking humility and being submitted to the authority of God's Word and one another is life-giving (Philippians 2:1–8).

Truth to Remember—I must understand and never forget: I cannot live as "more than a conqueror in Christ" unless I live under the authority of God's Word (Romans 8:37).

Thinking God in Reflecting—Before this study, have you ever done your due diligence to come to your own personal conviction about the Bible being God's perfect Word and trustworthy to be the authority for your life? Now that you have, how will your life be different (2 Timothy 3:16–17)?

Thinking God: Why Were You Created?

Memorize God's Word!

"The Lord is my shepherd; I shall not want. He makes me lie down in green pastures. He leads me beside still waters. He restores my soul. He leads me in paths of righteousness for his name's sake. Even though I walk through the valley of the shadow of death, I will fear no evil, for you are with me; your rod and your staff, they comfort me. You prepare a table before me in the presence of my enemies; you anoint my head with oil; my cup overflows. Surely goodness and mercy shall follow me all the days of my life, and I shall dwell in the house of the Lord forever" (Psalm 23:1–6).

"The Lord is my light and my salvation; whom shall I fear? The Lord is the stronghold of my life; of whom shall I be afraid? When evildoers assail me to eat up my flesh, my adversaries and foes, it is they who stumble and fall. Though an army encamp against me, my heart shall not fear; though war arise against me, yet I will be confident. One thing have I asked of the LORD, that will I seek after: that I may dwell in the house of the LORD all the days of my life, to gaze upon the beauty of the LORD and to inquire in his temple. For he will hide me in his shelter in the day of trouble; he will conceal me under the cover of his tent; he will lift me high upon a rock. And now my head shall be lifted up above my enemies all around me, and I will offer in his tent sacrifices with shouts of joy; I will sing and make melody to the LORD" (Psalm 27:1–6).

"I will bless the Lord at all times; his praise shall continually be in my mouth. My soul makes its boast in the Lord; let the humble hear and be glad. Oh, magnify the Lord with me, and let us exalt his name together! I sought the Lord, and he answered me and delivered me from all my fears. Those who look to him are radiant, and their faces shall never be ashamed. This poor man cried, and the Lord heard him and saved him out of all his troubles. The angel of the Lord encamps around those who fear him, and delivers them. Oh, taste and see that the Lord is good! Blessed is the man who takes refuge in him" (Psalm 34:1–8)!

"I waited patiently for the Lord; he inclined to me and heard my cry. He drew me up from the pit of destruction, out of the miry bog, and set my feet upon a rock, making my steps secure. He put a new song in my mouth, a song of praise to our God. Many will see and fear, and put their trust in the Lord. Blessed is the man who makes the Lord his trust, who does not turn to the proud, to those who go astray after a lie! You have multiplied, O LORD my God, your wondrous deeds and your thoughts toward us; none can compare with you! I will proclaim and tell of them, yet they are more than can be told" (Psalm 40:1–5).

"Trust in the Lord with all your heart, and do not lean on your own understanding. In all your ways acknowledge him, and he will make straight your paths. Be not wise in your own eyes; fear the LORD, and turn away from evil" (Proverbs 3:5–7).

"For the Lord will be your confidence and will keep your foot from being caught" (Proverbs 3:26).

"In the beginning was the Word, and the Word was with God, and the Word was God. He was in the beginning with God. All things were made through him, and without him was not anything made that was made. In him was life, and the life was the light of men. The light shines in the darkness, and the darkness has not overcome it" (John 1:1–5).

"He was in the world, and the world was made through him, yet the world did not know him. He came to his own, and his own people did not receive him. But to all who did receive him, who believed in his name, he gave the right to become children of God, who were born, not of blood nor of the will of the flesh nor of the will of man, but of God. And the Word became flesh and dwelt among us, and we have seen his glory, glory as of the only Son from the Father, full of grace and truth" (John 1:10–14).

"And there is salvation in no one else, for there is no other name under heaven given among men by which we must be saved" (Acts 4:12).

"Therefore, if anyone is in Christ, he is a new creation. The old has passed away; behold, the new has come. All this is from God, who through Christ reconciled us to himself and gave us the ministry of reconciliation" (2 Corinthians 5:17–18).

"And you were dead in the trespasses and sins in which you once walked, following the course of this world, following the prince of the power of the air, the spirit that is now at work in the sons of disobedience—among whom we all once lived in the passions of our flesh, carrying out the desires of the body and the mind, and were by nature children of wrath, like the rest of mankind. But God, being rich in mercy, because of the great love with which he loved us, even when we were dead in our trespasses, made us alive together with Christ—by grace you have been saved—and raised us up with him and seated us with him in the heavenly places in Christ Jesus, so that in the coming ages he might show the immeasurable riches of his grace in kindness toward us in Christ Jesus. For by grace you have been saved through faith. And this is not your own doing; it is the gift of God, not a result of works, so that no one may boast. For we are his workmanship, created in Christ Jesus for good works, which God prepared beforehand, that we should walk in them" (Ephesians 2:1–10).

"Whoever has the Son has life; whoever does not have the Son of God does not have life" (1 John 5:12).

ଚରଷ

In June of 2012, along with three other persons from our church and our translator, I was walking on a dirt road in the country side of Costa Rica going house to house saying, "Hello, I am Pastor Phil from the United States. We have come to tell you how much God loves you and how he proved that love in giving his son, Jesus Christ, for you. Has anyone ever told you how much Jesus loves you?" Most would reply "No one." Nearly run over the first day of our trip by motor scooters and vehicles speeding on the narrow roads, upon hearing a scooter or vehicle coming, I would face the oncoming person, hold my hand up, and hope they would slow down. Surprised, they did much better than just slow down. Most would stop, and I would state our purpose for being in their neighborhood.

One man, Pedro, replied, "I have fourteen children by ten different women, and I have a prostitute in a motel room waiting for me right now." I responded, "That's why we have come to tell you how much God loves you and how you can have a different life than you are living." A man in my group, Duwain, looked at him and said, "I can see the pain in your eyes." Pedro replied, "I am a liar." Duwain said, "I am too." Pedro said, "I am a cheater." Duwain said, "I am too." Both men began to weep as the Holy Spirit did what only the Holy Spirit can truly do: convict persons of guilt in regard to sin and righteousness and judgment (John 16:8). An hour later, Pedro discovered what he was created for: to become a new creation in Jesus Christ and be reconciled to begin Thinking God (2 Corinthians 5:17–18). On June 27, 2012, Pedro began a new journey in Jesus Christ of learning to know God better than anything else and to make him known more than anything else (Philippians 1:6).

After Pedro trusted Christ's death on the cross for the payment of his sins and repented in response to God's conviction to change his mind about his sinfulness (2 Corinthians 7:10), we showed him from the Bible his new position in Christ: "If then you have been raised with Christ, seek the things that are above, where Christ is, seated at the right hand of God. Set your minds on things that are above, not on things that are on earth. For you have died, and your life is hidden with Christ in God. When Christ who is your life appears, then you also will appear with him in glory. Put to death therefore what is earthly in you: sexual immorality, impurity, passion, evil desire, and covetousness, which is idolatry" (Colossians 3:1–5).

We explained to Pedro now as a new creation in Christ, the Holy Spirit was going to change his thinking from the inside out:

> "Therefore, if anyone is in Christ, he is a new creation. The old has passed away; behold, the new has come. All this is from God, who through Christ reconciled us to himself and gave us the ministry of reconciliation; that is, in Christ, God was reconciling the world to himself, not counting their trespasses against them, and entrusting to us the message of reconciliation. Therefore, we are ambassadors for Christ, God making his appeal through us. We implore you on behalf of Christ, be reconciled to God. For our sake he made him to be sin who knew no sin, so that in him we might become the righteousness of God."
>
> (2 Corinthians 5:17–21)

Now belonging to Christ, we showed Pedro why he needed to belong to a church family:

> "For just as the body is one and has many members, and all the members of the body, though many, are one body, so it is with Christ. For in one Spirit we were all baptized into one body—Jews or Greeks, slaves or free—and all were made to drink of one Spirit. For the body does not consist of one member but of many. If the foot should say, 'Because I am not a hand, I do not belong to the body,' that would not make it any less a part of the body. And if the ear should say, 'Because I am not an eye, I do not belong to the body,' that would not make it any less a part of the body. If the whole

body were an eye, where would be the sense of hearing? If the whole body were an ear, where would be the sense of smell? But as it is, God arranged the members in the body, each one of them, as he chose. If all were a single member, where would the body be? As it is, there are many parts, yet one body. The eye cannot say to the hand, 'I have no need of you,' nor again the head to the feet, 'I have no need of you.' On the contrary, the parts of the body that seem to be weaker are indispensable, and on those parts of the body that we think less honorable we bestow the greater honor, and our unpresentable parts are treated with greater modesty, which our more presentable parts do not require. But God has so composed the body, giving greater honor to the part that lacked it, that there may be no division in the body, but that the members may have the same care for one another. If one member suffers, all suffer together; if one member is honored, all rejoice together. Now you are the body of Christ and individually members of it."

(1 Corinthians 12:12–27)

We emphasized to Pedro how important it was for him to become and to stay connected to a local church fellowship for encouragement and accountability (Hebrews 10:24–25), so he could know the joy of growing in his new faith in Christ.

We encouraged Pedro to become a part of the new church we were starting that week. We showed him Matthew 28:18–20. "And Jesus came and said to them, 'All authority in heaven and on earth has been given to me. Go therefore and make disciples of all nations, baptizing them in the name of the Father and of the Son and of the Holy Spirit, teaching them to observe all that I have commanded you. And behold, I am with you always, to the end of the age.'" We explained the significance of a believer's baptism as an obedient act to his new Lord and of confessing God's ownership of his life as well as the joy of identifying with Christ's death, burial, and resurrection (Romans 6:3–11).

We gave Pedro a Spanish Bible and showed him how daily he should study God's Word to grow in the grace and knowledge of Thinking God (2 Peter 3:18). And there was much rejoicing as there always is when anyone comes to repent and receive Christ as one's Lord and Savior (Luke 15:10).

Regardless of how long you have been in church or what you have done in church, think about what the Bible teaches us about knowing God by trusting Jesus Christ to be our personal Lord and Savior.

God is creator and we are created by him and for him to be preeminent in our lives (Colossians 1:16–18).

God is holy and is separate from sin (Leviticus 11:44). In a relationship with him, God has commanded us to be holy (1 Peter 1:13–16).

God is just and demands sin must be paid for. In the Old Testament, God told Israel their sins must be atoned by the shed blood of a bull, goat, ram, or lamb (Leviticus 4–6). In the New Testament, the justice of God was satisfied by the shed blood of Jesus Christ (Romans 3:23–24; Hebrews 9:22).

God is love and is merciful, kind, full of grace, and he sent his Son, Jesus Christ, to be the lamb of God (John 1:36). Romans 5:8 tells us: "God demonstrated His love for us in that while we were yet sinners, Christ died for us." Ephesians 2:4–5 declares: "But God, being rich in mercy, because of the great love with which he loved us, even when we were dead in our trespasses, made us alive together with Christ—by grace you have been saved." 2 Corinthians 5:21 gloriously tells us: "For our sake he made him to be sin who knew no sin so that in him we might become the righteousness of God." God paid for your sin!

The first story about man in the Bible tells us about the problem we all have (Genesis 3). We like to be independent of God. We are prone to be rebellious to God and to each other. We like to do our own thing. The Bible calls it sin. Sin always leads to broken relationships with God and with one another. Broken relationships always bring great hurt, confusion, alienation, bitterness, unresolved anger, and unending blame. Sin always brings suffering. You may be living there right now.

Because God is holy, our sin separates us from having fellowship with God. Remember what we were created for—God. Without God, no matter what we can acquire, accomplish, or achieve in life, we stay empty on the inside, always searching for what is missing in our lives.

Until we are supernaturally transformed by the power of Jesus Christ, we remain independent, disobedient, and rebellious to God's authority in our lives. Lying, stealing, being unkind to others, and refusing to forgive are all examples of our rebellion to God. Because God is holy, that rebellion and disobedience to God has separated us from God. There is nothing we can ever do in or of ourselves to make that right. That is why all religions, regardless of their system of good works, fail and fall short of God's righteousness. None of us can do enough good works to satisfy the justice accomplished through the redemption that is in Christ Jesus (Romans 3:21–26).

That's why the good news of the Bible is so important for each of us to understand. In the kindness of God, we are given the grace of God, so we can be forgiven by the perfect and complete work of Jesus Christ (Ephesians 2:7–10). God loved us so much he sent his son, Jesus Christ, to live a perfect life and model for us the joy of servant-hearted relationships instead of self-centered relationships (John 13:1–15). Jesus did for us what we could not do for ourselves. He paid for our sin by dying on the cross as the sacrificial Lamb of God (John 1:36). Different than Buddha or Muhammad who are still in the tomb, three days after Jesus died God raised him from the dead. We need a living Lord to change our lives (1 Corinthians 15:14). We need a living Lord to have the assurance that we can have eternal life (1 Corinthians 15:17). Jesus is a living Lord who has "paid it all," so God can forgive our sins and change our lives (1 Corinthians 15:20). When Jesus returned to heaven after his resurrection, he promised his disciples he would send the Holy Spirit to be their Counselor (John 16:7). The first thing the Holy Spirit counsels us about is in convicting us of our sinfulness and our need to repent and receive Christ (John 16:8–11).

The greatest privilege of life is to experience what you were created for—to have a loving and freeing relationship with your Creator. If you have not already done so, would you like to trust Jesus Christ's death on the cross for the payment of your sins and know you can be forgiven and cleansed from all your sin (1 John 1:9)? Do not rob yourself of the love, joy, and peace of living your life in Christ—no more guilt, shame, fear, condemnation, and confusion of what your life was created for.

To trust Jesus Christ to be your Lord and Savior, you must repent of your sins. Repenting means changing your mind about living life your way—doing whatever you want to do. You now trust God's Word as the authority of your life because

God's way is perfect. God can do such a better job with your life than you can. Jesus wants to be your life, your love, your joy, your peace, your passion, your purpose. Jesus wants to take the fear out of your life as you surrender your life to him as the King of kings and Lord of lords (Revelation 19:16).

If you have not yet known the joyous privilege of trusting Jesus Christ to be your Lord and Savior, I would love to sit down with you and take you through the Bible so you are able to read the Scriptures for yourself and see who God is (Deuteronomy 6:4), who Jesus is (see list in following pages), and who the Holy Spirit is (John 16:7–11). Salvation truly is an "inexpressible gift" (2 Corinthians 9:15) you can have. Do not miss out on knowing why you were created—to know God through his son, Jesus Christ!

If I could, I would open the Bible to the following seven scriptures and help you understand twelve key words, giving you the biblical foundation to truly trust Jesus Christ to be your Lord and Savior.

If you already know Christ as your Lord and Savior, review the following, and I encourage you to know the joy of seeing many come to trust Christ as their Lord and Savior as you share God's Word with them.

I.   The Bible Tells Us

   1.   Mark 1:15, NIV—"The time has come," he said. "The kingdom of God is near. Repent and believe the good news!"

      a.   repent (metanoeo)—This word means "to change one's mind or purpose," always in the New Testament, involving a change for the better; both noun and verb denote a radical moral turn of the whole person from sin and to God. True repentance is proven by "bearing fruit" and "performing deeds" in keeping with "changing our mind and purpose" (Matthew 3:8; Acts 26:20).

b. sin (hamartia)—This word means "a missing of the mark; it is the most comprehensive term for moral deviation." We are sinners by choice because we are sinners by nature (Romans 3:23). Parents never teach their children to be selfish, to lie, to fight, or to be rebellious. Sin is that attitude of independent rebellion that says, "God, I don't care what you say, I am going to do it my way."

c. believe (pisteuo)—This word means "to entrust something to someone; to rely upon completely; to be convinced of; to accept as true; to have faith in or to trust in God."

Because of who Jesus Christ is, we must change our minds about our sinfulness— independent rebellion to God. Entrusting our lives to God, we put our complete confidence in obeying the Word of God as our new authority.

2. John 3:1–7, NIV—"Now there was a man of the Pharisees named Nicodemus, a member of the Jewish ruling council. He came to Jesus at night and said, 'Rabbi, we know you are a teacher who has come from God. For no one could perform the miraculous signs you are doing if God were not with him.' In reply, Jesus declared, 'I tell you the truth, no one can see the kingdom of God unless he is born again.' 'How can a

man be born when he is old?' Nicodemus asked. 'Surely he cannot enter a second time into his mother's womb to be born!' Jesus answered, 'I tell you the truth, no one can enter the kingdom of God unless he is born of water and the Spirit. Flesh gives birth to flesh, but the Spirit gives birth to spirit.' You should not be surprised at my saying, 'You must be born again.'"

  a. born again (gennao)—This word means "to beget: It is used metaphorically in the writings of the Apostle John of the gracious act of God in conferring upon those who believe, the nature and disposition of children, imparting to them spiritual life."

Even all religious good persons must be "born again" by the Spirit. We need God to do something for us, to us, and in us. Receiving Jesus Christ into our lives by the person of the Holy Spirit, we are born again.

3. Romans 1:16–17, NIV—"I am not ashamed of the gospel, because it is the power of God for the salvation of everyone who believes: first for the Jew, then for the Gentile. For in the gospel a righteousness from God is revealed, a righteousness that is by faith from first to last, just as it is written: The righteous will live by faith."

  a. gospel (euangelion)—This word means "good news. In the New Testament it denotes the good tidings of the kingdom of God and of salvation through Christ, to be received by faith, on the basis of his life, death, burial, resurrection and ascension."

b. power (dunamis)—This word means "power in action, when put forth in performing miracles; it occurs 118 times in the New Testament."

c. righteousness (dikaioune)—This word means "the character or quality of being right or just; it is used to denote an attribute of God; essentially the same as his faithfulness or truthfulness, that which is consistent with his own nature and promises."

d. faith (pistis)—This word means a "firm persuasion, a conviction, a trust, an obedience based upon hearing the Word of God."

Since the gospel is the power of God that saves us, what exactly is the gospel? The gospel is 4Ws and 2Rs. The gospel is who Jesus is, what Jesus has done for us, what we need to do—the 2Rs—repent from our sinfulness and receive the person of the Holy Spirit into our lives, making Jesus Christ the Lord of our lives, and would you like to trust Jesus Christ now to be your personal Lord and Savior? Read now the 4Ws and 2Rs. You will love it. I encourage you to memorize this presentation:

II. Who Jesus Christ Is

He is the Almighty who has all power to change your life!

He is the Bread of Life who only can really satisfy your soul!

He is the Comforter who can comfort you in every heartache of your life!

He is the Deliverer who can free you from the bondage of all sin!

He is the Everlasting Lord who can give you eternal life!

He is the Faithful One who loves you in all your unfaithfulness!

He is the Giver of everything good!

He is the Hope of Glory who can give your life direction and purpose like nothing else!

He is the Invincible and Immortal Lord who wants to save you from wasting your life!

He is Just and knew sin must be paid for and he died to pay for your sin!

He is the King of kings and Lord of lords and truly worthy to trust with your life!

He is the Lord of Love who loves you more than you can ever comprehend!

He is the Messiah, the Most High God who can sure do a lot better job with your life than you can!

He is indescribable—there is None like him!

He is Open to receive you right now!

He is the Prince of Peace and until you have Jesus, you will search for what is missing in your life!

He is Quick to forgive and wants you to know freedom from guilt and the joy of forgiveness!

He is the Rock of our salvation, the Redeemer of all mankind, and the Resurrection and the life!

He is the Savior of the world and wants to be your personal Savior!

He is the Truth who can set your life free from living a lie!

He Understands you like you don't even understand yourself and loves you!

He is Victory and wants to be your victory!

He is Wisdom and can save you from making a lot of bad choices!

He is Excellent in all the earth!

He Yearns that you would know him as your personal Lord and Savior!

He is Zealous that no one or nothing would be more precious to you than himself!

III. What Jesus Christ Did for Us

He showed us what God is like (John 1:1–5, 14; 10:30)!

He showed us what life is for—a humble, servant-hearted relationship with the Father and one another versus living arrogant toward God, selfish, and self-centered with one another (Matthew 11:28–30; John 13:1–17)!

He accomplished in his death what religion could never do—he paid for our sin (Romans 3:21–24; 5:8–11; 6:23; 2 Corinthians 5:21)!

He arose from the grave (1 Corinthians 15:1–17)!

He "showed himself to his apostles and gave many convincing proofs that he was alive. He appeared to them over a period of forty days and spoke about the kingdom of God" (Acts 1:3)!

He promised his apostles: "But you will receive power when the Holy Spirit comes on you; and you will be my witnesses in Jerusalem, and in all Judea and Samaria, and to the ends of the earth" (Acts 1:8)!

He went back to heaven to be at the right hand of the Father (Acts 1:9; Hebrews 1:3; 1 Peter 3:22)!

He waits for you to receive him into your life as your Lord and Savior (John 1:12)!

4. Romans 3:21–25, NIV—"But now a righteousness from God, apart from law, has been made known, to which the Law and the Prophets testify. This righteousness from God comes through faith in Jesus Christ to all who believe. There is no difference, for all have sinned and fall short of the glory of God, and are justified freely by his grace through the redemption that came by Christ Jesus. God presented him as a sacrifice of atonement, through faith in his blood."

a. justified (dikaioo)—This word means "the legal and formal acquittal from guilt by God as judge, the pronouncement of the sinner as righteous, who believes on the Lord Jesus Christ."

We are justified freely by Jesus Christ's death on the cross.

IV. What We Must Do to Have a Relationship with Jesus Christ

By faith, trust Christ's death on the cross for the payment of your sins, receiving him by the person of the Holy Spirit into your life as your personal Lord and Savior (Ephesians 2:1–10; John 3:1–7; Romans 1:16–17; 2 Corinthians 5:17–21).

Receiving Jesus Christ as your Lord and Savior means repenting of your sinfulness—turning from your control to trust Christ as King of kings and Lord of lords to take control of your life (Matthew 4:17; Mark 1:15; Luke 3:8–9; 13:3; Acts 3:19; 26:20; 2 Corinthians 7:10).

5. 2 Corinthians 5:17–21, NIV—"Therefore, if anyone is in Christ, he is a new creation; the old has gone, the new has come! All this is from God, who reconciled us to himself through Christ and gave us the ministry of reconciliation: that God was reconciling the world to himself in Christ, not counting men's sins against them. And he has committed to us the message of reconciliation. We are therefore Christ's ambassadors, as though God were making his appeal through us. We implore you on Christ's behalf: Be reconciled to God. God made him who had no sin to be sin for us, so that in him we might become the righteousness of God."

a. reconciled (katallasso)—This word means "to change, exchange; of persons, to change from enmity to friendship; with regard to the relationship with God and man, the use of this and connected words shows that primarily reconciliation is what God accomplishes, exercising his grace toward sinful man to change their attitude. Until this change of attitude takes place men are under condemnation, exposed to God's wrath."

Trusting Jesus Christ to be our Lord and Savior, "the old has gone" and "the new has come" into our lives for the purpose of changing our attitudes about God, ourselves, and others.

6. Ephesians 2:1–10, NIV—"As for you, you were dead in your transgressions and sins, in which you used to live when you followed the ways of this world and of the ruler of the kingdom of the air, the spirit who is now at work in those who are disobedient. All of us also lived among them at one time, gratifying the cravings of our sinful nature and following its desires and thoughts. Like the rest, we were by nature objects of wrath. But because of his great love for us, God, who is rich in mercy, made us alive with Christ even when we were dead in transgressions—it is by grace you have been saved. And God raised us up with Christ and seated us with him in the heavenly realms in Christ Jesus, in order that in the coming ages he might show the incomparable riches of his grace, expressed in his kindness to us in Christ Jesus. For it is by grace you have been saved, through faith—and this not from yourselves, it is the

gift of God—not by works, so that no one can boast. For we are God's workmanship, created in Christ Jesus to do good works, which God prepared in advance for us to do."

   a. grace (charis)—This word means "unmerited favor, loving kindness, graciousness, goodwill; with reference to God, there is an emphasis on its freeness and universality, its spontaneous character, its redemptive mercy, and the pleasure or joy he designs for the recipient; thus, it is set in contrast with debt, with works and with law."

Without Jesus Christ in our lives, we are dead in our sins, disobedient to God, depraved in our sinful nature, and doomed to live with unresolved anger. But because of his great love for us… by grace we can be saved through faith.

V. Would You Like to Trust Jesus Christ Right Now to Be Your Lord and Savior?

   You only have one life to live. Jesus said: "I am the way, and the truth, and the life. No one comes to the Father except through me" (John 14:6). Do not miss what you were created for—Jesus Christ!

   7. Revelation 3:20, NIV—"Here I am! I stand at the door and knock. If anyone hears my voice and opens the door, I will come in and eat with him, and he with me."

      a. door (thura)—Even though the context of this verse is about God's warning to the church of

Laodicea to repent, which had become lukewarm, this word picture of Jesus "standing at the door and knocking at an individual's door" is a powerful and applicable way to speak "of Christ's entrance into a repentant believer's life."

(All definitions are from *W.E. Vine's Expository Dictionary of New Testament Words* and *Mounce's Complete Expository Dictionary of Old and New Testament Words*.)

You can receive him or reject him. The door represents your free will. If you have not yet, would you like to trust Jesus Christ by the person of the Holy Spirit to come into your life right now and be your Lord and Savior? If yes, pray:

Dear God, thank you for loving me and allowing Jesus Christ to die on the cross to pay for my sins. I am a sinner and I desperately need your forgiveness. I repent. I change my mind about disobeying you. I change my mind about who is trustworthy to be my authority. You are Lord. I change my mind about my purpose for living. I want you Lord to be my life. I surrender my life to you as the King of kings and Lord of lords. I ask you by your Holy Spirit to come into my life and take control of my life. Thank you, God, for giving me a new life in Jesus Christ. Thank you, God, for giving me eternal life. I choose to trust you and follow you as my Lord and Savior for the rest of my life. I love you, Lord. Thank you for loving me and saving me. In Jesus's name, I pray. Amen.

On the authority of God's Word, I welcome you to the family of God. Praise the Lord!

Thinking God—Whereas Jesus wants to give you abundant life, sin leads to broken relationships and brings suffering (John 10:10).

Truth to Remember—Without God, no matter what we can acquire, accomplish, or achieve in life, we stay empty on the inside, always searching for what is missing in our lives (1 John 5:12).

Thinking God in Reflecting—Reading through the "Who Jesus Christ Is" list, isn't that who everyone is searching for? That's why I share Jesus with everyone I can. Are you sharing Jesus with others (Mark 1:17)?

Thinking God: Why Were You Saved?

Memorize God's Word!

"Blessed are the poor in spirit, for theirs is the kingdom of heaven. Blessed are those who mourn, for they shall be comforted. Blessed are the meek, for they shall inherit the earth. Blessed are those who hunger and thirst for righteousness, for they shall be satisfied. Blessed are the merciful, for they shall receive mercy. Blessed are the pure in heart, for they shall see God. Blessed are the peacemakers, for they shall be called sons of God. Blessed are those who are persecuted for righteousness' sake, for theirs is the kingdom of heaven. Blessed are you when others revile you and persecute you and utter all kinds of evil against you falsely on my account. Rejoice and be glad, for your reward is great in heaven, for so they persecuted the prophets who were before you. You are the salt of the earth, but if salt has lost its taste, how shall its saltiness be restored? It is no longer good for anything except to be thrown out and trampled under people's feet.

You are the light of the world. A city set on a hill cannot be hidden. Nor do people light a lamp and put it under a basket, but on a stand, and it gives light to all in the house. In the same way, let your light shine before others, so that they may see your good works and give glory to your Father who is in heaven" (Matthew 5:3–16).

"And you shall love the Lord your God with all your heart and with all your soul and with all your mind and with all your strength. The second is this: 'You shall love your neighbor as yourself.' There is no other commandment greater than these" (Mark 12:30–31).

"And he said to all, 'If anyone would come after me, let him deny himself and take up his cross daily and follow me'" (Luke 9:23).

"And he told this parable: 'A man had a fig tree planted in his vineyard, and he came seeking fruit on it and found none. And he said to the vinedresser, 'Look, for three years now I have come seeking fruit on this fig tree, and I find none. Cut it down. Why should it use up the ground?'" (Luke 13:6–7).

"And the Word became flesh and dwelt among us, and we have seen his glory, glory as of the only Son from the Father, full of grace and truth" (John 1:14).

"So Jesus said to the Jews who had believed him, 'If you abide in my word, you are truly my disciples, and you will know the truth, and the truth will set you free'" (John 8:31–32).

"My sheep hear my voice, and I know them, and they follow me" (John 10:27).

"Jesus said to her, 'I am the resurrection and the life. Whoever believes in me, though he die, yet shall he live'" (John 11:25).

"I am the vine; you are the branches. Whoever abides in me and I in him, he it is that bears much fruit, for apart from me you can do nothing. If anyone does not abide in me he is thrown away like a branch and withers; and the branches are gathered, thrown into the fire, and burned. If you abide in me, and my words abide in you, ask whatever you wish, and it will be done for you. By this my Father is glorified, that you bear much fruit and so prove to be my disciples" (John 15:5–8).

"But you will receive power when the Holy Spirit has come upon you, and you will be my witnesses in Jerusalem and in all Judea and Samaria, and to the end of the earth" (Acts 1:8).

"For in it the righteousness of God is revealed from faith for faith, as it is written, 'The righteous shall live by faith'" (Romans 1:17).

⁊

I n the summer of 1986, I had the privilege of going to Estes Park, Colorado to meet several Christian artists who I would enlist for the next several years to be a part of an annual state youth evangelism conference at the Forum in Worlds of Fun in Kansas City, Missouri. One such artist was Michael Peterson who was not only a talented singer but also had been trained as a member of the Power Team to perform incredible feats of strength. On this particular evening, Michael was blowing up with his mouth a hot water bottle guaranteed not to break or leak. Because Michael had stretched the water bottle before the event like you can do with any balloon before you blow it up to expand its capacity, this hot water balloon became four to five feet in diameter before it exploded like a bomb with him laying on it and blowing away. Completely amazed, I excitedly left my chair in the audience to go and meet Michael as he was leaving the stage.

Learning in our conversation that Michael had grown up and gone to high school the same time I had served in a church less than a mile from his school gave us an immediate connection. I invited Michael to be a part of a state youth evangelism conference at Worlds of Fun the following summer. Ministering together that summer, God gave us a heart and vision to work together much like Michael had previously done with the Power Team. Through my networking with Missouri Baptist pastors and youth pastors who had good relationships with the leadership of schools in their area, we would schedule a week of services with their church and a number of assemblies in area schools. Michael would do two to three assemblies a day in the schools demonstrating his incredible feats of strength before hundreds and sometimes thousands of students. Michael would also share parts of his life which were filled with great tragedy and brokenness, bringing many students to tears. This encouraging message was also always shared, "I have learned there is hope and healing for every hurt and heartache in our lives." At the close of each assembly, Michael would invite the students and faculty to bring their families and come each night to such and such church "to see more feats of strength and hear how you can know this hope and healing in your life and be the best you can possibly be." Hundreds came to each evening event.

Each night, Michael would begin the evening with more incredible feats, incorporating in his presentation how Jesus Christ had supernaturally and radically changed his life. After thirty to forty minutes of high energy and excitement, Michael would introduce me as a good friend who had the privilege of teaching thousands of students each year how Jesus Christ could change their lives.

I would preach the Word of God presenting the gospel of Jesus and extend an invitation to trust Jesus Christ as their

Lord and Savior. During those many invitations, I always encouraged the audience with the words, "Do not live beneath your privilege. Trust your life wholeheartedly to Jesus Christ!"

Think what your life would be like if you really began to live the following statements:

You were saved to be radically changed (Matthew 5:3–10).

You were saved to rejoice and be glad because great is your reward in heaven (Matthew 5:12).

You were saved to make a difference in this world (Matthew 5:13–15).

You were saved to bring glory to God (Matthew 5:16).

You were saved to experience the release and freedom of forgiveness from your heavenly Father (Matthew 6:14–15).

You were saved to serve one master, Jesus Christ. (Matthew 6:24).

You were saved not to worry but to seek first the reign of God in your life (Matthew 6:25–33).

You were saved to bear much fruit (Matthew 7:16, 20).

You were saved to practice the Lord's words (Matthew 7:24).

You were saved to build your life on the foundation of Jesus Christ (Matthew 7:25–27).

You were saved to be a worker in the Lord's harvest (Matthew 9:38).

You were saved to rest in the Lord (Matthew 11:28).

You were saved to learn from the Lord (Matthew 11:29).

You were saved to think humility (Matthew 18:3–4).

You were saved to forgive others just as you have been forgiven (Matthew 18:21–35).

You were saved to be a servant (Matthew 20:26–28).

You were saved to give to Caesar what is Caesar's, and to God what is God's (Matthew 22:21).

You were saved to live with a passion to faithfully please him (Matthew 25:21).

You were saved to go and make disciples of all nations (Matthew 28:19).

You were saved to be a fisher of men (Mark 1:17).

You were saved to have in mind the things of God rather than the things of men (Mark 8:33).

You were saved to deny yourself, take up your cross, and follow Christ (Mark 8:34).

You were saved to lose your life for Christ and for the gospel (Mark 8:35).

You were saved to not be ashamed of Christ and his words (Mark 8:38).

You were saved to be a servant of all (Mark 9:35).

You were saved to love the Lord God with all your heart, and with all your soul, and with all your mind, and with all your strength (Mark 12:30).

You were saved to love your neighbor as yourself (Mark 12:31).

You were saved to give the Lord your extravagant best, not your leftovers (Mark 14:9).

You were saved to obey the Lord just because he says so (Luke 5:5).

You were saved to do to others as you would have them do to you (Luke 6:31).

You were saved to love your enemies and do good to them (Luke 6:35).

You were saved to be merciful, just as your Father is merciful (Luke 6:36).

You were saved to give and it will be given to you (Luke 6:38).

You were saved to exercise great faith by living under the Lord's authority (Luke 7:9).

You were saved to deny yourself and die daily and follow Christ (Luke 9:23).

You were saved to never look back in being wholeheartedly committed to the Lord's service (Luke 9:62).

You were saved to be a faithful worker in the harvest (Luke 10:2).

You were saved to be a good neighbor to those in need (Luke 10:36–37).

You were saved to be humbly listening at the Lord's feet (Luke 10:42).

You were saved to be a prayer warrior (Luke 11:10).

You were saved to receive the Holy Spirit (Luke 11:13).

You were saved to not worry about what you say when you speak about the Lord (Luke 12:11).

You were saved to bear fruit showing your repentance (Luke 13:6–7).

You were saved because you entered through the narrow gate (Luke 13:24).

You were saved to go and share the gospel with others (Luke 14:23).

You were saved to count the cost and give up everything to be the Lord's disciple (Luke 14:28–33).

You were saved to serve God, not money (Luke 16:13).

You were saved to obey your Lord in everything (Luke 17:10).

You were saved to have the kingdom of God within you (Luke 17:21).

You were saved to always pray and not give up (Luke 18:1).

You were saved to see the Lord's glory (John 1:14).

You were saved to tell others about Jesus (John 1:41).

You were saved to have eternal life (John 3:16).

You were saved to live by the truth in the Lord's light (John 3:21).

You were saved so that Jesus might increase and you must decrease (John 3:30).

You were saved to be free of condemnation (John 8:11).

You were saved to hold to the Lord's teaching and be set free in his truth (John 8:31–32).

You were saved to have life and have it abundantly (John 10:10).

You were saved to know and listen to the Lord's voice (John 10:27).

You were saved to no longer fear death, trusting Jesus to be the resurrection and the life. (John 11:25).

You were saved to have loving and lasting relationships (John 13:34–35).

You were saved to bear much fruit and so prove to be the Lord's disciple (John 15:5–8).

You were saved to keep the Lord's commandments (John 15:10).

You were saved to receive the power of the Holy Spirit and be the Lord's witness (Acts 1:8).

You were saved to be filled with the Holy Spirit (Acts 2:4).

You were saved to be devoted to the Word of God (Acts 2:42a).

You were saved to be devoted to a church family (Acts 2:42b).

You were saved to be devoted to prayer (Acts 2:42c).

You were saved to stand strong in the courage of the Lord (Acts 4:13).

You were saved to be one in heart and mind with your brothers and sisters in Christ (Acts 4:32a).

You were saved to be a sacrificial giver (Acts 4:32b).

You were saved to testify with great power the resurrection of Jesus Christ (Acts 4:33).

You were saved to never stop teaching and proclaiming the good news that Jesus is the Christ (Acts 5:42).

You were saved to have breakthroughs in your understanding of life in Christ (Acts 10:34).

You were saved to keep your eyes on Jesus in your trials knowing the power of praise in the midnights of your life (Acts 16:25).

You were saved to use your needs as a means to minister instead of an excuse to minister (Acts 16:28–31).

You were saved to impact the world for Christ (Acts 17:6).

You were saved to be an encouragement to many (Acts 20:2).

You were saved to know the blessed life of giving (Acts 20:35).

You were saved to do anything to have the Lord's will be done in your life (Acts 21:12–14).

You were saved to not be ashamed of the gospel (Romans 1:16).

You were saved to live by faith (Romans 1:17).

You were saved by God's kindness to repent (Romans 2:4).

You were saved and were justified freely by Christ's grace through faith in his blood (Romans 3:23–24).

You were saved to rejoice in the hope of the glory of God (Romans 5:2).

You were saved to rejoice in your sufferings knowing suffering produces perseverance, character, and hope (Romans 5:3).

You were saved to humbly live your redeemed position in Jesus Christ (Romans 6:11).

You were saved to be controlled by the Spirit of God who lives in you (Romans 8:9).

You were saved to know that in all things God works for the good of those who love him, who have been called according to his purpose (Romans 8:28).

You were saved to be conformed to the likeness of Jesus Christ (Romans 8:29).

You were saved to rest in knowing, "if God is for you, who can be against you" (Romans 8:31).

You were saved to rest in God's sovereignty, knowing Jesus Christ is at the right hand of God interceding for you (Romans 8:34).

You were saved to be more than a conqueror through Jesus Christ regardless of your circumstances (Romans 8:37–39).

You were saved to rest and rejoice that nothing can separate you from the love of God (Romans 8:37).

You were saved to offer your body as a living sacrifice, holy and pleasing to God which is your reasonable worship to God (Romans 12:1).

You were saved to be transformed by Thinking God so you can live his good, pleasing, and perfect will (Romans 12:2).

You were saved to belong to the body of Christ (Romans 12:5).

You were saved to love (Romans 12:9a).

You were saved to hate what is evil and cling to what is good (Romans 12:9b).

You were saved to honor one another above yourselves (Romans 12:10).

You were saved to keep your spiritual fervor, serving the Lord (Romans 12:11).

You were saved to be joyful in hope, patient in affliction, and faithful in prayer (Romans 12:12).

You were saved to share with God's people who are in need (Romans 12:13).

You were saved to bless those who persecute you (Romans 12:14).

You were saved to rejoice with those who rejoice and mourn with those who mourn (Romans 12:15).

You were saved to live in harmony with one another (Romans 12:16a).

You were saved to not be proud or conceited (Romans 12:16b).

You were saved to not repay anyone evil for evil (Romans 12:17a).

You were saved to be careful to do what is right (Romans 12:17b).

You were saved as far as it depends on you, to live at peace with everyone (Romans 12:18).

You were saved to not take revenge knowing that belongs to the Lord (Romans 12:19).

You were saved to overcome evil with good (Romans 12:21).

You were saved to submit to governing authorities (Romans 13:1).

You were saved to pay the taxes you owe (Romans 13:7).

You were saved to pay your debts (Romans 13:8).

You were saved to put aside the deeds of darkness and put on the armor of light (Romans 13:12).

You were saved to not think about how to gratify the desires of the sinful nature (Romans 13:14).

You were saved to accept those whose faith is weak, without passing judgment on disputable matters (Romans 14:1).

You were saved to give an account of yourself to God (Romans 14:12).

You were saved to stop passing judgment on one another (Romans 14:13a).

You were saved to not put any stumbling block in your brother's way (Romans 14:13b).

You were saved to make every effort to do what leads to peace and to mutual edification (Romans 14:19).

You were saved to bear with the failings of the weak and not please yourself (Romans 15:1).

You were saved to live with endurance, encouragement of the Scriptures, and hope (Romans 15:4).

You were saved to be filled with all joy and peace as you trust in God (Romans 15:13a).

You were saved to be full of goodness (Romans 15:14a).

You were saved to instruct one another (Romans 15:14b).

You were saved to watch out for those who cause divisions and stay away from them (Romans 16:17).

You were saved to be wise about what is good and innocent about what is evil (Romans 16:19).

You were saved to be sanctified in Christ Jesus and called to be holy (1 Corinthians 1:2).

You were saved to be enriched in every way—in all your speaking and in all your knowledge (1 Corinthians 1:5).

You were saved to be kept strong to the end so you will be blameless on the day of our Lord Jesus Christ (1 Corinthians 1:8).

You were saved to know the power of God (1 Corinthians 1:18).

You were saved to have Christ's wisdom, righteousness, holiness, and redemption (1 Corinthians 1:30).

You were saved to boast in the Lord (1 Corinthians 1:31).

You were saved to have what "no eye has seen, no ear has heard, or no mind has conceived what God has prepared for you" (1 Corinthians 2:9).

You were saved to be a spiritual person who makes judgments about all things (1 Corinthians 2:15).

You were saved to have the mind of Christ (1 Corinthians 2:16).

You were saved to know that you are God's temple and that God's Spirit lives in you (1 Corinthians 3:16).

You were saved to be entrusted with the secret things of God and required to be faithful (1 Corinthians 4:1–2).

You were saved to honor God with your body (1 Corinthians 6:20).

You were saved to be defined by obeying God's commands (1 Corinthians 7:19b).

You were saved to run in such a way not to be disqualified, as to get the prize (1 Corinthians 9:24-27).

You were saved to bring glory to God (1 Corinthians 10:31).

You were saved to not seek your own good but the good of many, so that they may be saved (1 Corinthians 10:33).

You were saved to be a part of the body of Christ (1 Corinthians 12:27).

You were saved to live the most excellent way—love (1 Corinthians 13).

You were saved to follow the way of love and eagerly desire spiritual gifts (1 Corinthians 14:1).

You were saved to excel in gifts that build up the church (1 Corinthians 14:12).

You were saved to live in a fitting and orderly way (1 Corinthians 14:40).

You were saved to not be misled by bad company (1 Corinthians 15:33).

You were saved to be changed at death and be raised imperishable (1 Corinthians 15:53).

You were saved to live with victory through our Lord Jesus Christ (1 Corinthians 15:57).

You were saved to stand firm, always giving yourself fully to the work of the Lord (1 Corinthians 15:58).

You were saved to be comforted by God in all your troubles, so you can comfort those in any trouble (2 Corinthians 1:3–4).

You were saved to rely completely on God who raises the dead (2 Corinthians 1:9).

You were saved to set your hope on God who delivers you (2 Corinthians 1:10).

You were saved to stand firm in Christ (2 Corinthians 1:21).

You were saved with Christ's seal of ownership on you with his Spirit in your heart as a deposit guaranteeing what is to come (2 Corinthians 1:22).

You were saved to stand the test and be obedient in everything (2 Corinthians 2:9).

You were saved to not be outwitted by Satan's schemes (2 Corinthians 2:11).

You were saved to always be led in triumphal procession, and spread the fragrance of the knowledge of him everywhere (2 Corinthians 2:14).

You were saved to be competent as a minister of the new covenant (2 Corinthians 3:6).

You were saved to live in the freedom of the Lord (2 Corinthians 3:17).

You were saved to be transformed into Christ's likeness with ever increasing glory from the Lord (2 Corinthians 3:18).

You were saved to live with his perspective (2 Corinthians 4:18).

You were saved to be supernaturally and radically changed by God (2 Corinthians 5:17–18).

You were saved to be Christ's ambassadors (2 Corinthians 5:20).

You were saved to be the righteousness of God (2 Corinthians 5:21).

You were saved to not be yoked together with unbelievers (2 Corinthians 6:14).

You were saved to live in perfect holiness out of your reverence for God (2 Corinthians 7:1).

You were saved to live in repentance to sinfulness leaving no regret (2 Corinthians 7:10).

You were saved to give yourself first to the Lord and reflect that commitment in the rich generosity of your giving (2 Corinthians 8:2–5).

You were saved to be rich in the grace of the Lord Jesus Christ (2 Corinthians 8:9).

You were saved to do right in the eyes of the Lord and the eyes of your brothers and sisters in Christ (2 Corinthians 8:22).

You were saved to give, generously knowing you will reap generously (2 Corinthians 9:6, 8).

You were saved to give not reluctantly or under compulsion but with a hilarious heart (2 Corinthians 9:7).

You were saved to receive his inexpressible gift of grace in Christ Jesus (2 Corinthians 9:14–15).

You were saved to demolish arguments and pretentions that set themselves up against the knowledge of God (2 Corinthians 10:5a).

You were saved to take captive every thought to make it obedient to Christ (2 Corinthians 10:5b).

You were saved to know in your weakness Christ's power is made perfect (2 Corinthians 12:9).

You were saved to have grace and peace from God our Father and the Lord Jesus Christ (Galatians 1:3).

You were saved to be crucified with Christ and live by faith in the Son of God who loved you and gave himself for you (Galatians 2:20).

You were saved to all be one in Christ—Jew, Greek, slave, free, male, female (Galatians 3:28).

You were saved to belong to Christ, be Abraham's seed and heir according to the promise (Galatians 3:29).

You were saved to have the Spirit of his Son into your heart, crying "Abba! Father!" (Galatians 4:6).

You were saved to have freedom in Christ to stand firm and not be burdened again by a yoke of slavery (Galatians 5:1).

You were saved to run a good race in obeying the truth (Galatians 5:7).

You were saved to not use your freedom to indulge the sinful nature but serve one another in love (Galatians 5:13).

You were saved to live by the Spirit and not gratify the desires of the sinful nature (Galatians 5:16).

You were saved to experience the fruit of the Spirit (Galatians 5:22–23).

You were saved to restore those caught in sin gently (Galatians 6:1).

You were saved to carry each other's burdens and fulfill the law of Christ (Galatians 6:2).

You were saved to not be deceived and sow to please the Spirit (Galatians 6:8).

You were saved to not become weary and give up in doing good (Galatians 6:9).

You were saved to boast in the cross of our Lord Jesus Christ through which the world has been crucified to you (Galatians 6:14).

You were saved to be blessed in the heavenly realms with every spiritual blessing in Christ (Ephesians 1:3).

You were saved because you were chosen before the creation of the world (Ephesians 1:4).

You were saved to be adopted as his sons through Jesus Christ in accordance with his pleasure and will (Ephesians 1:5).

You were saved to the praise of his glorious grace (Ephesians 1:6).

You were saved to have redemption through his blood (Ephesians 1:7).

You were saved in accordance with the riches of God's grace that he lavished on us with all wisdom and understanding (Ephesians 1:8).

You were saved, having been predestined according to the plan of Christ who works out everything in conformity with the purpose of his will (Ephesians 1:11).

You were saved to be marked in Christ with a seal, the promised Holy Spirit (Ephesians 1:13).

You were saved to have the eyes of your heart enlightened so you may know the hope to which he has called you (Ephesians 1:18).

You were saved to have his mighty power and strength which was exerted in Christ when he was raised from the dead and seated at God's right hand in the heavenly realms (Ephesians 1:19–20).

You were saved to know God's grace expressed in his kindness in Christ Jesus (Ephesians 2:7–8).

You were saved to be God's workmanship created in Christ Jesus to do good works which God prepared in advance for you (Ephesians 2:10).

You were saved to know Christ as your peace (Ephesians 2:14).

You were saved to be a dwelling in which God lives by his Spirit (Ephesians 2:22).

You were saved to approach God with freedom and confidence (Ephesians 3:12).

You were saved to be strengthened with power through his Spirit (Ephesians 3:16).

You were saved to be rooted and established in love to grasp how wide and long and high and deep is the love of Christ (Ephesians 3:17–18).

You were saved to know the love of God that surpasses knowledge (Ephesians 3:19).

You were saved to have more done in you and through you than you could ask or imagine according to his power at work in you (Ephesians 3:20).

You were saved to live a life worthy of the calling you have received (Ephesians 4:1).

You were saved to be completely humble, gentle, and patient, bearing with one another in love (Ephesians 4:2).

You were saved to make every effort to keep the unity of the Spirit through the bond of peace (Ephesians 4:3).

You were saved to be prepared for works of service (Ephesians 4:12).

You were saved to become mature, attaining the fullness of Christ (Ephesians 4:13).

You were saved to grow up into Christ doing the work God saved you for (Ephesians 4:16).

You were saved to put off your old self and to put on the new self, created to be like God in true righteousness and holiness (Ephesians 4:24).

You were saved to not let the sun go down while you are still angry, giving the devil a foothold (Ephesians 4:26–27).

You were saved to build others up according to their needs (Ephesians 4:29).

You were saved to get rid of all bitterness, rage, and anger (Ephesians 4:31).

You were saved to be kind and compassionate to one another, forgiving each other, just as in Christ, God forgave you (Ephesians 4:32).

You were saved to be an imitator of God and live a life of love giving yourself as an offering and sacrifice to him (Ephesians 5:1–2).

You were saved to be filled with the Holy Spirit (Ephesians 5:17–18).

You were saved to speak to one another with psalms, hymns, and spiritual songs (Ephesians 5:19).

You were saved to give thanks to God for everything (Ephesians 5:20).

You were saved to submit to one another out of reverence for Christ (Ephesians 5:21).

You were saved to be strong in the Lord and in the strength of his might (Ephesians 6:10).

You were saved to put on the full armor of God so you can stand against the devil's schemes (Ephesians 6:11).

You were saved to be confident of making progress in your walk with God because of his working in you (Philippians 1:6).

You were saved to be able to discern what is best (Philippians 1:10).

You were saved to be filled with the fruit of the righteousness that comes through Jesus Christ (Philippians 1:11).

You were saved to know Christ and to die is gain (Philippians 1:21).

You were saved to conduct yourself in a manner worthy of the gospel of Christ (Philippians 1:27).

You were saved to do nothing out of selfish ambition, but in humility, to consider others better than yourself (Philippians 2:3).

You were saved to have the same attitude of humility as Christ (Philippians 2:5).

You were saved to work out your salvation with fear and trembling (Philippians 2:12).

You were saved to do everything without complaining or arguing (Philippians 2:14).

You were saved to shine as lights in the world, holding fast to the word of life (Philippians 2:15–16).

You were saved to know Christ's power (Philippians 3:10).

You were saved to press on to take hold of that for which Christ Jesus took hold of you (Philippians 3:12).

You were saved to forget what is behind and strain toward what is ahead (Philippians 3:13–14).

You were saved to rejoice in the Lord always (Philippians 4:4).

You were saved to let your meekness be evident to all (Philippians 4:5).

You were saved to not be anxious about anything but live with a grateful confidence in the Lord in all your circumstances (Philippians 4:6).

You were saved to be guarded with his peace (Philippians 4:7).

You were saved to think on those things that are true, noble, right, pure, lovely, admirable, excellent, and praiseworthy (Philippians 4:8).

You were saved to learn to be contented in the Lord in all your circumstances because of his strength in your life (Philippians 4:11–13).

You were saved to know all your needs will be met in Christ Jesus (Philippians 4:19).

You were saved to understand God's grace in all its truth (Colossians 1:6).

You were saved to be filled with the knowledge of God's will through all spiritual wisdom and understanding (Colossians 1:9).

You were saved to live a life worthy of the Lord in pleasing him in every way, bearing fruit in every good work, growing in the knowledge of God and being strengthened with his power (Colossians 1:10–11a).

You were saved to have great endurance and patience joyfully giving thanks to the Father (Colossians 1:11b–12).

You were saved to be rescued from the dominion of darkness to be brought into the kingdom of the Son God loves (Colossians 1:13).

You were saved to be held together by the person and power of Christ (Colossians 1:17).

You were saved to live with Christ's preeminence (Colossians 1:18).

You were saved to be reconciled to Christ from being an enemy in your mind to God and have his peace by the blood of his cross (Colossians 1:20–21).

You were saved to be established and firm in your faith (Colossians 1:23).

You were saved to have Christ in you, the hope of glory (Colossians 1:27).

You were saved to continue to live in Christ, rooted and built up in him, strengthened in the faith of God's Word and overflowing with thankfulness (Colossians 2:6–7).

You were saved to not be taken captive by any hollow and deceptive philosophy which depends on human tradition and the principles of this world, but rather on Christ (Colossians 2:8).

You were saved to have fullness in Christ over every power and authority (Colossians 2:10).

You were saved to be buried with him in baptism and raised with him through your faith in the power of God who raised him from the dead (Colossians 2:12).

You were saved to die with Christ to the basic principles of this world (Colossians 2:20).

You were saved to set your heart on things above (Colossians 3:1–2).

You were saved to have your life hidden with Christ in God (Colossians 3:3).

You were saved to appear with Christ in glory (Colossians 3:4).

You were saved to put to death whatever belongs to your earthly nature (Colossians 3:5).

You were saved to put on the new self, which is being renewed in knowledge in the image of its Creator through Christ (Colossians 3:10–11).

You were saved to clothe yourself with compassion, kindness, humility, gentleness, and patience (Colossians 3:12).

You were saved to forgive as the Lord forgave you (Colossians 3:13).

You were saved to let the peace of Christ rule in your heart (Colossians 3:15).

You were saved to let the word of Christ dwell in you richly as you teach and admonish one another (Colossians 3:16).

You were saved to do everything in the name of the Lord Jesus giving thanks to God the Father through him (Colossians 3:17).

You were saved in whatever you do, to work at it with all your heart as working unto the Lord, not for men (Colossians 3:23).

You were saved to wrestle in prayer for others that they may stand firm in all the will of God (Colossians 4:12).

You were saved to work because of your faith, to labor because of your love, and to endure because of your hope in the Lord Jesus Christ (1 Thessalonians 1:3).

You were saved to not have a life of only words but to live with the power of the Holy Spirit and deep conviction (1 Thessalonians 1:5).

You were saved to be a model to other believers (1 Thessalonians 1:7).

You were saved to turn from idols to serve the living and true God (1 Thessalonians 1:9).

You were saved to not please men but God, who tests our hearts (1 Thessalonians 2:4).

You were saved to not be unsettled by your trials (1 Thessalonians 3:3).

You were saved to have your love increase and overflow for one another (1 Thessalonians 3:12).

You were saved to have your heart strengthened so you will be blameless and holy in the presence of your God and Father when our Lord Jesus comes with all his holy ones 1 (Thessalonians 3:13).

You were saved to be sanctified and avoid sexual immorality (1 Thessalonians 4:3).

You were saved to learn to control your own body in a way that is holy and honorable (1 Thessalonians 4:4).

You were saved to live a holy life (1 Thessalonians 4:7).

You were saved to live your daily life so it would win the respect of outsiders and not be dependent on anybody (1 Thessalonians 4:12).

You were saved to not grieve like the world who have no hope (1 Thessalonians 4:13).

You were saved to live encouraged knowing we will be with the Lord forever (1 Thessalonians 4:17–18).

You were saved to be alert and self-controlled, putting on faith and love as a breastplate (1 Thessalonians 5:6, 8).

You were saved to encourage and build each other up (1 Thessalonians 5:1).

You were saved to be kind to each other, not paying anybody wrong for wrong (1 Thessalonians 5:15).

You were saved to pray without ceasing and give thanks in all circumstances confident your God is in charge of everything (1 Thessalonians 5:16–18).

You were saved to not put out the Spirit's fire (1 Thessalonians 5:19).

You were saved to test everything and hold onto the good and avoid every kind of evil (1 Thessalonians 5:21).

You were saved to be sanctified through and through and kept blameless at the coming of the Lord Jesus Christ (1 Thessalonians 5:23).

You were saved to persevere in your faith in all persecutions and trials (2 Thessalonians 1:4).

You were saved to share in the glory of your Lord Jesus Christ (2 Thessalonians 2:14).

You were saved to stand firm and hold to the teachings of God's Word (2 Thessalonians 2:15).

You were saved to be encouraged in your heart and be strengthened in every good deed and word (2 Thessalonians 2:17).

You were saved to be strengthened and protected from the evil one (2 Thessalonians 3:23).

You were saved to work and be a model to others to follow (2 Thessalonians 3:7–9).

You were saved to never tire of doing what is right obeying the Word of God (2 Thessalonians 3:13).

You were saved to have peace from the Lord of peace at all times (2 Thessalonians 3:16).

You were saved because you were shown mercy and unlimited patience as an example of those who would believe (1 Timothy 1:16).

You were saved to fight the good fight, holding on to faith, and a good conscience (1 Timothy 1:18–19).

You were saved to know God wants all men to be saved and come to a knowledge of truth (1 Timothy 2:4).

You were saved to lift up holy hands in prayer without anger or disputing (1 Timothy 2:8).

You were saved to train yourself to be godly (1 Timothy 4:7).

You were saved to put your hope in the living God (1 Timothy 4:10).

You were saved to watch your life and doctrine closely and persevere in them (1 Timothy 4:16).

You were saved to care for your own family and so repaying your parents and grandparents for their care for you (1 Timothy 5:4).

You were saved to keep yourself pure (1 Timothy 5:22).

You were saved to flee from the temptation to love money and pursue righteousness, godliness, faith, love, endurance and meekness (1 Timothy 6:11).

You were saved to be generous and willing to share (1 Timothy 6:18).

You were saved to not live with a spirit of fearfulness but with the Spirit of power, love, and self-control because God is in control of your life (2 Timothy 1:7).

You were saved to live a holy life because of Christ's own purpose and grace (2 Timothy 1:9).

You were saved to not be ashamed of Jesus, because you know whom you have believed and are convinced that he is able to guard what you have entrusted to him (2 Timothy 1:12).

You were saved to guard the good deposit that was entrusted to you (2 Timothy 1:14).

You were saved to be strong in the grace that is in Christ Jesus (2 Timothy 2:1).

You were saved to endure hardship like a good soldier of Christ Jesus (2 Timothy 2:3).

You were saved to know when you are faithless, Christ Jesus will be faithful (2 Timothy 2:13).

You were saved to present yourself to God as one approved, a workman who does not need to be ashamed and who correctly handles the word of truth (2 Timothy 2:15).

You were saved to avoid godless chatter (2 Timothy 2:16).

You were saved to not have anything to do with foolish and stupid arguments, because they produce quarrels (2 Timothy 2:23).

You were saved to be thoroughly equipped for every good work by Thinking God according to his Word (2 Timothy 3:16–17).

You were saved to be prepared in season and out of season (2 Timothy 4:2).

You were saved to fight the good fight, finish the race and keep the faith (2 Timothy 4:7).

You were saved to receive the crown of righteousness which the Lord will award to you on his appearing (2 Timothy 4:8).

You were saved to be in everything an example by doing what is good (Titus 2:7).

You were saved to be peaceable and considerate and to show true humility toward all men (Titus 3:2).

You were saved to become God's heir having the hope of eternal life (Titus 3:7).

You were saved to avoid foolish controversies and arguments and quarrels about the law (Titus 3:9).

You were saved to not be a divisive person (Titus 3:10).

You were saved to be active in sharing your faith (Philemon 6).

You were saved to refresh the hearts of your brothers and sisters in Christ (Philemon 7).

You were saved to encourage other brothers and sisters in Christ when they struggle to live the truth of God's Word (Philemon 10).

You were saved to forgive others freely because you have been forgiven freely (Philemon 17).

You were saved to be sustained by his powerful Word (Hebrews 1:3).

You were saved to not drift away (Hebrews 2:2).

You were saved to be perfected through suffering (Hebrews 2:10).

You were saved to be made holy (Hebrews 2:11).

You were saved to be helped when you are tempted (Hebrews 2:18).

You were saved to share in the heavenly calling, so fix your thoughts on Jesus (Hebrews 3:1).

You were saved to be God's house and to hold on to your courage and the hope of which you boast (Hebrews 3:6).

You were saved to not harden your heart (Hebrews 3:8).

You were saved to be transformed by the Word of God which is living and active, sharper than any double-edged sword (Hebrews 4:12).

You were saved to have everything uncovered and laid bare before the Lord whom you must give an account (Hebrews 4:12).

You were saved to approach the throne of grace with confidence, so you may receive mercy and find grace to help you in your time of need (Hebrews 4:16).

You were saved to learn obedience from what you suffer (Hebrews 5:8).

You were saved to grow and leave the elementary teachings about Christ and go on to maturity (Hebrews 6:1).

You were saved to take hold of the hope of Christ as an anchor for your soul, being firm and secure (Hebrews 6:19).

You were saved to have Jesus, the guarantee of a better covenant (Hebrews 7:22).

You were saved to have Jesus, a high priest who meets our need—one who is holy, blameless, pure, set apart from sinners, exalted above the heavens (Hebrews 7:26).

You were saved by the shedding of the blood of Christ (Hebrews 9:22).

You were saved to face judgment knowing you are forgiven (Hebrews 9:27).

You were saved to draw near to God with a sincere heart in full assurance of faith (Hebrews 10:22).

You were saved to hold unswervingly to the hope we profess in Christ (Hebrews 10:23).

You were saved to spur one another on toward love and good deeds (Hebrews 10:24).

You were saved to not give up meeting together with brothers and sisters in Christ to be encouraged (Hebrews 10:25).

You were saved to having done the will of God, to receive what he has promised (Hebrews 10:36).

You were saved to please God by being a person of faith—submitted to the authority of his Word (Hebrews 11:6).

You were saved to throw off everything that hinders you and the sin that so easily entangles you and run with perseverance the race marked out for you (Hebrews 12:1).

You were saved to fix your eyes on Jesus (Hebrews 12:2).

You were saved to not grow weary and lose heart (Hebrews 12:3).

You were saved to be disciplined by your Lord (Hebrews 12:6).

You were saved to endure hardship as discipline (Hebrews 12:7).

You were saved to make every effort to live in peace with all men and to be holy (Hebrews 12:14).

You were saved to have no bitter root grow up in you causing trouble and defiling many (Hebrews 12:15).

You were saved to keep on loving each other as brothers (Hebrews 13:1).

You were saved, you who are married, to keep the marriage bed pure (Hebrews 13:4).

You were saved to keep your life free from the love of money and be content with what you have (Hebrews 13:5).

You were saved to imitate your leader's faith, knowing Christ Jesus is the same yesterday, and today, and forever (Hebrews 13:7-8).

You were saved to be equipped with everything good for doing God's will (Hebrews 13:21).

You were saved to count it all joy when you meet trials of various kinds because you know that the testing of your faith produces steadfastness (James 1:2-3).

You were saved to become mature and complete, not lacking anything (James 1:4).

You were saved to ask God for wisdom (James 1:5).

You were saved to not doubt God at his Word (James 1:6).

You were saved to be blessed and faithful in your trials (James 1:12).

You were saved to not be deceived in your temptations (James 1:16).

You were saved to be a kind of first fruits of all God created (James 1:18).

You were saved to be quick to listen, slow to speak, and slow to become angry (James 1:19).

You were saved to get rid of moral filth and the evil that is so prevalent and humbly accept the Word planted in you (James 1:21).

You were saved to not merely listen to the Word and so deceive yourself but do what it says (James 1:22).

You were saved to have freedom and be blessed in doing God's Word (James 1:25).

You were saved to keep a tight rein on your tongue (James 1:26).

You were saved to look after orphans and widows in their distress and to keep yourself from being polluted by the world (James 1:27).

You were saved to not show favoritism toward people (James 2:1).

You were saved to be merciful (James 2:12).

You were saved to show your faith by your deeds (James 2:17).

You were saved to put away envy and selfish ambition, disorder, and every evil practice (James 3:17).

You were saved to stop fighting and quarreling with others (James 4:1).

You were saved to submit yourself to God (James 4:7).

You were saved to humble yourself before God and he will lift you up (James 4:10).

You were saved to be patient until the Lord's coming (James 5:7).

You were saved to confess your sins to each other and pray for each other so that you may be healed (James 5:16).

You were saved in his great mercy to be given a new birth into a living hope through the resurrection of Jesus Christ (1 Peter 1:3).

You were saved into an inheritance that can never perish, spoil, or fade—kept in heaven for you (1 Peter 1:4).

You were saved to have a faith of greater worth than gold to be proved genuine and bring praise, glory, and honor when Jesus Christ comes again (1 Peter 1:7).

You were saved to be filled with an inexpressible and glorious joy (1 Peter 1:8).

You were saved to be holy because God is holy (1 Peter 1:16).

You were saved to grow up in your salvation now that you have tasted the Lord is good (1 Peter 2:2–3).

You were saved to be a part of a chosen people, a royal priesthood, a holy nation, a people belonging to God that you may declare the praises of him who called you out of darkness into his wonderful light (1 Peter 2:9).

You were saved to do good and silence the ignorant talk of foolish men (1 Peter 2:15).

You were saved to endure when suffering for doing good (1 Peter 2:20).

You were saved to live in harmony with one another being sympathetic, loving, compassionate, and humble (1 Peter 3:8).

You were saved to not repay evil with evil or insult with insult but to bless others, so you may inherit a blessing (1 Peter 3:9).

You were saved to always be prepared to give an answer to everyone who asks you to give a reason for the hope that you have with gentleness and respect (1 Peter 3:15).

You were saved to above all else love each other deeply because love covers over a multitude of sins (1 Peter 4:8).

You were saved to offer hospitality to one another without grumbling (1 Peter 4:9).

You were saved to humble yourself under God's mighty hand that he may lift you up in due time (1 Peter 5:6).

You were saved to cast all your anxiety on him because he cares for you (1 Peter 5:7).

You were saved to be self-controlled and alert because the devil prowls around like a roaring lion looking for someone to devour (1 Peter 5:8).

You were saved to resist the devil and stand firm in your faith (1 Peter 5:9).

You were saved to rest in his divine power that has granted you all things that pertain to life and godliness through the knowledge of him (Thinking God) (2 Peter 1:3).

You were saved by Thinking God through his very great and precious promises, to participate in the diving nature of God and escape the corruption in the world caused by evil desires (2 Peter 1:4).

You were saved to be a slave to God (2 Peter 2:19).

You were saved to wholesome thinking—Thinking God (2 Peter 3:1).

You were saved to know God is patient, and not wanting anyone to perish, but everyone to come to repentance (2 Peter 3:9).

You were saved to live a holy and godly life as you look forward to the day of God and speed its coming (2 Peter 3:12).

You were saved to make every effort to be found spotless, blameless, and at peace with the coming Lord (2 Peter 3:14).

You were saved to stay on your guard, so you do not fall away (2 Peter 3:17).

You were saved to stay faithful in the process of growing in the grace and knowledge of him (2 Peter 3:18).

You were saved to walk in God's light and have fellowship with one another (1 John 1:7).

You were saved to confess your sins to God and be forgiven (1 John 1:9).

You were saved to walk as Jesus did (1 John 2:6).

You were saved to not love the world or anything in the world (1 John 2:15).

You were saved to not be led astray to keep sinning (1 John 3:6).

You were saved to love one another (1 John 3:11).

You were saved to lay down your life for your brothers (1 John 3:16).

You were saved to know the one, Jesus Christ, who is in you who is greater than the one who is in the world (1 John 4:4).

You were saved to have your fearfulness replaced by the power of God's love (1 John 4:18).

You were saved to obey his promises (1 John 5:3).

You were saved to overcome the world living in the victory of your faith (1 John 5:4).

You were saved to know without a doubt you have life and eternal life in the Son (1 John 5:13).

You were saved to live with the confidence that if you ask anything according to his will, he hears you (1 John 5:14).

You were saved to walk in obedience to the Lord's commands (2 John 6).

You were saved to walk in love (2 John 7).

You were saved to continue in the teaching of Christ (2 John 9).

You were saved to be faithful to the truth and walk in the truth (3 John 3).

You were saved to build yourself up in your most holy faith and praying in the Holy Spirit (Jude 20).

You were saved to be merciful to those who doubt (Jude 22).

You were saved to snatch others from the fire and save them (Jude 23).

You were saved to be kept from falling and be presented before God's glorious presence without fault and with great joy (Jude 24).

You were saved to see one day the coming of the Lord (Revelation 1:7).

You were saved to know the Lord as your first love (Revelation 2:4).

You were saved to not fear in your suffering for the Lord (Revelation 2:10).

You were saved to be true to the Lord's name (Revelation 2:13).

You were saved to trust and obey the Lord who is faithful and true (Revelation 3:14).

You were saved to be rebuked and be disciplined (Revelation 3:19).

You were saved to overcome (Revelation 3:20).

You were saved to live and eternally declare, "You are worthy, our Lord and God, to receive glory and honor and power, for you created all things, and by your will they were created and have their being" (Revelation 4:11).

You were saved to overcome the devil, your accuser, by the blood of the Lamb, by the word of your testimony, and not loving your life so much as to shrink from death (Revelation 12:11).

You were saved to endure all suffering with patient endurance and faithfulness (Revelation 13:10).

You were saved to have your name written in the Book of Life (Revelation 20:15).

You were saved to know the inexpressible joy of a new heaven and a new earth (Revelation 21:1).

You were saved to have everything made new (Revelation 21:5).

You were saved to live in the light of God not knowing anymore night (Revelation 22:15).

You were saved to live Thinking God now and eternally knowing God's Word is trustworthy and true (Revelation 22:6).

You were saved to worship God (Revelation 22:9).

This is certainly not a complete list, but long enough to thrillingly overwhelm you of the supernatural and radically changed, indescribable, abundant, and victorious life Jesus Christ has saved you to live. And remember, there are over five thousand promises and commands in the Bible outlining for us the inexpressible abundant life God has saved us to experience. You may be thinking, *The Christian life is hard.* The Christian life is not hard. The Christian life is impossible to live apart from living the Spirit-filled life (Ephesians 5:17–18).

You were saved to live the Spirit-filled life (Ephesians 5:17–18). Every promise and command of God has a purpose and a privilege for you to enjoy "Christ in you, the hope of glory" (Colossians 1:27), but you can only do it surrendered to the presence of the power of the Holy Spirit!

So I must ask you: Are you living out why you were saved? I encourage you to be courageously honest, considering the Apostle Paul's admonition to the church at Corinth: "Examine yourselves, to see if you are in the faith. Test yourselves. Or do you not realize this about yourselves that Jesus Christ is in you?—unless indeed you fail to meet the test" (2 Corinthians 13:5)!

If you failed the test, humbly ask yourself these three questions:

1. Have I truly ever had God break my heart over my rebellion toward him, so I repented of my sinfulness to God and changed my mind about my disobedience to God (2 Corinthians 7:10)?

2. Have I ever truly surrendered my life to the authority of Jesus Christ as the Lord of my life, or do I still justify and tolerate sin in my life (Matthew 7:21-23)?

3. Does my life have fruit that shows the evidence of repentance as Jesus said his followers would have (Luke 13:3–7)?

The first word Jesus ever taught about experiencing his presence and power in our lives was "repent" (Mark 1:15). The first word Peter said in answering the people after he and the apostles were asked, "Brothers, what shall we do?" (to be saved) was "repent" (Acts 2:37–38).

Yes, we need to ask God to forgive us, and he will cleanse us of all our sins (1 John 1:9), but if we are not brought by God to repent (Luke 13:3; Acts 3:19)—change our minds about our sinfulness and turn to God—nothing changes in our lives because we just keep on sinning. Remember, our behavior does not change until our thinking changes. We must repent.

I believe an ignorance of and absence of repentance is what is missing in most professing Christian's lives. An absence of repentance leaves us living our lives with a belief system but lacking a transformed life in Christ as God's Word clearly and emphatically promises (2 Corinthians 5:17–18).

If you sense the Lord's working in your life to repent, go back to chapter two and review the presentation on how to be saved and truly repent and receive Jesus Christ as King of kings and Lord of lords of your life. Praise the Lord for his grace, greatness, and goodness in your life. Praise the Lord for a new beginning in your life. Tell or call someone and rejoice with them about this new work of grace and truth in your life!

If you have already repented of your sinfulness and received Jesus Christ as your Lord and Savior, but you are not living out what God has saved you for—the Spirit-filled life, I encourage you with a story that could be told about millions of professing Christians.

During my first pastorate, a man, Ray, said to me after I had invited him to attend a men's Bible study, "The reason I don't come to those Bible studies or come to church that much is I have enough pressures at home and work to keep me stressed out. I don't need any more pressure trying to do all of those things in the Bible." Like the majority of Christians I have known, Ray, who professed to have been a Christian for many years, did not understand he was saved, not to keep living in his best efforts, but to die to his old sinful nature and yield his life to the presence and the power of the Holy Spirit (Romans 6:1-11). Not Thinking God, Ray was confused about what the Christian life is.

Let me repeat what you read earlier. The Christian life is not hard. The Christian life is impossible to live apart from living the Spirit-filled life. Stop trying harder. Give up and give in to the Lord's authority in your life by surrendering your life completely to him.

Remember what Jesus told his disciples after predicting his betrayal by Judas (John 13:18–30) and Peter's denial of him (John 13:36–38). He would "ask the Father, and he will give you another Counselor to be with you forever—the Spirit of truth" (John 16:13). Following his resurrection and before his ascension back to heaven, Jesus declared, "And behold, I am sending the promise of my Father upon you. But stay in the city until you are clothed with power from on high" (Luke 24:49).

Without the powerful control of the Holy Spirit in your life, you are guaranteed failure, frustration, and condemnation. You were saved to be "equipped with everything good for doing God's will" (Hebrews 13:21). You were saved to "count it all joy when you meet trials of various kinds because you know that the testing of your faith produces steadfastness" (James 1:2–3). You were saved to "become mature and complete, not lacking anything" (James 1:4). You were saved to "ask God for wisdom" (James 1:5). You were saved to "not doubt God at his Word" (James 1:6).

When you think or say, "I can't do that" to the Word of God, you are right! You cannot! But God did not ask you to give your best to him. God asked you to bring your best and your worst to him. Remember, even your best is "as filthy rags" (Isaiah 64:6) to God because he is holy. God asked you to come to your end and let him, by the Holy Spirit, take over your life (Romans 6:11). God wants to take over your life by the presence and power of the Holy Spirit.

As a Christian, you will live every moment of your life by one of two ways: under the Spirit's control or by the control of your sinful nature (Galatians 5:16–18). Understand what many do not seem to understand—no matter how long you have been a Christian, your sinful nature does not improve. Time in itself does not produce spiritual maturity or Christ-like character. We must learn to live under the Spirit's control (Galatians 5:16–17).

Compare the acts of the sinful nature with the fruit of the Spirit: "Now the works of the flesh are evident; sexual immorality, impurity, sensuality, idolatry, sorcery, enmity, strife, jealousy, fits of anger, rivalries, dissensions, divisions, envy, drunkenness, orgies, and things like these, I warn you, as I warned you before, that those who do such things will not inherit the kingdom of God. But the fruit of the Spirit is love, joy, peace, patience, kindness, goodness, faithfulness, gentleness, self-control; against such things there is no law" (Galatians 5:19–23). Until you choose to humble yourself moment by moment to surrender your life to the Holy Spirit, you will waste your life in frustration, hearing God's promises and commands but not experiencing the love, joy, and peace of living God's promises and commands.

Regardless of what Jesus had done for the apostles or with the apostles during the time they had been together during his earthly ministry, they continued to be faithless and frustrated in their failures. Therefore, Jesus spent another forty days with them following his resurrection, and before he went back to heaven, he told the apostles, "But you will receive power when the Holy Spirit has come upon you, and you will be my witnesses in Jerusalem and in all Judea and Samaria, and to the end of the earth"(Acts 1:8). Jesus was reemphasizing to them what he had already said to them, "you can do nothing apart from me" (John 15:5).

Realize this profound truth for your life so many Christians miss: Receiving Christ is not just a great addition to your life. Receiving Christ is to be a transformational takeover in your life. The Christian life is to be an end of you being in control. The Christian life is to be an end of you trying to manage and fix everything. The Christian life is the beginning of a new life with Christ in control and Thinking God (Colossians 3:1–7).

Since there is so much confusion about what it means to be filled with the Holy Spirit, let's study Ephesians 5:17–18 and learn about this very important teaching of Thinking God for each of us. Learn and apply these ten life-transforming truths:

First Life-Transforming Truth

"Therefore do not be foolish, but understand what the will of the Lord is." *It is senseless to think being filled with the Spirit is an option.*

Being filled with the Spirit is not an option. It is God's will for every Christian. Trying to live otherwise is foolish. Foolish means senseless. Since you were created by God and for God and Jesus Christ is to be preeminent in your life (Colossians 1:16–18), and since you were redeemed and reconciled to be a supernatural and radically changed person by God (2 Corinthians 5:17–18), the only way this miracle can occur in your life or anyone else's life is by the power of the Holy Spirit. You will only frustrate yourself and everyone around you until you learn to humbly live surrendered to the power of the Holy Spirit. Just as Jesus told his apostles, "Do not leave Jerusalem until you are clothed with power from on high" (Luke 24:49), hear the Lord say to you right now, "stop trying to live the Christian life without being clothed with the power of the Holy Spirit." It is senseless.

Second Life-Transforming Truth

"Be filled." It is in the passive voice.

"Be filled" in Greek is *pleroo*. It means "to make full or to fill to the full." *We need God to do in us and for us what we cannot do for ourselves.*

Third Life-Transforming Truth

"Be filled." It is in the present tense.

It is a moment by moment yielding of ourselves completely to the Spirit's control. Just as you need to keep breathing air to stay alive, you must remember your position in Christ (Romans 6:11) moment by moment so you will have his power to live his promises and commands always victoriously (2 Corinthians 2:14).

Fourth Life-Transforming Truth

"Be filled." It is plural in its number.

It is for all Christians. This truth is for you to be set free (John 8:32) and have the abundant life promised in Christ (John 10:10). There are no second-class citizens in the kingdom of God. Stop living beneath your privilege in Christ.

Fifth Life-Transforming Truth

"Be filled." It is in the imperative mood.

It is a command. Hear this loud and clear: This is not an option for Christians. It is God's perfect will for your life.

Have you figured it out yet that you can sin all you want, but you cannot choose your consequences. The consequences of sin will always bring you hurt and will hurt those you love. When you sin, you suffer and you bring suffering to those you love. That's why I have come to hate sin in my life and in everyone else's life. Sin brings hurt and suffering. Yes, we all have a sinful nature that is easily deceived and is tempted to sin continually (James 1:13–16). Yes, we are in a spiritual battle with the devil who schemes against us to bring ruin to us (Ephesians 6:10–13). And yes, we live in a fallen world where "the cravings of sinful man, the lust of his eyes and the boasting of what he has and does—comes not from the Father but from the world" (1John 2:16). But remember, "The world and its desires pass away, but the man who does the will of God lives forever" (1John 2:17). Know the joy and peace of living your life without regret and shame as you live your life filled with the Holy Spirit.

Sixth Life-Transforming Truth

"Be filled." *It is what you were saved for.*

Being filled with the Holy Spirit leads us to desire his preeminence (Colossians 1:18). Being filled with the Holy Spirit leads us to seek his perspective (2 Corinthians 4:18). Being filled with the Holy Spirit leads us to trust his patience (Romans 5:3–5). Being filled with the Holy Spirit leads us to experience his power (Acts 1:8). Being filled with the Holy Spirit leads us to rest in his provision (1 Thessalonians 5:16–19). Being filled with the Holy Spirit leads us to be ruled by his peace (Colossians 3:15). Being filled with the Holy Spirit leads us to live out his purpose with perseverance (Hebrews 12:1–2).

Until you learn to "be filled with the Spirit," you will not enjoy living out God's promises and obeying God's commands, leaving you confused, frustrated, and miserable. Throughout the book of Acts and the epistles, think about the characteristics of the early church once they were "filled with the Spirit" (Acts 2:4) and lived "clothed with power from on high" (Luke 24:49):

1. They became an empowered church.
2. They became a witnessing church.
3. They became an obeying church.
4. They became a praying church.
5. They became a devoted church.
6. They became a giving church.
7. They became a preaching/teaching church.
8. They became a growing church.
9. They were an unexplainable church.
10. They were a persecuted and persevering church.
11. They were an overcoming church.
12. They were a mission-minded church.

Seventh Life-Transforming Truth

"Be filled." *You will be filled with something or someone.*

Until you learn to "be filled with the Spirit," you will stay full of other powers (your sinful nature, pressures, bitterness, blame, and/or shame), leaving you struggling, failing, defeated, and suffering. First Corinthians 2:14-3:4 instructs us about the three kinds of persons who are in the world. Which one are you?

1. The natural person who "does not accept the things of the Spirit of God, for they are folly to him, and he is not able to understand them because they are spiritually discerned" (1 Corinthians 2:14).

2. The spiritual person who lives under the authority of God's Word, surrendered to the presence and power of the Holy Spirit to live out God's promises and commands to his glory (1 Corinthians 2:15-16).

3. The infant in Christ, having said he has trusted Christ to be his Lord and Savior, but still lives by the flesh, thinking and acting like the natural person (1 Corinthians 3:1–4).

Which of these describe you?

Eighth Life-Transforming Truth

"Be filled." *Be fruitful, be fulfilled, and be faithful in the Spirit's control.*

Until you learn to "be filled with the Spirit," you will not become fulfilled or be able to do what you want with all your heart because when you received Christ in your life, he gave you the desire to know him and please him above everything (2 Corinthians 5:18). Until you are filled with the Spirit, you will live empty, knowing something is missing in your life. It is not something. It is experiencing the abundance and victory of living in the power of being surrendered to the control of Christ's lordship in your life.

Ninth Life-Transforming Truth

"Be filled." *Enjoy loving and lasting servant-hearted relationships.*

Until you learn to "be filled with the Spirit," you will not enjoy servant-hearted life, leaving yourself missing the joy of loving and lasting relationships. If you are wounding others by your selfishness and arrogance in relationships, *stop*! Don't you think it's time to start living the victorious life God saved you for? This truly can be the first day of the rest of your life, if…

Tenth Life-Transforming Truth

Resolve you are going to "be a doer of the word, and not a hearer only, deceiving yourself" (James 1:22).

These insights about being filled with the Holy Spirit will only transform your life if you do them (James 1:22). Do it to the glory of God. Do it for your joy. Do it for the good of everyone close to you. Do it for the good of the church you belong to. Do it so your children will want to repeat your life. Do it so one day you will hear your Lord say, "Well done, good and faithful servant. You have been faithful with a few things; I will put you in charge of many things. Come and share your master's happiness" (Matthew 25:21)! Daily, moment by moment, live your life by Thinking God in accomplishing the purpose for your salvation—"be filled with the Spirit" and live out the promises and commands of God's Word to the glory of God!

Thinking God—You were saved to be filled with the power of the Holy Spirit enabling you to live out God's promises and commands to the glory of God (Ephesians 5:17–21).

Truth to Remember—You will live every moment of your life by one of two ways: under the Spirit's control or by the control of your sinful nature. Live by the Spirit (Galatians 5:16–26).

Thinking God in Reflecting—You only have one life to live! Being filled with the Holy Spirit will transform your life to be faithful, fruitful, and fulfilled. Will you live beneath your privilege and power in Christ (Ephesians 3:19–20)?

PART II

BECAUSE RELATIONSHIPS ARE SO IMPORTANT

THINKING GOD: MARRIAGE

Memorize God's Word!

"Then the Lord God said, 'It is not good that the man should be alone; I will make him a helper fit for him'" (Genesis 2:18).

"Therefore a man shall leave his father and his mother and hold fast to his wife, and they shall become one flesh. And the man and his wife were both naked and were not ashamed" (Genesis 2:24–25).

"Did he not make them one, with a portion of the Spirit in their union? And what was the one God seeking? Godly offspring. So guard yourselves in your spirit, and let none of you be faithless to the wife of your youth" (Malachi 2:15).

"And the rain fell, and the floods came, and the winds blew and beat on that house, but it did not fall, because it had been founded on the rock. And everyone who hears these words of mine and does not do them will be like a foolish man who built his house on the sand. And the rain fell, and the floods came, and the winds blew and beat against that house, and it fell, and great was the fall of it" (Matthew 7:25–27).

"But whoever would be great among you must be your servant, and whoever would be first among you must be your slave, even as the Son of Man came not to be served but to serve, and to give his life as a ransom for many" (Matthew 20:26–28).

"And calling the crowd to him with his disciples, he said to them, 'If anyone would come after me, let him deny himself and take up his cross and follow me'" (Mark 8:34).

"Do you not know that all of us who have been baptized into Christ Jesus were baptized into his death? We were buried therefore with him by baptism into death, in order that, just as Christ was raised from the dead by the glory of the Father, we too might walk in newness of life. For if we have been united with him in a death like his, we shall certainly be united with him in a resurrection like his. We know that our old self was crucified with him in order that the body of sin might be brought to nothing, so that we would no longer be enslaved to sin. For one who has died has been set free from sin. Now if we have died with Christ, we believe that we will also live with him. We know that Christ, being raised from the dead, will never die again; death no longer has dominion over him. For the death he died he died to sin, once for all, but the life he lives he lives to God. So you also must consider yourselves dead to sin and alive to God in Christ Jesus. Let not sin therefore reign in your mortal body, to make you obey its passions. Do not present your members to sin as instruments for unrighteousness, but present yourselves to God as those who have been brought from death to life, and your members to God as instruments for righteousness. For sin will have no dominion over you, since you are not under law but under grace" (Romans 6:3–14).

"For those who live according to the flesh set their minds on the things of the flesh, but those who live according to the Spirit set their minds on the things of the Spirit" (Romans 8:5).

"If I speak in the tongues of men and of angels, but have not love, I am a noisy gong or a clanging cymbal. And if I have prophetic powers, and understand all mysteries and all knowledge, and if I have all faith, so as to remove mountains, but have not love, I am nothing. If I give away all I have, and if I deliver up my body to be burned, but have not love, I gain nothing. Love is patient and kind; love does not envy or boast; it is not arrogant or rude. It does not insist on its own way; it is not irritable or resentful; it does not rejoice at wrongdoing, but rejoices with the truth. Love bears all things, believes all things, hopes all things, endures all things. Love never ends. As for prophecies, they will pass away; as for tongues, they will cease; as for knowledge, it will pass away. For we know in part and we prophesy in part, but when the perfect comes, the partial will pass away. When I was a child, I spoke like a child, I thought like a child, I reasoned like a child. When I became a man, I gave up childish ways. For now we see in a mirror dimly, but then face to face. Now I know in part; then I shall know fully, even as I have been fully known. So now faith, hope, and love abide, these three; but the greatest of these is love" (1 Corinthians 13:1–13).

"But I say, walk by the Spirit, and you will not gratify the desires of the flesh. For the desires of the flesh are against the Spirit, and the desires of the Spirit are against the flesh, for these are opposed to each other, to keep you from doing the things you want to do. But if you are led by the Spirit, you are not under the law. Now the works of the flesh are evident: sexual immorality, impurity, sensuality, idolatry, sorcery, enmity, strife, jealousy, fits of anger, rivalries, dissensions, divisions, envy, drunkenness, orgies, and things like these. I warn you, as I warned you before, that those who do such things will not inherit the kingdom of God. But the fruit of the Spirit is love, joy, peace, patience, kindness, goodness, faithfulness, gentleness, self-control; against such things there is no law. And those who belong to Christ Jesus have crucified the flesh with its passions and desires. If we live by the Spirit, let us also keep in step with the Spirit. Let us not become conceited, provoking one another, envying one another" (Galatians 5:16–26).

"Be angry and do not sin; do not let the sun go down on your anger, and give no opportunity to the devil" (Ephesians 4:26–27).

"Let no corrupting talk come out of your mouths, but only such as is good for building up, as fits the occasion, that it may give grace to those who hear. And do not grieve the Holy Spirit of God, by whom you were sealed for the day of redemption. Let all bitterness and wrath and anger and clamor and slander be put away from you, along with all malice. Be kind to one another, tenderhearted, forgiving one another, as God in Christ forgave you" (Ephesians 4:29–32).

ഇ⊃രോ

My wife, Roni, and I first met at a winter youth retreat in Hayden Lake, Idaho. Roni was seventeen and a junior in high school, and I was eighteen and a freshman at Eastern Washington State College. I had been asked by my pastor to come and share at this retreat what it was like to live for Christ on a state college campus. After the service, Roni and I began to visit, and I thought, *This is the most beautiful girl I have ever met.* When I got back to my apartment, I told my roommates, "I met the most amazing girl. She loves the Lord with all her heart. She is beautiful!" My roommates asked me, "Are you going to take her out?" I replied disappointedly, "She is only a junior in high school with the emphasis on high school, and she lives thirty-five miles from here." (I did not have a car at school.)

A year later, I was invited to be the pianist at a city-wide crusade in the Spokane Coliseum. At that time (1970), every big crusade had a big choir. When Roni heard from a visiting pastor at her church, who was recruiting persons for the crusade choir, that Phil Hunter is going to be the pianist, she signed up for the choir.

At the close of the first service of the crusade which was on a Sunday evening, Roni came up to me on the stage and said, "Do you remember me?" When I could only remember her brother's name because I had some classes with him and said, "I remember your brother's name is John," she quickly helped me with, "Roni."

As we talked, I thought, *She is a year older and I now have my own car at school*, so I said as we were departing, "Come see me again tomorrow night if I don't see you." (There were hundreds in the choir and thousands attending the crusade.) We visited the next night, and I met her parents. On Tuesday evening, I asked her if she would like me to take her home Friday, and she said she would ask her parents. The next night, she said, "That would be great!"

Roni was a beautiful young woman. She is now a beautiful older woman and grandmother of nine. Roni also had a beautiful singing voice and was taking voice lessons at Whitworth College. I started taking piano lessons at the age of five, and having been the pianist for all of the Northwest Baptist Conventions and Northwest Baptist Evangelism Conferences from 1970—73, I built a reputation in the Northwest as a classical concert pianist who could *wow* my audiences with my improvisations of hymns and praise choruses. After a few months of dating, we began to do concerts throughout the Northwest and became accustomed to having standing ovations and hearing how great we were.

After dating for almost two years, we married on March 17, 1973. Being only twenty-one and Roni being twenty left us with many challenges to overcome. Our success, pride, immaturity and selfishness were a bad combination for a young newly wedded couple! When we got married our pastor friends were so impressed about what God was doing through us, they did not counsel us about the challenges of marriage, assuming everything would be just fine. That proved to be an unwise assumption. Praise the Lord we did have an understanding of covenant marriage that gave us a bulldog resolve and strength we needed to persevere in all our "growing up" years we had before us. We knew in our heads, when we did not feel it in our hearts, "When God has called you to do his will, there is no rest in quitting but only in finishing!"

In a covenant marriage, you do not quit, knowing God is greater than any failure or faithlessness. In a covenant marriage, you do not throw in the towel, knowing God is in the business of redeeming messes. In a covenant marriage, you do not bag it and get someone else you think is better, knowing nothing is too hard for God. In a covenant marriage you do not give up allowing the devil to win, knowing you have victory in Christ and are living to give God the glory.

God has used our greatest failures and sorrows as the very best times in our lives (Romans 8:28–29) because that's when God taught us how truly desperate we were for him to transform our lives. It has been in the "midnights" of our lives God has graciously and faithfully shown us our total inadequacies apart from him (John 15:5) and our desperateness to "walk by the Spirit and not by the flesh" (Galatians 5:16). In the darkest and most difficult times caused by the blindness of our pride, immaturity, and selfishness, we have realized it is not our beauty or good looks, it is not our ability, it is not our giftedness, it is not my biblical knowledge or anything God by his grace and mercy has done through us in ministry that makes the difference in our marriage.

What makes a difference in our marriage is humbling ourselves before God and each other and allowing God to transform our character. What makes a difference in any marriage is when a husband and a wife move from saying and doing all the right things in public, and they say privately before God as Isaiah did, "Woe is me! For I am lost; for I am a man (and a woman) of unclean lips, (because of my heart) and I dwell in the midst of a people of unclean lips; for my eyes have seen the King, the LORD of hosts" (Isaiah 6:5)! And God touches them and transforms them, and they see like they have never truly seen before.

When we see the LORD like Job saw the LORD, we truly make him first in our lives (Exodus 20:3; Matthew 6:33). Being first, God does his work he has promised to do in our lives. He radically and deeply changes us because of our desire to be deeply changed. Because God meets us at the level of our desire, God works mightily in our lives. In God's grace and mercy, he gives us the vision to see our sinfulness with disgust, and despising our condition in light of God's holiness, there is great repentance with many tears (Job 42:5–6).

You have already read of repenting several times in this book, and you may have said you have repented, but have you ever seen the LORD so that in the light of his holiness, you became disgusted and despised at your sinfulness? (That is so much deeper than being sorrowful over the consequences from your sinfulness.) When that happens, your life will never be the same again, and the transformational truth of Thinking God changes you and your marriage. You finally "get it"— "We got married to serve one another because we are first serving the one LORD God." A husband serves his wife by "loving her as Christ loved the church and gave himself up for her" (Ephesians 5:25), unconditionally assuring her she is secure in his care which is a wife's greatest need. A wife serves her husband by "respecting him" (Ephesians 5:33), assuring him of his adequacy to be the leader of their home which is a husband's greatest need.

You start serving each other with no rights or expectations because as servants of the Master Lord Jesus, you have no rights (1 Corinthians 6:19–20). You only want to please your Lord (2 Corinthians 5:9). When any husband and any wife truly understand and live this truth, everything for their good and God's glory will change in their marriage.

Let me reemphasize: When any husband and any wife truly understand and live what they were married for—to serve one another in covenant love as unto the one LORD God in obedience to him (John 13:14–17), everything changes for their good, their children's good, their church's good, the world's good, and, of course, the glory of God (Matthew 5:16). And you get to live out the privileges of God's love described in 1 Corinthians 13. And you grow up in the process we should all be making progress described in 1 Corinthians 13:11: "When I was a child, I reasoned like a child. When I became a man, I gave up childish ways." Isn't it time to grow up and be a servant?

You may be thinking because hurting and bitter husbands and wives discouragingly have said to me through the years, "Pastor, you don't know my hurts. You don't know what we have been through. I don't trust him. I cannot stand her." I only ask you what God asked Abraham when he and Sarah had become hopeless of having God's promised son: "Is anything too hard for the LORD" (Genesis 18:14)? Of course, God's answer is, "Nothing is too hard for the LORD."

Genesis 21:1–2 declares: "Now the LORD was gracious to Sarah as he had said, and the LORD did for Sarah what he had promised. Sarah became pregnant and bore a son to Abraham in his old age, at the very time God had promised him."

I promise you on the authority of God's Word, there is nothing God cannot make new (Revelation 21:5) if you and your spouse will only humble yourselves before him and each other (1 Peter 5:5–6). Do not allow your pride to rob you of what God has planned for you in learning the privilege of serving one another. Do not allow your pride to confuse, hurt, and put a hole in your children's hearts for the rest of their lives by quitting on your marriage. Stop trying to change your spouse. Focus on humbling yourself before God and letting him change you. Give up and give in to God right now.

In our marriage, it has been a forty-one year journey through the ups and downs of life—overcoming all kinds of pride, immaturity, selfishness, and hurt; having and raising three sons, Phillip (38), Joshua (37) and Matthew (29); having times when the doctors thought in each of their lives they might die or have cancer; moving across the country three times to attend seminary to further our equipping; struggling how we would at times buy food for our babies during those seminary years and working different jobs at minimum wage; living in three different states serving in five churches as minister of music and youth as we were attending college and seminary; having an arsonist burn our church building to the ground during our first full-time ministry while we were on vacation; moving two thousand miles away from our parents, brothers and their families, and all our extended family members to follow God's call in ministry; being away from home several weeks at a time, traveling across Missouri and the country for seven years, preaching and teaching God's Word; leading two churches through major building programs as pastor; starting a new church, West County Community Church, twenty-one years ago; being in three serious car wrecks that left us in months of pain and rehabilitation; my wife going through three major surgeries; having nodules on my vocal cords and not being able to preach for over a year without often losing my voice; the heartbreak of three brothers serving time in jail or prison; caring for my mom for almost two years after she suffered a stroke and severe paralysis and thinking I was going to die from exhaustion before she was of old age; burying each of our parents and two of our brothers; and "apart from other things, there is the daily pressure on me" (2 Corinthians 11:28) of being a pastor—*but we have not lost heart and quit* because we have learned in a covenant relationship with God how to be "renewed day by day" (2 Corinthians 4:16) in the Lord's satisfaction (Matthew 5:6), sufficiency (2 Corinthians 12:9–10), and strength (Philippians 4:11–13) in our lives. Thinking God, we understand marriage is a covenant with God and one another, not just a contract we will keep if everything works out good and it is agreeable with our feelings and circumstances.

Always remember:

1. Whatever God intended to be most important in your life, the devil wants you to think it is less important (2 Corinthians 2:11).

2. Whatever God intended to give you as the greatest enrichment, to be most precious to you, and to be the greatest blessing in your life, the devil wants to steal from you (John 10:10).

3. Whatever newness God brought to you in Christ, the devil wants it to fade and become old in you (2 Corinthians 5:17).

4. The devil wants you to get over God and everything good God has done for you (1 Peter 2:23).

The Bible teaches marriage is to be a permanent relationship, a covenant between one man and one woman completely committed to each other as companions for life (Matthew 19:1–8). Marriage is so much more than a contract. Even though a contract and a covenant may sound similar in meaning and intent, they are in reality much different. Whereas a contract is usually a written agreement based on distrust, outlining the conditions and consequences if broken, a covenant is a verbal commitment based on trust, assuring someone your promise is unconditional and good for life.

In Christian marriage, a covenant is spoken out of love between a husband-to-be and a wife-to-be before witnesses and before God. A covenant is for the benefit of others and comes with unlimited responsibility. It has no expiration date. It is until "death do us part." A covenant is intended to be unbreakable, reflecting God's unbreakable promises to us as his redeemed and reconciled children (Matthew 28:20; John 14:1–3; 2 Timothy 2:13).

A contract is much different in that it is self-serving and comes with limited liability. It establishes a time for certain conditions to be met and accomplished. A contract can be broken with mutual consent.

Christian marriage is to be the strongest covenant on earth between two people, the pledge of a man and woman to establish a love that is unconditional and lasts a lifetime because they have already made a covenant with Jesus Christ as their Lord and Savior (Hebrews 9:13–15). In marriage, your wedding ring represents your covenant vows to each other, not merely commitments you hope to keep, but a covenant with God and those family members and friends who witnessed your vows to one another. Always remember, how you treat your spouse is a reflection of your commitment and walk with your God (1 Corinthians 6:19–20). *Mounce's Complete Expository Dictionary Of Old & New Testament Words* provides us with many of the following insights concerning the meaning of "covenant."

The Hebrew noun for covenant is *beriyth* which was used two hundred eighty seven times in the Old Testament. It means "a solemn agreement with binding force." God is a covenant God. The Bible is a covenant book. Its table of contents bears the title "the Old Testament" and "the New Testament." Synonyms for the word *testament* are covenant and agreement. The Bible contains several major covenants as part of the unfolding story of God's people. God's first covenant was with Noah after the flood, where God promised not to destroy the earth again (Genesis 9:9–17). God established a covenant with Abram, where he promised to make Abram's name great and to give him a descendant from whom a great nation would arise (Genesis 15:18; 17:1–8). God made a covenant with Moses, declaring the people of Israel would be God's permanent possession (Exodus 19:3–6). God made a covenant with David, promising a ruler would sit on his throne forever (2 Samuel 7:7–16). In each of these covenants, God established the terms, and he was the one who vowed to keep a series of promises. In the covenant at Mount Sinai, God set the terms (his law), but he called on the Israelites to agree to those terms (Exodus 24:1–8). As his covenant people, Israel promised to obey his revealed laws, but repeatedly, they were not faithful in their agreement to keep their word. God promised to live among his people in "the ark of the covenant" (Numbers10:33). Throughout the Old Testament, a covenant was used to show the seriousness and significance of the solemn agreement in the relationship being established.

The Hebrew verb for covenant is *karat* which was used two hundred eighty nine times. The majority of the uses of *karat* have to do with making (cutting) a covenant, either between human beings (Genesis 21:27, 32; Joshua 9:11, 15) or between God and his people (Exodus 34:10; Deuteronomy 4:23). Two different backgrounds have been suggested for this use of the word relative to covenant/treaties. Most scholars relate it to a rite of ratification for a covenant, in which the parties of the covenant walked through dismembered parts of a sacrificed animal (see Genesis 15:9-10, 17-21; Jeremiah 34:18-20). The tacit announcement made through this event was: "Let it be done to me as has been done to this beast if I fail to keep my pledge of covenant loyalty." Other scholars have noted how many ancient treaties were cut into pieces of stone, so that there was a permanent record of the treaty.

In the New Testament, the Greek word for covenant is *diatheke* which was used thirty-three times. God made a "new covenant" by the blood of Christ, establishing an unending and unchanging legacy of forgiven sins and eternal life for those who repent and believe in him (Hebrews 9:15). Jesus is the mediator of the new covenant (Hebrews 8:6; 12:24). The blood he shed on the cross and symbolized in the cup of the Lord's Supper is "the blood of the new covenant" (Luke 22:20; 1 Corinthians 11:25). In Christ, we are a covenant people. Covenant is the foundational concept upon which all Scripture is built.

A covenant marriage is described powerfully in Genesis 2:24: "Therefore a man shall leave his father and his mother and hold fast to his wife and they shall become one flesh" (Genesis 2:24).

The words "leave," "hold fast," and "become one flesh" provide us incredible insight and life-changing perspective we must understand and live out in our marriage if we are going to enjoy the loving and lasting relationship God intended when he gave us the gift of marriage for the purpose of raising godly offspring (Genesis 2:18; Malachi 2:15).

1. "leave"—The moment we are married, the marriage relationship becomes primary and all other relationships, including with parents, become secondary.

2. "hold fast"—The Hebrew word for "hold fast" presents the idea of two things being glued together permanently. It means wholehearted commitment and absolute loyalty from each person making the covenant. The husband is to remain a one-woman man until the

death of his wife. The wife is to remain a one-man woman until the death of her husband.

3. "become one flesh"– I becomes we. I and mine are replaced by us and ours. Even though each person in the marriage is a very special, unique, and gifted person, together with your spouse, you become more than you are by yourself. When our "I" becomes "we," each of us is in a stronger position because our spouse's strengths compensate for our weaknesses and vice versa. The biblical image of two becoming one is not about a loss of identity. It is about an enhancement of identity through the joining together of two lives. That's why Jesus said, "So they are no longer two but one flesh. What therefore God has joined together let no man separate" (Matthew 19:6).

If you are married or one day plan to be married, God wants you to experience a covenant relationship where you share the love and commitment God has for each of you described in 1 Corinthians 13:4–8a. Regardless of one another's failures or faithlessness to each other, each of you will suffer long, if that is needed, and be faithful to love and care for one another's needs. No matter how selfish or unkind either one of you might be to each other, you will not treat one another as your sins deserve, but will give one another what each of you need—kindness, grace, and truth with gentleness and respect. When one of you is successful, he or she will remember to be grateful and humble before God and your spouse and with a servant-hearted attitude continue to be an encouragement by serving and blessing. Regardless of any frustrations, hurts, or fears that may arise in your relationship, grace and forgiveness will be given to each other to restore your relationship. No matter how many years the relationship lasts or how difficult the circumstances might become in the relationship, each of you can rest assured there will be a persevering commitment in each of your hearts and minds to live Thinking God in living out God's promises and commands for each other's good and to God's glory. The husband will love his wife "as Christ loved the church and gave himself up for her" (Ephesians 5:25) and the wife will "respect her husband" (Ephesians 5:33) as the spiritual leader of the home (Ephesians 5:23). Both husband and wife in these roles will be "submitting to one another out of reverence for Christ" (Ephesians 5:21). In that covenant love, you will live in the assurance of God's protection, confidence, and hope knowing your relationship will endure and grow— because such "love never fails" (1 Corinthians 13:8a).

Tragically, covenant love as I just described based on 1 Corinthians 13 has not been understood or practiced by many where the husband and wife profess to be Christians, including many church leaders who faithfully serve in their church and say they "love the Lord with all their hearts." If you are presently struggling in your marriage, it does not have to stay that way. God is greater than any sin and can forgive any sin (1 John 1:9). God can comfort any heartache and heal any heart (2 Corinthians 1:3–4). God can transform your life and your marriage (Romans 12:1–2). God can reconcile any relationship because he is God (2 Corinthians 5:17–18).

Three of the most joyful experiences of my life have been to lead the ceremony and preach the message at each of my son's weddings. On June 28, 2003, Joshua married Julie Griffith. On June 9, 2005, Phillip married Shelly Ruth. On May 30, 2008, Matthew married Lauren Waeckerle. As I was praying and preparing for Matt and Lauren's wedding, God began to pour through my mind the ways he had taught Roni and me through all our challenges how to live out a covenant marriage that has so enriched and blessed our lives and produced three godly sons (Malachi 2:15).

I shared a list of those ways as "my prayer" for Matt and Lauren right before we witnessed their vows to each other as husband and wife. All three of my sons and several in my church family who had been at each of my son's weddings told me following the wedding, "Dad, (Pastor), that's the most powerful wedding message you have ever done, and I want a copy of that list." One person at the wedding, Deidre Pujols said, "Pastor, I want a wedding just like that."

A year and a half later in Kansas City, Missouri, Albert and Deidre Pujols celebrated their ten-year anniversary on January 1, 2010 by renewing their vows before over six hundred family members and friends. I had the privilege of sharing with them and their guests what I have come to understand are God's ways to live out a covenant marriage to the glory of God. I promise you on the authority of God's perfect Word (Psalm 19:7–8), if you will apply these principles in your life and marriage, God will do exceedingly abundantly more than you could ever imagine or think in you and through you to the glory of God (Ephesians 3:20–21)!

† Humble yourselves daily before the Lord and one another as his servants remembering your position in Christ, dead to sin and alive to God in Christ Jesus (Philippians 2:5–8; Romans 6:11).

† Love, encourage, and forgive each other and others as if you have never been hurt (Ephesians 4:26–5:2).

† Be deeply rooted in the Word of God so you will always know the Lord greater than any trouble, test, temptation, or triumph in your lives (Ephesians 3:16–19; Proverbs 3:5–7).

† Learn and grow in the school of prayer so you can rest and rejoice in God's presence and promises in the worst of times, and stay fixed on God's purpose and perspective in the best of times (Romans 8:28–29; 2 Corinthians 4:17–18).

† Love the Lord your God with all your heart and with all your soul and with all your mind and with all your strength (Mark 12:30).

† Be defined by the Word of God and daily settle the issue of whose you are (1 Corinthians 6:19–20).

† Above all else, guard your heart for it is the wellspring of life (Proverbs 4:23).

† Learn and grow in your understanding of how to make each other know and feel most loved and special to each other (Ephesians 5:17–33).

† Learn and grow in your understanding of how to relate to each other and others in the Lord's grace and truth (John 1:17).

† Learn and grow in the grace of giving (2 Corinthians 8:1–7; 9:6–8).

† Live with the power and passion of God's conviction, confidence, and courage, persevering in all your difficulties, failures, questions, challenges, and successes, keeping your eyes fixed on Jesus (Ephesians 5:17–21; Hebrews 12:1–3).

† Keep the priority to always do the best things: Know the Lord your God first in your life and make him known by leading others to Jesus Christ and discipling them in his Word to do the same (Matthew 6:33; Mark 1:17).

† Following the will of God will not lead you where the grace of God will not keep you, stay confident and courageous in the Lord (2 Peter 1:3–4; Joshua 1:6–9).

† Knowing Jesus is enough to cover every sin, comfort every heartache and complete every life, rest in him (Matthew 11:28–30).

† There is no substitute for obedience to the Lord your God if you want to know his love, joy and, peace (1 John 5:3–4).

† Attempt great things for God and expect great things from God (Ephesians 3:20–21).

† Laugh a lot, play a lot, sing a lot, and dance a lot enjoying the abundant privilege of living your lives together as husband and wife in Jesus Christ (Proverbs 17:22; Ecclesiastes 4:9–12).

At the close of the service, Albert and Deidre stood before all their family and friends and proclaimed with great conviction, confidence, and courage, "As for me and my house, we will serve the LORD" (Joshua 24:15). I encourage you with all my heart to proclaim and live likewise.

As you live in a covenant relationship with each other, God will be honored, your children will be blessed and will want to repeat your lives and your marriage, and everyone who knows you will be encouraged in seeing what God intended marriage to be—a covenant relationship. To God be the glory for the great things he is going to do in and through all of us who are married!

Thinking God—Christian marriage is to be the strongest covenant on earth between two people, the pledge of a man and woman to establish a love that is unconditional and lasts a lifetime because they have already made a covenant with Jesus Christ as their Lord and Savior (Matthew 19:1–8; 1 Corinthians 6:19–20).

Truth to Remember—In a covenant marriage you do not quit, knowing God is greater than any failure or faithlessness; you do not throw in the towel, knowing God is in the business of redeeming messes; you do not bag it and get someone else you think is better, knowing nothing is too hard for God; and you do not give up allowing the devil to win, knowing you have victory in Christ and are living to give God the glory (Galatians 6:9; 2 Peter 1:3–4).

Thinking God in Reflecting—Are you living out the ways you just read that God has used to transform my life and marriage? If not, let this be the first day of the rest of your life to the glory of God (1 Corinthians 10:31).

Thinking God: Parenting

Memorize God's Word!

"You shall have no other gods before me" (Exodus 20:3).

"And these words that I command you today shall be on your heart. You shall teach them diligently to your children, and shall talk of them when you sit in your house, and when you walk by the way, and when you lie down, and when you rise. You shall bind them as a sign on your hand, and they shall be as frontlets between your eyes" (Deuteronomy 6:6–8).

"Only be strong and very courageous, being careful to do according to all the law that Moses my servant commanded you. Do not turn from it to the right hand or to the left, that you may have good success wherever you go. This Book of the Law shall not depart from your mouth, but you shall meditate on it day and night, so that you may be careful to do according to all that is written in it. For then you will make your way prosperous, and then you will have good success" (Joshua 1:7–8).

"Whoever spares the rod hates his son, but he who loves him is diligent to discipline him" (Proverbs 13:24).

"Grandchildren are the crown of the aged, and the glory of children is their fathers" (Proverbs 17:6).

"Train up a child in the way he should go; even when he is old he will not depart from it" (Proverbs 22:6).

"The father of the righteous will greatly rejoice; he who fathers a wise son will be glad in him. Let your father and mother be glad; let her who bore you rejoice" (Proverbs 23:24–25).

"Did he not make them one, with a portion of the Spirit in their union? And what was the one God seeking? Godly offspring. So guard yourselves in your spirit, and let none of you be faithless to the wife of your youth" (Malachi 2:15).

"And you will know the truth, and the truth will set you free" (John 8:32).

"There is therefore now no condemnation for those who are in Christ Jesus" (Romans 8:1).

"Do not be deceived: God is not mocked, for whatever one sows, that will he also reap. For the one who sows to his own flesh will from the flesh reap corruption, but the one who sows to the Spirit will from the Spirit reap eternal life" (Galatians 6:7–8).

"Children, obey your parents in the Lord, for this is right. 'Honor your father and mother' (this is the first commandment with a promise), 'that it may go well with you and that you may live long in the land.' Fathers, do not provoke your children to anger, but bring them up in the discipline and instruction of the Lord" (Ephesians 6:1–4).

T his is a challenging chapter to write because as I said in the preface of the book, I want to encourage and equip you to live in the Lord's victory, Thinking God in every way. However, if you have not had the blessing as a parent of raising godly children and you are already living with great heartache, guard your heart (Proverbs 4:23) as you read this chapter. Do not allow the devil to lie to you (John 8:44) and make you think the intent of this chapter is to condemn you because of past failures. Always remember in hearing the perfect truth of God's Word that sets us free (John 8:32), the Holy Spirit works in our lives to convict us (John 16:8–11) and guide us into all truth (John 16:13). The Holy Spirit does not condemn us (Romans 8:1) and leave us without hope (Romans 15:13). God wants parents and their children to know the joyous reality of Proverbs 23:24–25: "The father of the righteous will greatly rejoice; he who fathers a wise son will be glad in him. Let your father and mother be glad; let her who bore you rejoice." Our walk with the Lord is to be a learning process. Wherever you are in that journey, God is a redeeming, reconciling, and restoring God.

By God's grace and working in our lives (Romans 12:3) and after watching several parents, including our own, struggle greatly in heartache when their children walked away from the Lord during their high school and college years, Roni and I made it a priority in our lives to seek the Lord humbly with all our hearts to learn from God's Word how to raise godly children. God taught us an indescribably powerful truth that influenced our three sons greatly to be godly teenagers and adults. Raising godly children to be godly teenagers and godly adults is not only one of life's greatest joys, it is also God's intended purpose for every parent (Malachi 2:15).

The good news is most Christian parents are not surprised when they hear this indescribably powerful truth. Furthermore, parents know that living this truth out before their children would have a powerful impact upon them for their good. The bad news is many parents after learning this truth either underestimate the powerful influence of doing this or do not discipline themselves to do this in making a profound difference in their children's lives. This blessed way of raising your children for their good, your joy, and God's glory almost seems like a "secret" since it is not modeled by many pastors and church leaders or practiced by many professing Christian parents. This "secret" is a biblical principal practiced throughout God's Word in men and women who trusted and obeyed God wholeheartedly demonstrating life-changing and often history-changing faith. If you are a parent or one day will be a parent, I want you to know and practice this "secret" and know the joy of raising godly children.

I asked Dr. Holly Brand, chair of our church's Living Water Academy Board, to give me a list of those things Christian psychologists recommend as crucial in raising godly children. She gave me the following guidelines. As you read over these, I'm sure you will agree with me, this is a very insightful list and everything on it is biblical, important, good, and needed in raising godly children. They all hint at the "secret" but it still leaves the "secret" out. See if you can identify the "secret" after you read through the list:

Best Practices in Parenting:
Tips for Raising Godly Children

Love unconditionally—show it and say it.

- Play! Children spell "love" T-I-M-E.

- Rules without relationship = rebellion.

- Shepherd the hearts of children, don't just correct behavior. For example, most parents who see two children fighting over an object will treat it as an issue of fairness (i.e. who had it first?). Rather it is an issue of two little sinners who are both deeply selfish. This is when a parent should shepherd the hearts of the children by illuminating their pride and selfishness and their need for a Savior and a heart change.

- Teach children there is no substitute for obedience—first time obedience.

- Teach children to respond to God with "Yes, sir" not "Yes, but."

- Teach and model for children the principle of "first fruits"-giving.

- Children need discipline—the Lord disciplines those he loves.

- Parents are the largest influence on a child's self-concept—every word that proceeds from a parent's mouth should fulfill Ephesians 4:29.

- The three fondest memories young adults have of their childhood are: family meals, time playing outside together with parents, and family vacations.

- Walk your talk—teens are excellent hypocrisy detectors and it is one of the primary reasons that college students fall away from the church.

- Model Christ-like character. More is caught than taught. Be the person you want your children to become.

- Model and teach children self-control.

- Let your children see you pray.

- Pray with your children.

- Pray for your children. Pray Scripture over them.

- Know your children's friends and love on them too.

- Three most important things to avoid adolescent rebellion: between the ages of birth and age four, children must be taught respect for authority; between ages five and eleven, children must be taught strong character; during the teen years they must be taught their identity is found only through a relationship with Christ.

- The success of discipline is determined by consistency.

- The central focus of parenting is the gospel.

- Show respect to children and don't exasperate them.

- Never withhold affection in order to punish children.

- Never shame a child.

- Never spank in anger—always follow the Biblical model of spanking.

- One's parenting goal cannot simply be well behaved children—they must understand why they sin and how to recognize internal change lest they become "white-washed" tombs.

- Teach children the meaning of repentance and let them see evidence of it in your life.
- Ask children for forgiveness when you sin against them.
- Teach children absolute truth and a Biblical worldview.
- Teach children their daily purpose: to love and serve God and love and serve others.
- Overtly teach children how to avoid and resist temptation.
- Teach children to hide God's Word in their hearts. Model it for them.
- Communicate effectively with children:

  - Honesty
  - Affirmation
  - Encouragement
  - Listening
  - Empathizing with temptation
  - Relating to them
  - Nonjudgmental

- *Hug them tight!*

Isn't that an incredible list? As insightful and great as it is though, it only hints at the "secret" but does not state it emphatically as the Bible teaches and models it throughout the Old and New Testaments. If parents do not know the "secret" and more importantly, live out the "secret" before their children, when many children leave home, they fall to "loving the world and the things in the world" (1 John 2:15).

I know you want me to tell you the "secret" now, but I want you to come to realize what the "secret" is yourself. Please do not turn to the end of the chapter to see what it is and rob yourself of discovering this for yourself.

Telling you my journey and learning about my heartaches, doubts, and questions in my journey to discover the "secret" will hopefully help you come to know what the "secret" is. I pray God uses this chapter for a great breakthrough in your life and in your parenting.

When I was seven or eight, I overheard a conversation between my parents and our pastor and his wife one Sunday night after the evening service. Their son had gone to college and become a "prodigal son" (Luke 15:11-24), and they were brokenhearted over his choice to turn away from the Lord and the biblical values they thought they had taught him throughout his life. They could not believe how he had "squandered his property in reckless living" (Luke 15:13), given away his purity, and said he no longer considered himself a Christian.

Hearing their anguish with many tears as they shared this with my parents (none of them knew I had walked in the room next to them with "big ears"), I thought this must really be an exception to what most often happened in families where the children supposedly grow up loving the Lord and faithfully serving the Lord in their church. Going through my middle school and high school years, I continued to learn of other pastor's children and church leader's children walking away from the faith they had been taught by their parents and raised in church to say they accepted as their own. In time, I learned this tragedy was much more common than the exception.

When I went away to college, every professing Christian, but one I had known during my high school years and who chose to attend the same college as me, walked away from their faith in Christ and fell into a life of drugs or drunkenness and sexual immorality within a few months of their freshman year. One of the worst heartaches of my college years came when I discovered my older brother who was two years ahead of me in school had also been living this type of rebellious lifestyle at college. When I confronted him, "Doug, how can you be living like this and call yourself a Christian?" He replied, "If you ever tell Dad or Mom, I'll kill you." I knew my brother loved me, and I did not think he would do such a thing, but it did scare me enough that I went through my freshman year never telling my parents out of fear of what he might do to me if I did. Praise the Lord, in the spring of my freshman year, Doug trusted Christ to be his Lord and Savior!

After college graduation, I became a student at Southwestern Baptist Theological Seminary in Fort Worth, Texas. One day in a class, the topic of "what truly is most important in your life" was discussed. During the discussion, our professor, who was very respected and loved because of his heart for the LORD and his commitment to teach the authority of God's Word, shared: "As important as my teaching is here at seminary and my speaking at many churches and conferences is, as important as all of my degrees are, as important as everything I am esteemed for accomplishing, all my titles and honors, I would give it all up to have my sons walk faithfully with the Lord." He went on to tell us how his sons had walked away from their faith when they had gone away to college and how when his children were in middle school and high school, he was often away from home, over committed in earning his seminary degrees and out of town for speaking engagements. Taking his glasses off and wiping his tears away, he said, "Men, do not lose your children. Know what is most important in your life." From what I had already experienced, I was greatly shaken in my heart, hearing this story from a man who had such a humble heart and commitment to God. I began to carry a heavy burden in my heart wondering, *Is it really possible to raise godly children in this world in which we live?*

Following graduation from Southwestern, I served in a church as minister of music and youth. Not long after I was there, one of my pastor's sons committed suicide. Six months earlier, Roni and I had become parents of our first son. After having my brokenhearted pastor tell me of his son's death and grieving with him, I went into my office, shut the door, got on my face before the LORD, and prayed, "Father, whatever you do in and through my life, I ask you to show me how to be a godly dad to raise godly children."

The Father graciously answered that prayer. By God's greatness, goodness, and grace in my life, I consider, other than my salvation, my greatest blessing in life to be what God has done in my marriage and my three sons. Seeing what God has done and is doing in my marriage and my sons through the years, I could not tell you how often I have had other pastors, professors, and the people I have been privileged to pastor for the last twenty-one years say, "Phil, you are a blessed man."

The first thing the LORD did in my heart was to assure me that based on his purpose stated in his Word, Roni and I could raise "godly offspring" (Malachi 2:15). Always remember, God does not tell us to do anything we cannot do when we humble ourselves before him, submitting ourselves to the authority of his Word and surrendering ourselves to the presence of the Holy Spirit. This was huge in my heart because with everything I have shared, I had also been brokenhearted over my two younger brothers who had also walked away from their commitment to Christ and the authority of his Word during their high school years. For years, I had listened often to my mom's concerns regarding my brothers' struggles, and I had hurt with her and my dad through many tears over my brothers' waywardness and all the heartache and suffering that had followed their choices to disobey the Lord (Galatians 6:7–8).

Let me say again, whatever you have seen and experienced, God never commands or promises us anything he does not intend for us to experience to his glory. I especially want to encourage you if you are a young parent, "God did not give you a spirit of fearfulness, but of power and love and self-control" (2 Timothy 1:7) to know the joy of raising godly children.

So what is the "secret?" *God has given parents an indescribable powerful influence upon their children and in that influence, commands them to live their lives defined by the Word of God, not just influenced by the Word of God!* When parents throughout their lives are experiencing, living, modeling, and communicating Thinking God in everything they are and do, they *create a desire* in their children to be and do likewise by *leaving no doubt* whose they are and what they are for—the LORD's!

This "secret" is taught throughout God's Word. Here are seven examples:

A. It's what Deuteronomy 6:4–9 is all about: "Hear, O Israel: The LORD our God, the LORD is one. You shall love the LORD your God with all your heart and with all your soul and with all your might. And these words that I command you today shall be on your heart. You shall teach them diligently to your children, and shall talk of them when you sit in your house, and when you walk by the way, and when you lie down, and when you rise. You shall bind them as a sign on your hand, and they shall be as frontlets between your eyes. You shall write them on the doorposts of your house and on your gates."

Do you see the "secret" of raising godly children in Deuteronomy 6:4–9? It is "Love the LORD our God with all your heart…all your soul…all your might!" When we do not do that by wholehearted obedience or we obey as if it is a burden or our Christian duty (1John 5:3), we confuse our children.

Confused children live with great conflict when they hear their parents say that "God's Word is perfect truth," and then they see their parents compromising and disobeying the authority of God's Word. Confused children in conflict, with a sinful nature, in a sinful world, bombarded with lies from a 24/7 media, in a war with the devil and spiritual forces of evil (Ephesians 6:11–12), easily fall to the lies of the devil (John 8:44) and the temptations of their flesh to "love the world or the things in the world" (1 John 2:15).

Remember what God had against the church in Ephesus, even though they had "good works, faithful service, patient endurance, and sound doctrine" (Revelation 2:2–3). God said, "You have abandoned the love you had at first" (Revelation 2:4). "Remember therefore from where you have fallen; repent and do the works you did at first" (Revelation 2:5).

Remember what God said to the church in Laodicea, "I know your works: you are neither cold nor hot. Would that you were either cold or hot! So, because you are lukewarm, and neither hot nor cold, I will spit you out of my mouth. For you say, I am rich, I have prospered and I need nothing, not realizing that you are wretched, pitiable, poor, blind, and naked" (Revelation 3:15–17).

Understand: Just as God "spits those who are lukewarm out of his mouth," children spit out their parent's teaching and faith regardless of how many "good works, faithful service, patient endurance, and sound doctrine" they have if their love/ affection for the one LORD God does not leave any doubt who is first in their lives. It is very confusing to children when parents go back and forth on who or what they are worshiping in their lives. (A god is whatever is most important in your life.) *Leave no doubt* who is most important in your life—the LORD God (Exodus 20:3)!

Think about the wholehearted intentionality of these commands: "These words that I command you today shall... be on your heart...teach them diligently...talk of them when you sit...when you walk...when you lie down...when you rise...bind them as a sign on your hand...as frontlets between your eyes...write them on the doorposts and your gates" (Deuteronomy 6:6–9). When we live 24/7 experiencing, living, modeling, and communicating the Word of God to our children and to others, they see our lives as defined by the Word of God. That is radically different than teaching or telling our children about God or teaching them it is important to learn the Word of God.

Just as Jesus warned his disciples about the Pharisees, "Everything they do is done for men to see so do not do what they do" (Matthew 23:1–5), parents must not have a faith that is only seen when we are at church or with Christian leaders or friends we want to impress. That is very confusing to children if parents act one way in certain places and situations but not the same way with them all the time. The word for that behavior is *hypocrite*. We must have a faith that is wholeheartedly authentically lived before our children during our greatest days of success, our darkest days of difficulty, and all the days in between in every season of life. Such a walk of faith will *create a desire* in their hearts to likewise be defined by the Word of God and *leave no doubt* on whose they are and what they are for—the Lord's!

B. It's what Joshua 24:14–15 is all about: "Now therefore fear the Lord and serve him in sincerity and in faithfulness. Put away the gods that your fathers served beyond the River and in Egypt, and serve the Lord. And if it is evil in your eyes to serve the Lord, choose this day who you will serve, whether the gods your fathers served in the region beyond the River, or the gods of the Amorites in whose land you dwell. But as for me and my house, we will serve the Lord."

Here is the "secret" again. If you are going to serve the Lord, you must fear the Lord and wholeheartedly obey the Lord. Parents must stop arrogantly mocking the Lord and confusing their children by what they do during the week and then going and serving in their church on Sunday acting as if everything is fine. Put away your gods—serve the Lord! Be defined by the Word of God and not just influenced by the Word of God. *Leave no doubt!*

Understand: Parents, hear me loud and clear, the intent of this chapter is *not* to make you feel bad, condemned, or shamed about your past. The intent for you and your children is to be awakened to the same reality Joshua was calling Israel out on. In our culture with its temptations and the hundreds of lies and confusing messages of the media our children face weekly, we cannot be compromising and comfortable in our faith. The cost is too high—our children! *Leave no doubt* of whose you are and what you are for—the LORD's!

C. It's what Proverbs 22:6 and Psalm 100:2 are all about: "Train up a child in the way he should go; even when he is old he will not depart from it." "Serve the LORD with gladness! Come into his presence with singing!"

The word *train* in this verse is the Hebrew word *chanak* which carries the ideas of instructing, dedicating, disciplining, and creating an appetite. Because of our children's sinful nature and everything our children face and must overcome in living out their faith, all four of these ingredients are needed— much instruction, extreme dedication, biblical discipline, and creating an appetite by parents to lead them to know and love God better than anything else. Therefore, we must do the following:

1. *Instruct* our children by Thinking God in our modeling and teaching God's Word to them with a heart of rejoicing, prayerfulness, and thankfulness (1 Thessalonians 5:16–18).

2. *Dedicate* ourselves to live before our children a persevering faith, never growing weary in modeling

Christ-like character in the trials and the triumphs of life (Hebrews 12:1–2).

3. *Discipline* our children, not growing weary in exercising consistent biblical discipline; teaching our children there is right and wrong, and there are great blessings for obedience, and there are painful consequences for disobedience to God and to godly authority (Ephesians 6:4).

4. *Create an appetite* in our children's hearts by letting them see in us through all the seasons of life an "abiding life in Christ" (John 15:1–11), a "witnessing life in the power of the Holy Spirit" (Acts 1:8), a "happy life of giving because of Christ" (Acts 20:35), a "victorious life in Christ" (Romans 8:28–39), a "loving life in Christ" (Romans 12:9–21), and an "overflowing life in Christ" with love, peace, and thankfulness" (Colossians 3:1–17).

If we do not do instruct, dedicate, and discipline, the "creating an appetite" in our children's hearts to know, love, and live in Christ can be lacking. Lacking leads to doubting. Doubting leads to being distracted. Distracted leads to being discouraged. Doubting, distracted, and discouraged children can easily fall to the lusts of the flesh and walk away from their faith. We must be defined by the Word of God and *leave no doubt* whose we are and what we are for—the LORD's!

Understand this "secret" of "creating an appetite." Many parents teach their children about God, and they want their children to obey God's Word when what is really needed is for the parents to model joyful obedience to God to their children as they teach. Since more is caught than is taught by our children,

children must see this joyful obedience in their parents in every season of life. When parents serve the LORD without gladness and live much of their lives complaining rather than living with a song of thankfulness in their hearts (Ephesians 5:19–20), they confuse their children because their teaching and modeling of faith does not match. Just as the midwives would rub the palate of a newborn with olive oil in order to give the new baby a taste, creating an appetite for the baby to suck, we create an appetite for our children to feed on the LORD as they see our gratefulness and gladness in the LORD. *Leave no doubt* whose you are and what you are for—the LORD's!

D. It's what Daniel 3:16–18 is all about: "Shadrach, Meshach, and Abednego answered and said to the king, 'O Nebuchadnezzar, we have no need to answer you in this matter. If this be so, our God whom we serve is able to deliver us from the burning fiery furnace, and he will deliver us out of your hand, O king. But if not, be it known to you, O king, that we will not serve your gods or worship the golden image that you have set up.'"

Remember the situation: King Nebuchadnezzar made an image of gold ninety-feet high (Daniel 3:1). Everyone was given the decree upon "hearing the sound of the horn, flute, harp, lyre, and psaltery, in symphony with all kinds of music, shall fall down and worship the golden image. Whoever does not fall down and worship shall be cast into a burning fiery furnace" (Daniel 3:10–11). Shadrach, Meshach, and Abednego had the conviction, confidence, and courage in the one LORD God to not compromise even if it would cost them their lives to not bow down to the image of gold.

Remember what they said:

1. "Our God whom we serve"—The three knew what Jeremiah knew, "The LORD who made the earth, formed it, and established it—the LORD is his name (Jeremiah 33:2) and is all powerful! "Nothing is too hard for the LORD" (Genesis 18:14).

2. "Is able to deliver us"—The three young men trusted in the LORD with all their heart, and did not lean on their own understanding" (Proverbs 3:5).

3. "But if not"—The three young men, surrendered to the sovereignty of the LORD, rested in his wisdom and working in their lives. Life or death, they were the LORD's (Philippians 1:21).

Understand: Years ago I heard Dr. Adrian Rogers say, "A faith that cannot stand much of a testing is not much of a faith. You can tell a lot about a person's faith in what it takes to make him quit on God." Children are encouraged, more than their parents ever know, when they see in the darkest and most difficult times of life their parents standing firm in the Lord rather than shrinking to be comfortable with the crowd and living lives of compromise. Compromise in parents always confuses children. Confusion leads to conflict. We must be defined by the Word of God and *leave no doubt* about whose we are and what we are for—the LORD's!

As parents, we all have those times when we are challenged to bow down and compromise to biblical principles or stand firm in the authority of God's Word. Our children are always watching and listening. You know the old saying, "The apple doesn't fall far from the tree." "Therefore, my beloved brothers, be steadfast, immovable, always abounding in the work of the LORD, knowing that in the Lord your labor is not in vain" (1 Corinthians 15:58). *Leave no doubt* whose you are and what you are for—the LORD's!

E. It's what Luke 1:26–38 is all about: "In the sixth month the angel Gabriel was sent from God to a city of Galilee named Nazareth, to a virgin betrothed to a man whose name was Joseph, of the house of David. And the virgin's name was Mary. And he came to her and said, 'Greetings, O favored one, the Lord is with you!' But she was greatly troubled at the saying, and tried to discern what sort of greeting this might be. And the angel said to her, 'Do not be afraid, Mary, for you have found favor with God. And behold, you will conceive in your womb and bear a son, and you shall call his name Jesus. He will be great and will be called the Son of the Most High. And the Lord God will give to him the throne of his father David, and he will reign over the house of Jacob forever, and of his kingdom there will be no end.' And Mary said to the angel, 'How will this be, since I am a virgin?' And the angel answered her, 'The Holy Spirit will come upon you, and the power of the Most High will overshadow you; therefore the child to be born will be called holy—the Son of God. And behold, your relative Elizabeth in her old age has also conceived a son, and this is the sixth month with her who was called barren. For nothing will be impossible with God.' And Mary said, 'Behold, I am the servant of the Lord; let it be to me according to your word.' And the angel departed from her."

This is one of my favorite passages of Scripture in the Christmas narratives found in Matthew 1–2 and in Luke 1–2. Nothing made any sense in anything the angel said to Mary (Luke 1:28–37). Yet, being defined by the Word of God, notice how Mary humbly listened, trusted, and obeyed the Lord, *leaving no doubt* about whose she was and what she was for—the LORD's:

1. "Greetings, O favored one, the Lord is with you" (Luke 1:28)! Mary, as a common person, did not think of herself as anyone extra special and therefore was greatly troubled at the angel's appearance and declaration. What the angel told Mary was totally contrary to everything she knew about her circumstances. Yet, Mary humbly listened, trusted, and obeyed the Lord. Do you live by the Word of the Lord or by your circumstances?

2. "Do not be afraid, Mary, for you have found favor with God. And behold, you will conceive in your womb and bear a son, and you shall call his name Jesus. He will be great and will be called the Son of the Most High. And the Lord God will give to him the throne of his father David, and he will reign over the house of Jacob forever, and of his kingdom there will be no end." And Mary said to the angel, "How will this be, since I am a virgin" (Luke 1:30-34)? "And the angel answered her, 'The Holy Spirit will come upon you, and the power of the Most High will overshadow you; therefore the child to be born will be called holy—the Son of God. And behold your relative Elizabeth in her old age has also conceived a son and this is the sixth month with her who was called barren. For nothing will be

impossible with with God'" (Luke 1:35–36). This all seemed impossible to Mary because Mary knew it was impossible! But Mary, defined by the Word of God and not just influenced by the Word of God, continued to humbly listen, trust, and yielded herself to the Lord. Knowing nothing was impossible with God, Mary said, "Behold, I am the servant of the Lord; let it be to me according to your word" (Luke 1:38). Do you live by the Word of the Lord, or do you have a lot of impossibilities in your life because you say "yes, but?"

Understand: As parents model this kind of faith of humbly listening, trusting, and yielding themselves to the Lord even when nothing makes sense in their lives or their children's lives, God mightily uses their witness of trusting God according to his Word regardless of their circumstances or feelings to *create a desire* in their children's heart to do likewise. Defined by God's Word, parents *leave no doubt* whose they are and what they are for—the LORD's!

As a parent, if you have lived most of your Christian life only influenced by God's Word rather than being defined by God's Word, do not let the devil succeed in condemning you for your past. Remember, condemnation is not from the LORD and only paralyzes you to live in guilt and shame. The Holy Spirit convicts us with a "godly grief producing a repentance that leads to salvation without regret" (2 Corinthians 7:10). If there is a need to repent, repent and let this be the first day of the rest of your life to God's glory, your joy, and your children's good. Be defined by the Word of God and *leave no doubt* how you are going to live your life this day forward. Plan a special time to tell your children of this new beginning in your life and their lives.

F. It's what Matthew 26:6–13 is all about: "Now when Jesus was at Bethany in the house of Simon the leper, a woman came up to him with an alabaster flask of very expensive ointment, and she poured it on his head as he reclined at a table. And when the disciples saw it, they were indignant, saying, 'Why this waste? For this could have been sold for a large sum and given to the poor.' But Jesus, aware of this, said to them, 'Why do you trouble the woman? For she has done a beautiful thing to me. For you always have the poor with you, but you will not always have me. In pouring this ointment on my body, she has done it to prepare me for burial. Truly, I say to you, wherever this gospel is proclaimed in the whole world, what she has done will also be told in memory of her.'"

Notice how Jesus described this extravagant act toward him as "a beautiful thing to me." Nowhere else is Jesus ever recorded to say, "wherever this gospel is proclaimed in the whole world, what she has done will also be told in memory of her." I love it!

Understand: When parents demonstrate extravagant giving to the Lord before their children, they provide them with precious memories. Those expressions of love and devotion linger in their children's minds. Because so many Christians live confused in their selfish thinking that "life is all about them" instead of they were "created by God and for God" (Colossians 1:16), they have never come to learn and live the liberating truth Jesus said: "It is more blessed to give than to receive" (Acts 20:35). When you were redeemed by the Lord, you were to be reconciled from your selfishness to become an extravagant and hilarious giver (2 Corinthians 9:7). You have probably heard the wise statement, "You can give without loving because you can give out of duty, but you cannot love without giving." It confuses children greatly when they hear their parents say and sing how they love the Lord but do not demonstrate that in their giving. Children figure out at a young age, the more you love someone, the more you give to them. (Just ask my grandchildren.)

One of my greatest joys of being a pastor is leading several men's weekly Bible studies. Knowing the impact upon children when their parents are extravagant givers to the Lord and his work, and how children take notice by the aroma of such giving, I have asked men this question for many years, "How many of you when telling your children how much you love the Lord have told them of your joy of giving your tithes and offerings to your church and other kingdom work?" Sadly, many have not known that joy. When you do, I cannot tell you how much that influences your children to *leave no doubt* in their lives to do likewise. As they say, "money talks."

G. It's what Luke 14:25–35 is all about: "Now great crowds accompanied him, and he turned and said to them, 'If anyone comes to me and does not hate his own father and mother and wife and children and brothers and sisters, yes, and even his own life, he cannot be my disciple. Whoever does not bear his own cross and come after me cannot be my disciple. For which of you, desiring to build a tower, does not first sit down and count the cost, whether he has enough to complete it? Otherwise, when he has laid a foundation and is not able to finish, all who see it begin to mock him, saying,

'This man began to build and was not able to finish.' Or what king, going out to encounter another king in war, will not sit down first and deliberate whether he is able with ten thousand to meet him who comes against him with twenty thousand? And if not, while the other is yet a great way off, he sends a delegation and asks for terms of peace. So therefore, any one of you who does not renounce all that he has cannot be my disciple. 'Salt is good, but if salt has lost its taste, how shall its saltiness be restored? It is of no use either for the soil or for the manure pile. It is thrown away. He who has ears to hear, let him hear.'"

I first remember hearing this passage of Scripture being taught at a Northwest Baptist Youth Conference in Seattle, Washington when I was fourteen. I know that is hard to believe that I would remember. It is in fact the only message I remember in detail from my teenage years. The speaker was very passionate in his teaching and unreserved in detailing the costs of following Christ as he led us through this passage of Scripture. After he read and explained the meaning of each of the Lord's statements, he challenged us with questions like:

- "Are you willing to walk alone with the Lord or do you always want to be a part of the crowd?"

- "Is the Lord truly first in your life even above family where you would be willing to move thousands of miles away from your parents if that is where the Lord leads you to follow and serve him?"

- "Have you come to understand that trusting Jesus Christ as your Lord and Savior is not an addition to your life—it is to be the end of your old life and the beginning of a new life in Christ?"

- "Have you counted the cost truly of following Jesus, or when the cost seems too high, do you run?"
- "Do your friends back at school know that Jesus is good because they can see his goodness in your life?"
- "What do you hear the Lord saying to you today?"

During the invitation, the Holy Spirit broke my heart with how much God loved me and how he longed for me to truly surrender everything to him. I wept in brokenness, repentance, gratitude, and love for my Lord. Not long after that, during an invitation in a Sunday night service in my church, I made a public confession of my surrendered life to love and serve the Lord in vocational Christian ministry. I had no idea what that meant, but I knew I was the LORD's and I would *leave no doubt* for the rest of my life whose I was and what I was for—the LORD's! And forty-nine years later, "Thanks be to God for his inexpressible gift" (2 Corinthians 9:15) of being loved and able to love, learn, serve, and share him! For years I have told my sons, "If I had ten zillion lives to live on this earth, I would live every day for Jesus Christ!" *Leave no doubt* whose you are and what you are for—the LORD's!

Understand: More is caught than is taught. Therefore, I encourage you to be courageously honest as you answer these three questions:

1. Do you tell your children to not be selfish and then show them, "it is more blessed to give than to receive" (Acts 22:35) by being a grateful and hilarious giver of

your time, talents, and tithes and offerings to God's work (2 Corinthians 9:6–8)? During each year and/or at the end of each year in the attitude of gratitude, do you share with your children the joy you have to be able to sacrificially give to the Lord's work? Have you ever told them how much you extravagantly gave during the past year to the Lord and his work?

Create a desire in their lives—*leave no doubt* by telling them and showing them how much you give because of the priority of your heart to seek the Lord first (Matthew 6:19–33) and love the LORD the most (Matthew 22:37) in your life. When you do, I promise you they will know your love for God is genuine because they know you cannot love deeply without giving greatly. The greater you love someone, the more you will give to that person.

2. Do you tell your children how important God is in your life and then show them by often sharing the gospel of Jesus Christ with others? If your children are already eighteen or when your children reach the age of eighteen, how many times have they seen or will they see you show the importance of God in your life because you have to tell others about his love for them? It is very confusing to your children if you are always taking them to church and worshipping God, learning about God, acting and talking about how God is so important in your life and yet you never or rarely speak about him to those who do not yet know Christ as their Lord and Savior.

Create a desire in their lives—*leave no doubt* by sharing Jesus with others on a daily basis. Make weekly appointments with others to share Christ and take your children with you so they can see your priority and passion for others to know Christ.

3. Do you tell your children how important it is to forgive others, and then do you show them in your deepest hurts and wounds from others by modeling forgiveness as you yield your life to the power of the Holy Spirit, submitting your life to the authority of God's Word by "letting all bitterness and wrath and anger and clamor and slander be put away from you along with all malice, being kind to one another, tenderhearted, forgiving one another, as God in Christ forgave you" (Ephesians 4:31–32)? Are your children aware of any situation in your life where someone has deeply hurt you, betrayed you, deeply offended you, wounded you, and/or caused you great loss, and you have confused them about what you have taught them about forgiveness when you have not forgiven?

Create a desire—*leave no doubt* by humbling your life before God, so you can receive his grace to live the Spirit-filled life before your children "being doers of the word, and not hearers only, deceiving yourselves" (James 1:22) and your children. Forgive!

Understand: As children see the goodness of the Lord (Psalm 34:8) being lived in and through their parents in every season of life through wholehearted obedience to God's Word, a growing desire is created in them to be like their dad and mom and *leave no doubt* whose they are and what they are for—the LORD's!

In finishing this chapter, I know there are still many questions with "what if" and "what about." I have listened to them through the years and still do. I have often been asked, "What about you? With all three of your brothers falling away from their faith in their high school or college years, why didn't you?" It is a mystery of God's greatness, grace, and goodness in my life just as I have known some children who have grown up with no witness of Christ from their parents and yet, they have humbly trusted Christ to change their lives and have become mighty champions of God with the encouragement and equipping by others in the church. They have remained faithful to the Lord through their high school and college years and are now serving the Lord fruitfully as adults.

I love my parents with all my heart and will forever be grateful for everything they did in doing their best to bless my life indescribably in every way they knew possible. But my parents did make compromises in their lives that confused my brothers and led them to have much more conflict in their lives than I did. Being the pianist of my church since I was fourteen and having the privilege of playing for state evangelism conferences and other large Christian events since I was nineteen, I was extremely blessed to have many pastors and seminary professors love me, pray with me, encourage me, and mentor me through my teenage and young adult years. I have no idea how all of that love, prayer, encouragement, and mentoring from godly men has impacted my life for my good. But I do know, "Everyone to whom much was given, of him much will be required, and from him to whom they entrusted much, they will demand the more" (Luke 12:48). I have been given much.

I must give one final encouraging word as a grandparent to every parent of children who are now adults, married, and have started their own families and are parenting their children. Always remember, God is the one who is restorer "to you the years that the swarming locust has eaten" (Joel 2:25). Do not ever underestimate the power of being defined by God's Word in your life to encouragingly influence your children to be defined by the Word of God, *creating a desire—leaving no doubt* in your children and/or grandchildren regardless of their age. God is in the business of "making all things new" (Revelation 21:5)!

When our children are married, we must give them away (Genesis 2:24), but God still has invested in us, as their parents, the incomprehensible power of influencing them by the way we live our lives and by the words we speak to them. During the past year our son, Matt, was ordained to the Gospel Ministry. In that service, I read these words and had them framed to hang on his office wall to always remind him his dad and mom wanted him by God's grace in his life to *leave no doubt* of whose he was and what he was for—the LORD's:

> To Matthew, Our Dear Son,
>
> We are filled with joy as we think of your sincere faith you have had since you were a little boy. Always remember, God did not give us a spirit of fearfulness, but a spirit of power, of love, and of self-control. What you have learned from us, keep as the pattern of sound teaching with faith and love in Christ Jesus.

Daily surrendering your life to God's presence, you will continue to be strong in the grace and truth of Jesus Christ! Continue to make disciples for Jesus Christ who will reach and disciple others for Christ. Teach God's Word as the trustworthy authority for life. In your disappointments and difficulties, God is faithful! There is no rest in quitting, but only in finishing when God calls! Run the race God has marked out for you with perseverance staying fixed on Jesus, the author and finisher of your faith!

You are the fragrance of the knowledge of Christ in a world where the lost are blind to seeing the light of the gospel of the glory of Christ. Stay prepared in season and out of season. Keep on loving as if you have never been hurt. Keep on teaching and preaching as if you have never been frustrated. Keep on serving as if you have never been disappointed. Keep on giving as if you have never needed. When you are persecuted for living a godly life in Christ Jesus, continue in what you have learned and are convinced is the perfect truth of God's Word. Always remember, whatever God has taught you in the light, it does not change in the dark!

Never leave a doubt whose you are or what you are for! Jesus said, "Follow me and I will make you fishers of men." When you are fishing:

- You are pleasing the Father in obeying him.
- You are carrying out the Lord's mission of seeking and saving those who are lost.
- You are seeing and caring for others with compassion, as Christ did.

- You are coming to "have a full understanding of every good thing we have in Christ."

Don't ever become too busy to make appointments to share Christ every week with those who need him!

Keep your head in all situations. How you think will determine your faithfulness to do the Father's will, so think according to the Word of God! What you need to be and do publicly comes from what you are privately with the Father, so remember your most important time each day is alone with the Father. How you see people makes all the difference, so have a daily check-up with the Father— whatever you are filled with will determine how you see others.

There are no words to express our love for you! May our God continue to do "immeasurably more than all we ask or imagine, according to his power that is at work within you" (Ephesians 3:20).

Dad and Mom

Presenting this to Matt was such a blessing to him and his wife, I found a special time in Phillip and Josh's life to also give them a framed copy of this to bless them and leave no doubt whose we are and what we are for—the Lord's! I plan to also give a copy of this to each of our grandchildren as they begin their middle school years.

Thinking God—God has given parents an indescribable powerful influence upon their children and in that influence, commands them to live their lives defined by the Word of God to *leave no doubt* of whose they are and what they are for—the LORD's (James 1:22)!

Truth to Remember—When parents are experiencing, living, modeling, and communicating Thinking God in everything they are and do, they create a desire in their children to be and do likewise by leaving no doubt whose they are and what they are for—the LORD's (Proverbs 22:6)!

Thinking God in Reflecting—Always remember, God is the one who is the restorer "to you the years that the swarming locust has eaten" (Joel 2:25)! Do not underestimate the power of being defined by God's Word in your life to encouragingly influence your children and/or grandchildren to be defined by the Word of God no matter how old they are. God is in the business of "making all things new" (Revelation 21:5)!

Thinking God: Sharing Jesus with Others

Memorize God's Word!

"Then he said to his disciples, 'The harvest is plentiful, but the laborers are few; therefore pray earnestly to the Lord of the harvest to send out laborers into his harvest'" (Matthew 9:37–38).

"And Jesus came and said to them, 'All authority in heaven and on earth has been given to me. Go therefore and make disciples of all nations, baptizing them in the name of the Father and of the Son and of the Holy Spirit, teaching them to observe all that I have commanded you. And behold, I am with you always, to the end of the age'" (Matthew 28:18–20).

"And Jesus said to them, 'Follow me, and I will make you become fishers of men'" (Mark 1:17).

"For he and all who were with him were astonished at the catch of fish that they had taken, and so also were James and John, sons of Zebedee, who were partners with Simon. And Jesus said to Simon,

'Do not be afraid; from now on you will be catching men'" (Luke 5:9–10).

"He first found his own brother Simon and said to him, 'We have found the Messiah' (which means Christ)'" (John 1:41).

"For God so loved the world, that he gave his only Son, that whoever believes in him should not perish but have eternal life" (John 3:16).

"The thief comes only to steal and kill and destroy. I came that they may have life and have it abundantly" (John 10:10).

"Jesus said to him, 'I am the way, and the truth, and the life. No one comes to the Father except through me'" (John 14:6).

"But you will receive power when the Holy Spirit has come upon you, and you will be my witnesses in Jerusalem and in all Judea and Samaria, and to the end of the earth" (Acts 1:8).

"And there is salvation in no one else, for there is no other name under heaven given among men by which we must be saved" (Acts 4:12).

"And every day, in the temple and from house to house, they did not cease teaching and preaching that the Christ is Jesus" (Acts 5:42).

"Now those who were scattered went about preaching the word" (Acts 8:4).

"For I am not ashamed of the gospel, for it is the power of God for salvation to everyone who believes, to the Jew first and also to the Greek. For in it the righteousness of God is revealed from faith for faith, as it is written, 'The righteous shall live by faith'" (Romans 1:16–17).

"For all have sinned and fall short of the glory of God" (Romans 3:23).

"But God shows his love for us in that while we were still sinners, Christ died for us" (Romans 5:8).

"For the wages of sin is death, but the free gift of God is eternal life in Christ Jesus our Lord" (Romans 6:23).

"There is therefore now no condemnation for those who are in Christ Jesus" (Romans 8:1).

"Because, if you confess with your mouth that Jesus is Lord and believe in your heart that God raised him from the dead, you will be saved. For with the heart one believes and is justified, and with the mouth one confesses and is saved" (Romans 10:9).

"For the word of the cross is folly to those who are perishing, but to us who are being saved it is the power of God" (1 Corinthians 1:18).

"For the kingdom of God does not consist in talk but in power" (1 Corinthians 4:20).

"Therefore, we are ambassadors for Christ, God making his appeal through us. We implore you on behalf of Christ, be reconciled to God" (2 Corinthians 5:20).

"Praying at all times in the Spirit, with all prayer and supplication. To that end keep alert with all perseverance, making supplication for all the saints, and also for me, that words may be given to me in opening my mouth boldly to proclaim the mystery of the gospel" (Ephesians 6:19).

"But I am not ashamed, for I know whom I have believed, and I am convinced that he is able to guard until that Day what has been entrusted to me" (2 Timothy 1:12).

"And I pray that the sharing of your faith may become effective for the full knowledge of every good thing that is in us for the sake of Christ" (Philemon 1:6).

"And I heard a loud voice in heaven, saying, 'Now the salvation and the power and the kingdom of our God and the authority of his Christ have come, for the accuser of our brothers has been thrown down, who accuses them day and night before our God. And they have conquered him by the blood of the Lamb and by the word of their testimony, for they loved not their lives even unto death'" (Revelation 12:10–11).

෩ාༀ

Sharing Jesus Christ with others as you go through your day and leading others to trust him as their Lord and Savior is normal Christianity when you read the New Testament. I pray God will use my story and the teaching of God's Word to lead you to experience what you were saved for: "that you may be active in sharing your faith, so that you will have a full understanding of every good thing we have in Christ" (Philemon 6, NIV).

Growing up, my mom worked in the admissions and billing office of Bradley County Medical Center, the one hospital in Warren, Arkansas. My earliest memories in life were going with her to various homes to visit some family or man to inform them, "I'm sorry, but the hospital is going to have to deduct some of your pay each month to pay for your hospital bill that has become delinquent." Since my mom did not like to go into homes by herself, knowing there might be tension and possibly even conflict since nobody wants to hear what she had to say, she would often take me with her as a "security blanket." After the business part of the visit was completed, my mom would say, (using "Jones" for the name) "Mr. Jones, I want you to know how much God loves you and proved that love by giving his son, Jesus, to die on the cross to pay for your sins. John 3:16 says, 'For God so loved the world that he gave his only begotten Son, that whosoever believeth in him should not perish, but have everlasting life.' Do you know, Mr. Jones, that you are a sinner and need God's forgiveness?" Mr. Jones would most often respond, "Yes, I know that." A conversation would develop about family, interests, and the challenges of life. I would listen and watch my mom lead a stranger who had been upset about a deduction in their pay "travel over a bridge" (using friendship evangelism techniques I would be taught in seminary twenty years later) from not knowing about the love of Christ and failing miserably in life to listening intently to the saving message of Jesus Christ. Some of them trusted Jesus Christ to be their Lord and Savior!

There was always great rejoicing "with the angels" (Luke 15:10) that followed. My mom knew the importance of follow-up and would do her best to help each person and/ or family become involved in a local church to be encouraged and grow in their new relationship with Christ. I believe it is because of the great rejoicing that followed, which often included many tears and even shouting in the deliverance of the Lord, that I can remember some of these events so vividly, even though I was only four or five.

At the same time that I was experiencing the joy of seeing my mom share her faith with others trusting Christ as their Lord and Savior, it was common in my church, First Baptist Church, to have a one, two, or even three-week revival meeting every fall and spring. During every revival meeting, it was emphasized for everyone to share Jesus with their family members and friends who did not yet know the joy of trusting him as their personal Lord and Savior. We would often have early morning services, noon services, and evening services during the revival meetings. Sometimes, the guest evangelist stayed in our home. If he didn't stay in our home, he almost always had a meal with our family and the conversation always focused on my mom and him talking about the joy of leading others to Christ. Because of school, I could only attend the morning and evening services. It did not matter whether it was my pastor or a guest evangelist speaking, they all had the same message, "If you love Jesus and care about people, you should be sharing Jesus with them. It was our Lord's mission (Luke 19:10). It was the early church's mission (Acts 1:8). It is our mission (Matthew 28:18–20)."

Living in such an environment and watching my mom share her faith throughout the year whether there was a revival meeting or not, I grew up thinking it was normal Christianity to share Jesus with everyone. Seeing my mom make appointments with persons to take them through the Scriptures, so they could know how to trust Jesus as their Lord and Savior was just as normal for my mom and me to do as it was for me to go to school. It was just normal. Hearing my pastors, Sunday school teachers, and Mom teach me God's Word, I also saw it was normal everywhere in the New Testament. If you followed Jesus as your Lord, you were telling others about him (Matthew 28:18–20; Mark 1:17; Luke 5:10; Acts 1:8; Acts 5:42).

Therefore, when I trusted Jesus to be my Lord and Savior at the age of seven and God gave me that desire he promises to give in everyone's life who receives him, "Come ye after me, and I will make you to become fishers of men" (Mark 1:17,

KJV), it was just normal that I went to school the next day and I had to tell the meanest boy (at least that was what I thought) in my class, Tommy Thomas, about Jesus. That was the power of the Holy Spirit in me (Acts 1:8; 4:13; 5:42) because up to that day even with the teaching and example of my mom, my pastor, and my Sunday school teachers, I was afraid of Tommy and would not even go around him because he was taking boxing lessons. Tommy had a reputation for sometimes getting into trouble for hitting persons.

That's what Jesus does when he comes into our lives—he gives us the power of his love for others and a passionate courage to overcome our fearfulness (2 Timothy 1:7). I invited Tommy to go to the revival we were having. He agreed to go with me, saying, "No one has ever invited me to go to church." Each day at school we would talk about the meaning of what the evangelist had said the night before. Without Jesus, Tommy was living in the darkness of sin and did not understand spiritual things (2 Corinthians 4:4). At the end of that week, Tommy trusted Jesus to be his Lord and Savior. Tommy became one of my best friends, and for the next six years until my family moved to Washington, everyone in my school knew if they were going to give me trouble, they would have trouble with Tommy.

Moving to Ephrata, Washington in 1964, where there was no Southern Baptist Church, my parents started one in our home. Every Sunday, everyone in our family would dress up—Dad and we four boys in our suits, and my mom in one of her Sunday dresses. We would walk from our bedroom to the living room to have a Bible study with ten to fifteen others and then a worship service. After six months, we rented a Seventh-day Adventist Church to use for our Sunday ministries, and we didn't complain as much about putting a suit on since we were now able to go somewhere for church.

Things were no different for my mom just because she had moved from the "Bible Belt" to one of the most liberal and "un-churched" states in our nation. I would often hear her in a conversation with a new acquaintance say, "Has anyone ever told you how much God loves you?" When conversations would continue, she would often make an appointment to share Christ with them. Sometimes my dad would go with her. Often, I would go with my dad and mom or with just my mom.

Throughout her life, my mom never got over the thrill of sharing Jesus with others. After sharing Jesus with someone and making an appointment for us to go to their home and take them through the Scriptures, she would come home and excitedly say to me, "We have another one!" And I would reply, "Who with?" Through these experiences, my mom taught me a very important truth about sharing Jesus with others: "Sharing Jesus will always take us out of our way to be on God's way because God's love always cares enough to go out of its way." Until we went to see this person or family, I would begin to hear my mom pray for these persons that they would come to see the joy of trusting Jesus Christ to be their Lord and Savior.

Once the time for the appointment came, and we entered the home my mom would make the person or family feel loved, comfortable, and special. She was gifted in this ability. She called everyone "sweetie," "honey," or "sugar." Asking questions about the person or their family and sharing about our family and asking questions about their interests, she would find a way she needed this person's help. When I asked her why she did this, she explained, "Persons need to feel needed and important instead of what often they have come to feel and believe without the Lord, worthless, empty, guilty and hopeless in life." Asking questions about their church background and finding things we all had in common, she continued to teach me how to do friendship evangelism by "just doing it" (James 1:22). "Building the bridge" as she called it from being a stranger to becoming a friend with this person or family, she would wait for the Lord to bring himself up often reminding me before we went for our appointment, "God will open the door for us to present his Word and then the Spirit will do his work of opening their eyes to see the truth of surrendering their lives to Jesus." And I would watch it happen over and over again.

Adapting her presentation to each person's unique background and needs, she would use Scriptures to "scratch where people itched." (You can tell I am from Arkansas.) A more dignified way to say it is to "touch people where they hurt." She would begin by telling her own story of coming to know Jesus as her Lord and Savior. She would say, (using the person's first names) "Bill and Ann, when I was a young girl in Oklahoma, I was invited by a neighbor family to go with them in a wagon to a little country church. The first verse I ever learned was John 3:16. It says, 'For God so loved the world that he gave his only begotten Son that whosoever believeth in him should not perish but have everlasting life.'" Asking them if they had ever heard that, hearing their response, answering any questions they had about God's love, and explaining why Jesus had to die because of God's justice and sin needing to be paid for was usually a lengthy discussion of twenty minutes to an hour. If my mom was invited for a visit, she was never in a hurry. She would continue to say, "The Bible tells us, 'For all have sinned and come short of the glory of God' (Romans 3:23), 'But God demonstrated his love toward us, in that, while we were yet sinners, Christ died for us'" (Romans 5:8). She would keep going, "The wonderful good news is even though the wages of sin is death, the gift of God is eternal life through Jesus Christ our Lord" (Romans 6:23). Depending on the situation, she would often add, "Jesus said, I am the way, the truth, and the life: no man cometh unto the Father, but by me" (John14:6), or "Therefore if any man be in Christ, he is a new creature: old things are passed away; behold, all things are become new" (2 Corinthians 5:17), or "By grace are you saved through faith; and that not of yourselves: it is the gift of God: not of works, lest any man should boast, For we are his workmanship, created in Christ Jesus unto good works, which God hath before ordained that we should walk in them" (Ephesians 2:8–10).

As my mom would answer questions with "this is what the Bible tells us" and quote the Scripture and/or show the person the Scriptures to read for themselves, she would assure every person "God is sufficient to meet every need you have." She was always very loving, gracious, and kind, but forthright in her sharing about the need for repentance and surrender to anyone making a commitment to trust Christ as one's Lord and Savior. I would prayerfully wait for her to ask the question that with the right response can always change everything: "Bill and Ann, would you like to trust Jesus Christ to be your Lord and Savior?" When the answer was "yes" or following some questions and answers from God's Word and the answer was "yes," we would all get on our knees, and I would watch my mom lead some more precious persons to begin a new relationship with Christ with the promise: "Being confident of this very thing, that he which hath begun a good work in you will perform it until the day of Jesus Christ" (Philippians 1:6). And there was always great rejoicing "with the angels of God over more sinners who had repented" (Luke 15:10).

If the persons we had shared the gospel with were not ready to surrender their lives to Christ, my mom assured them of our prayers for God to continue to work in their lives to see the privilege of trusting Christ. She would always invite them to come to our Bible study hour and our worship services each Sunday at our new church to learn more about the Lord's indescribable love for them and his purpose for their lives. Leaving, she would encouragingly say, "I am always available to help you in any way, and I want to see you in church this Sunday!"

In chapter four, I mentioned the challenge of caring for my mom following a stroke that left her paralyzed and unable to walk unassisted the last two and a half years of her life. During that time in the midst of all her challenges and adjustments, she never got over the joy of sharing Christ with others. I would encourage her on her "hard days" of missing the blessings of having good health, of being independent, and able to do the many things she had enjoyed to remember she was on a special mission to caregivers, nurses, and doctors just as the apostle Paul would often find himself on a special mission to the Roman guards when he was imprisoned. By God's grace in our lives, there was never a caregiver, nurse, or doctor who cared for her during her last two years of life on earth who did not hear of the love, joy, and peace of trusting Jesus Christ as their Lord and Savior. Some of them came to trust Jesus as their Lord and Savior. Six months before she died, she suffered, according to her doctor, several more little strokes. The day came after a visit with the doctor when he told me, "Your mom will probably live only two to three more months." After a couple of visits to the hospital where she did not enjoy their care because it always included embarrassing tests and needles, she told me, "Honey, don't take me back to the hospital anymore." During her "last weeks," we had hospice care for her twenty-four hours a day.

I assured her, "Mom, some of these ladies are going to come to know Jesus before you die." She would smile at me and nod her weak little head in agreement with me. The night before she died, and she had gone into a "sleep" most of the time, I had the joy of leading one of her caregivers, Cara, to trust Christ as her Lord and Savior. I took Cara to my mom's bedside, and said, "Mom, Mom, wake up, Mom, wake up! Cara just trusted Jesus to be her Lord and Savior! I told you it would happen!" Her eyes barely opened. She smiled. She could not speak. I said, "Mom it's okay, I will keep sharing Jesus. Your grandsons will keep sharing Jesus. I will teach your great-grandchildren to share Jesus. It's time for you to go on home. Go home, Mama." She shut her eyes. Those were the last words I was privileged to speak to my mom. Those were the last words I was able to say to the one who had showed me and taught me the joy of sharing Jesus with others is just normal Christianity!

If you do not yet know the joy of sharing Jesus daily with others and making appointments with others to take them through the Scriptures and see the Holy Spirit convict, convince, and draw them to a saving knowledge and surrender to Christ, this can be the first day of the rest of your life. Do not accept yesterday's failures as today's finals for your life. Failure is final only if you let it be final. Remember, the purpose of you becoming a new creation in Jesus Christ was to begin Thinking God (2 Corinthians 5:17–18)—that means "you will be my witnesses in Jerusalem and in all Judea and Samaria, and to the end of the earth" (Acts 1:8).

Thinking God, think how normal it should be for each of us who say we are following Christ to daily share Christ with others (Mark 1:17; Acts 1:8). Throughout the New Testament, the following Scriptures demonstrate how telling others what Jesus had done in their lives was so expected by the Lord and modeled by everyone who followed the Lord:

In Matthew 4:12–19—"Now when he heard that John had been arrested, he withdrew into Galilee. And leaving Nazareth he went and lived in Capernaum by the sea, in the territory of Zebulun and Naphtali, so that what was spoken by the prophet Isaiah might be fulfilled: 'The land of Zebulun and the land of Naphtali, the way of the sea, beyond the Jordan, Galilee of the Gentiles—the people dwelling in darkness have seen a great light, and for those dwelling in the region and shadow of death, on them a light has dawned.' From that time Jesus began to preach, saying, 'Repent, for the kingdom of heaven is at hand.' While walking by the Sea of Galilee, he saw two brothers, Simon (who is called Peter) and Andrew his brother, casting a net into the sea, for they were fishermen. And he said to them, 'Follow me, and I will make you fishers of men.'"

In Mark 1:14–18—"Now after John was arrested, Jesus came into Galilee, proclaiming the gospel of God, and saying, 'The time is fulfilled, and the kingdom of God is at hand; repent and believe in the gospel.' Passing alongside the Sea of Galilee, he saw Simon and Andrew the brother of Simon casting a net into the sea, for they were fishermen. And Jesus said to them, 'Follow me, and I will make you become fishers of men.' And immediately they left their nets and followed him."

In Luke 5:9–11—"For he and all who were with him were astonished at the catch of fish that they had taken, and so also were James and John, sons of Zebedee, who were partners with Simon. And Jesus said to Simon, 'Do not be afraid; from now on you will be catching men.' And when they had brought their boats to land, they left everything and followed him."

In Matthew, Mark, and Luke, of all the important things Jesus could have told them that it was meant for them to follow him—worship him, love him, trust him, obey him, serve him, and he did tell them to do each of these very important things. Yet, Jesus told them from the beginning in following him, "I will make you become fishers of men." There could not be a clearer message given by the Lord in Matthew, Mark, and Luke to anyone who chooses to follow him. That's why the greatest mystery of all mysteries to me is how so few Christians out of the millions who say they love Jesus with all their hearts and say they are following him as their Lord do not do what he first told them to do and what he promised to do in their lives—"I will make you become fishers of men" (Mark 1:17). You may have heard it said, and rightfully so when you read the New Testament, "If you are following Jesus, you are fishing! If you are not fishing, you are either backslidden or lost."

In Matthew 28:18–20—"And Jesus came and said to them, 'All authority in heaven and on earth has been given to me. Go therefore and make disciples of all nations, baptizing them in the name of the Father and of the Son and of the Holy

Spirit, teaching them to observe all that I have commanded you. And behold, I am with you always, to the end of the age.'"

We cannot make disciples until we first lead them to trust Christ to be their Lord and Savior. We cannot baptize them in the name of the Father and of the Son and of the Holy Spirit until we first lead them to trust Christ to be their Lord and Savior. We cannot teach them to obey everything the Lord has commanded until we first lead them to trust him to be their Lord and Savior. Let's start sharing Christ daily! In your prayer time each day, start asking God to give you opportunities to make appointments to lead others to trust Christ to be their Lord and Savior.

Remember his promise when you ask according to the Lord's will: "And this is the confidence that we have toward him, that if we ask anything according to his will he hears us. And if we know that he hears us in whatever we ask, we know that we have the requests that we have asked of him" (1 John 5:14–15). Thinking God, if you ask God for appointments, he will give them to you. He gives them to me all the time. He gave another one to me today.

In Luke 19:10—"For the Son of Man came to seek and to save the lost."

If we love Jesus, we are going to love what he loves and hate what he hates. Jesus loves people so much "that though he was rich, yet for your sake he became poor, so that you by his poverty might become rich" (2 Corinthians 8:9). How can we be or do any less but to seek out the lost, and do everything we can so they will come to Christ?

In Luke 14:15–23—"When one of those who reclined at the table with him heard these things, he said to him, 'Blessed is everyone who will eat bread in the kingdom of God!' But he said to him, 'A man once gave a great banquet and invited many. And at the time for the banquet he sent his servant to say to those who had been invited, 'Come, for everything is now ready.' But they all alike began to make excuses. The first said to him, 'I have bought a field, and I must go out and see it. Please have me excused.' And another said, 'I have bought five yoke of oxen, and I go to examine them. Please have me excused.' And another said, 'I have married a wife, and therefore I cannot come.' So the servant came and reported these things to his master. Then the master of the house became angry and said to his servant, 'Go out quickly to the streets and lanes of the city, and bring in the poor and crippled and blind and lame.' And the servant said, 'Sir, what you commanded has been done, and still there is room.' And the master said to the servant, 'Go out to the highways and hedges and compel people to come in, that my house may be filled.'"

Again, how could the Lord's command to us be any clearer: "Go out to the highways and hedges and compel people to come in that my house may be filled" (Luke 14:23). Yes, many in their blindness of being lost will have excuses that sound good to them. It's easy to become discouraged and even feel rejected when people keep giving excuses to you. Aren't you grateful though that the Lord has "unlimited patience" and mercy for you (1 Timothy 1:16). If Jesus has truly changed your life, you know there is no good excuse for you not to be sharing him with others. Keep loving, keep praying, keep going, keep telling, keep encouraging, and keep inviting others to trust Jesus Christ to be their Lord and Savior!

In John 1:41–42—"He first found his own brother Simon and said to him, 'We have found the Messiah (which means

Christ). He brought him to Jesus. Jesus looked at him and said, 'You are Simon the son of John. You shall be called Cephas (which means Peter).'"

Once Andrew found Jesus, he had to tell his brother, Simon, about Jesus. Simon became Peter and he became the leader of the early church. Peter preached the first sermon following Pentecost and three thousand were saved, baptized, and added to the church (Acts 2:41). Simon Peter carried the baton for the early church for the first twelve chapters of Acts before God handed it off to Paul. Do you think Andrew had any idea what God had prepared for his brother the day he told him about Jesus? Every time you bring someone to Jesus, you have no idea what God has prepared to do in and through that person. Remember when you received Jesus Christ into your life, you had to tell someone about the new love, the new hope, the new joy, the new peace, and the new purpose in your life. That is normal Christianity. If you are not doing that now, what happened? Going through the gospel according to John, before Andrew had to tell someone, John the Baptist had to tell someone because he came as a witness to bear witness about the light (John 1:6–7, 29, 35). John had to tell Andrew (John 1:40). Then Andrew had to tell his brother Simon (John 1:41–42), and Phillip had to tell Nathaniel (John 1:45). Mary, the mother of Jesus, had to tell the servants (John 2:3-5). The Samaritan woman had to tell the people of her town (John 4:28–29). After the invalid at the Bethesda pool was healed, he had to tell the Jews (John 5:15). After the blind man was healed, he had to tell his neighbors (John 9:8–11). Mary had to tell her family and friends (John 12:1–3). Every day, will you tell someone about Jesus?

In John 14:5–6—"Thomas said to him, 'Lord, we do not know where you are going. How can we know the way?' Jesus said to him, 'I am the way, and the truth, and the life. No one comes to the Father except through me.'"

Do you really believe that? Is Jesus the only way to the Father? Is Jesus the only way to have abundant and eternal life? If we indeed believe what Jesus emphatically told his disciples, then we must tell others about Jesus. I know there is hard ground, rocky ground, and thorny ground, but there is good ground too (Mark 4:1–8). Always remember, we are not responsible for how they respond to the gospel. We are only responsible to love, pray, care, and share the gospel with others and then trust the results of convicting, convincing, drawing, cleansing, and saving to God.

In Acts 1:8—"But you will receive power when the Holy Spirit has come upon you, and you will be my witnesses in Jerusalem and in all Judea and Samaria, and to the end of the earth."

Consider the many promises Jesus could have given his apostles upon receiving the power of the Holy Spirit. Yet, the promise he gave them was "you will be my witnesses in Jerusalem and in all Judea and Samaria, and to the end of the earth." Throughout the book of Acts, whenever you find persons "filled with the Holy Spirit," you will find persons sharing Jesus. "Gratifying the desires of the flesh rather than walking by the Spirit" (Galatians 5:16) is the one and only biblical reason why we don't share Jesus everywhere with everyone. Spirit-filled, his presence, power, purpose, and passion gives us:

1. The Lord's compassion that compels us to overcome our apathy (Matthew 9:36);

2. The Lord's courage that calms our fears (2 Timothy 1:7);

3. The Lord's consciousness that calls our attention of doing his will (Mark 1:17);

4. The Lord's conviction that commits us to obedience (John 16:8–10); and

5. The Lord's confidence that assures us we can do whatever he asks us to do (Luke 12:11–12).

Do you see it is impossible to be Thinking God and not have the Lord's priority and passion of sharing Jesus with others all the time everywhere?

In Acts 4:12—"And there is salvation in no one else, for there is no other name under heaven given among men by which we must be saved."

Have you ever thought as a Christian, *if I don't share Jesus with this person, who will?* Throughout the book of Acts, they shared Jesus "everyday, in the temple and from house to house, they did not cease teaching and preaching that the Christ is Jesus" (Acts 5:42). How can we who are Christians, be or do any less?

In Acts 8:1–4—"And Saul approved of his execution. And there arose on that day a great persecution against the church in Jerusalem, and they were all scattered throughout the regions of Judea and Samaria, except the apostles. Devout men buried Stephen and made great lamentation over him. But Saul was ravaging the church, and entering house after house, he dragged off men and women and committed them to prison. Now those who were scattered went about preaching the word."

If you are a Christian and have reasons for not sharing Christ with others—fearfulness, you don't feel like you know enough of God's Word, and/or you don't think you have time—how do these reasons compare with the challenges the early church had—persecution, imprisonment, and possibly death. Yet "those who were scattered went about preaching the word" (Acts 8:4). How can we who are Christians be or do any less?

In 2 Corinthians 5:20—"Therefore, we are ambassadors for Christ, God making his appeal through us. We implore you on behalf of Christ, be reconciled to God."

We are not Christ's secret agents. We are Christ's ambassadors, God's resident representatives on earth of his own government, that is, of his kingdom (Matthew 6:33), who have been appointed, authorized, empowered, and entrusted as his messengers to tell the good news of Jesus Christ to others and implore them, earnestly call on them, and pray for as many as we can on behalf of Christ. This must be a priority and passion in our lives because only we, the redeemed, walk in the light of God's kindness and grace (Ephesians 2:7–8). Remember the cost Jesus paid that we might be redeemed— "though he was rich, yet for our sake he became poor, so that we by his poverty might become rich" (2 Corinthians 8:9), and "for our sake he made him to be sin who knew no sin, so that in him we might become the righteousness of God" (2 Corinthians 5:21). We must tell them because the "love of Christ controls us, because we have concluded this: that one has died for all, therefore all have died; and he died for all, that those who live might no longer live for themselves but for him who for their sake died and was raised" (2 Corinthians 5:14–15).

In Ephesians 6:18–20—"Praying at all times in the Spirit, with all prayer and supplication. To that end keep alert with all perseverance, making supplication for all the saints, and also for me, that words may be given to me in opening my mouth boldly to proclaim the mystery of the gospel, for which I am an ambassador in chains, that I may declare it boldly, as I ought to speak."

If the Apostle Paul struggled with fearfulness and needed others to pray for him that he might declare the gospel boldly, of course, we need others to pray for us in our struggles with fearfulness. It amazes me after all these years and with everything I have experienced in knowing the joy of sharing Jesus and all I have learned about the presence and power of the Holy Spirit and the Father's faithfulness in my life of how fearful I can still become at certain times in an opportunity to share Christ with someone. Knowing though that "God gave us a spirit not of fearfulness but of power and love and self-control" (2 Timothy 1:7), I must choose Thinking God to overcome that fearfulness and share Christ. This request by the apostle Paul should encourage each of us, knowing he too struggled with fear. Always remember, struggling to obey God and disobeying God are two radically different things. Thinking God, we walk by faith and are "not ashamed of the gospel, for it is the power of God for salvation to everyone who believes, to the Jew first and also to the Greek. For in it the righteousness of God is revealed from faith for faith, as it is written, 'The righteous shall live by faith'" (Romans 1:16–17).

In Philemon 6—"I pray that you may be active in sharing your faith, so that you will have a full understanding of every good thing we have in Christ" (NIV).

I will always be grateful to Dr. Howard Ramsey for his modeling, mentoring, and encouraging ministry in my life from the time I was fourteen. Howard preached my ordination message. As the director of evangelism of the Northwest Baptist Convention, he gave me the opportunity to be the pianist for the Northwest Baptist Evangelism Conference during my college years and be encouraged in sharing my faith by guest speakers like Dr. Roy Fish, Dr. E. V. Hill, Dr. Richard Jackson and Dr. John Sullivan. These men and others like them modeled sharing Jesus with others while I watched and listened during lunches and dinners we shared together. In 1987, as the director of personal evangelism for the Home Mission Board of the Southern Baptist Convention (now the North American Mission Board), Howard shared at a national evangelism conference with all the nation's state evangelism directors and associate directors how Philemon 6 had encouraged him greatly in sharing his faith: "Coming to understand the great truth that is taught in this verse— as I am sharing Christ with others, God is actually teaching me more of every good thing I have in him compels me to share Christ with everyone I can because I sure need to know every good thing I have in Christ." Listening to Howard, God convicted me, "Every struggle, discouragement and/or defeat I have—pride, temptation, worry, fearfulness, bitterness—it's because I do not yet fully understand everything I have in my relationship with Jesus Christ!" Remember, we are promised: "His divine power has granted to us all things that pertain to life and godliness, through the knowledge of him who called us to his own glory and excellence" (2 Peter 1:3).

That's when I made a commitment to share Jesus everyday with everyone I could. I went back to Missouri and started a statewide campaign called "I'm One." For several years, I led "I'm One" rallies and thousands of Christians made commitments to tell someone everyday about Jesus, and it was amazing how many were saved through that ministry. It was also thrilling how so many called our office or wrote us saying, "It works. When you share Christ everyday with others, it is unbelievable what God does in your life!"

Will you become one more "I'm One" person today? If you will, "God will do far more abundantly than all that you could ever ask or think according to the power at work within you" (Ephesians 3:20).

In 1 Peter 3:14–15—"But even if you should suffer for righteousness' sake, you will be blessed. Have no fear of them, nor be troubled, but in your hearts honor Christ the Lord as holy, always being prepared to make a defense to anyone who asks you for a reason for the hope that is in you; yet do it with gentleness and respect, having a good conscience, so that, when you are slandered, those who revile your good behavior in Christ may be put to shame."

Suffering for living for Christ and sharing Christ was common in the New Testament. The Apostle Paul reminded his son in the faith, Timothy: "Indeed, all who desire to live a godly life in Christ Jesus will be persecuted" (2 Timothy 3:12). This teaching to encourage you to always be prepared to share Jesus Christ daily and make appointments with others to lead them to trust Christ as their Lord and Savior would not be complete without warning you, as this Scripture does, of the trouble you can find yourself in, when sharing Christ with others. If you know much about me, you know I have gotten in more trouble over the past forty-four years as a youth minister, pastor, and when I was serving in the evangelism office of the Missouri Baptist Convention for challenging parents, church leadership, and denominational leaders to share their faith with those who do not yet know Christ than anything else I have ever done or said. But always remember Peter's words of encouragement after his warning of "even if you should suffer for righteousness' sake, *you will be blessed.*" If you have not yet known the joy of sharing Jesus with others on a daily basis and seeing them often come to trust Christ as their Lord and Savior, I cannot describe to you the happiness and joy you are being robbed of because the Lord promised: "By this my Father is glorified, that you bear much fruit and so prove to be my disciples. As the Father has loved me, so have I loved you. Abide in my love. If you keep my commandments, you will abide in my love, just as I have kept my Father's commandments and abide in his love. These things I have spoken to you, that my joy may be in you and that your joy may be full" (John 15:8–11). Always remember Peter's words: "*Have no fear of them, nor be troubled, but in your hearts honor Christ the Lord as holy, always being prepared to make a defense to anyone who asks you for a reason for the hope that is in you.*" When we love the Lord, our greatest desire will be to honor him. This verse tells us to honor our Lord by being prepared—empowered in the Spirit and equipped in the Word—to share the reason we live with hope with others. And how do we share? Always with gentleness and respect, seeing God's worth in every person regardless of their sin, never condemning or condescending. Each of us should see ourselves as one beggar who has found the "bread of life" (John 6:35), sharing with another beggar who needs the "bread of life."

In 2 Peter 3:9—"The Lord is not slow to fulfill his promise as some count slowness, but is patient toward you not wishing that any should perish, but that all should reach repentance."

Thinking God, think how much God loves people! The Apostle Paul prayed that we, the redeemed, would be able "to know the love of Christ that surpasses knowledge" (Ephesians 3:19), implying it is impossible for us to ever comprehend how much God loves us. Since God has chosen us to be his hands, his feet, and his voice to show and tell others how much God loves them, how can we not show and tell them considering how much God loves them? We must show them. We must tell them.

In Revelation 12:10–11—"And I heard a loud voice in heaven, saying, "Now the salvation and the power and the kingdom of our God and the authority of his Christ have come, for the accuser of our brothers has been thrown down, who accuses them day and night before our God. And they have conquered him by the blood of the Lamb and by the word of their testimony, for they loved not their lives even unto death."

I refer to this passage as "God's prescription for overcoming the devil." With any prescription, what does the doctor tell you? "You need to take all of it." Are you taking all three parts of this "prescription to overcome?" Here they are:

1. "The blood of the Lamb"—we know it is impossible to know the overcoming power of God apart from the mercy, kindness, and grace demonstrated through the redemption that is in Christ Jesus (Romans 3:21–24)

and we gratefully sing: "What can wash away my sin, nothing but the blood of Jesus."

2. "By the word of their testimony"—most have never come to understand what God does in their lives as they are sharing Jesus with others as promised in Philemon 6: "the sharing of your faith may become effective for the full knowledge of every good thing that is in us for the sake of Christ."

3. "They loved not their lives even unto death"—most have not come to this point of commitment and surrender to Christ as the Lord of their lives, or the often used reason of fearfulness given by so many for not trusting and obeying the authority of God's Word would not be so common. You only have one life. Take all of your "medicine" and overcome to the glory of God (1 John 5:4).

So how in the world can so many pastors, church staff, and Bible professors at Christian universities and seminaries know everything you have just read and still not know the joy of sharing Jesus with others on a daily basis? I asked my mom that question when I was in college after hearing my pastor say based on a survey he had read that "Ninety-five percent of Christians live and die and never know the joy of leading one person to Christ and less than ten percent of pastors, church staff, and Bible professors at Christian universities and seminaries share their faith on a daily basis with the lost outside the church or the classroom." She replied tearfully, "Honey, I grew up in a lost family. I know how bad life can be without Jesus. I know what a broken heart is without Jesus.

I know what hopelessness is without Jesus. I know what emptiness is without Jesus. Since I received Jesus into my life, I have had a lot of heartaches and been brokenhearted many times, but with the Lord, I have never been hopeless or empty. That's why we have to share Jesus with everyone we can."

It was during my freshman year in college that God broke my heart for persons who do not know Christ as their Lord and Savior. Even though my roommates were doing the best they knew how, not knowing and living in the truth and freedom of Christ (John 8:32–36), I daily watched their lives go in a downward spiral of suffering and destruction just as God's Word promises: "Do not be deceived: God is not mocked, for whatever one sows, that will he also reap. For the one who sows to his own flesh will from the flesh reap corruption, but the one who sows to the Spirit will from the Spirit reap eternal life" (Galatians 6:7–8). Having memorized that passage of Scripture in the fourth or fifth grade and seeing it lived out in my roommates gave me a burden and a passion to share Christ with those who are lost and hopeless without him.

As I mentioned in chapter four, discovering my older brother and my two other roommates (who had all told me they were Christians before I moved in with them) lived for the weekend party and everything that went with it, let me see firsthand that you can make any choice you want in life, but you cannot choose the consequences of suffering and heartache that go with those choices. As undesirable of living in a sea of alcohol and immorality was, as lonely as it was, as hard as it was to be challenged everyday by three older guys and their friends to compromise in my convictions, and as many tears as I shed that year, I am so grateful in God's providence, he let me live in that "desert storm" so I could see firsthand, the deadness, disobedience, and depravity of man spoken about in Ephesians 2:1–3. I no longer needed to be challenged by anyone to share my faith. I had to share my faith!

God has continued to break my heart through the years for those who do not know Christ as their Lord as he has increasingly shown me what being lost, empty, searching, and brokenhearted can be without the Lord. Let me ask you a real soul-searching question? How long has it been since you have shed tears over someone being lost because you were brokenhearted that they did not know Jesus (Luke 19:10)?

After being privileged for fourteen years of leading, serving, teaching, and preaching in churches in Washington, Texas, California, and Oregon (only a journey the Lord could have orchestrated because before I served in these churches, I knew no one outside the state of Arkansas and Washington), I was asked to serve in the evangelism office of the Missouri Baptist Convention in 1984 as an associate and a few years later as the director until August of 1991.

It was seven years in which I was able to pray, love, lead, preach, teach, encourage, equip, and serve with the Missouri Baptist Convention staff, the Home Mission Board staff, Southern Baptist seminary and college staff, and hundreds of pastors, worship and student pastors in ministering to their people. It was seven glorious years of reaching many for Christ and then making disciples in partnering with pastors and student pastors across Missouri and the nation. Preaching eight-to-ten-week revivals each year in churches, serving as interim pastor for several churches for a six month period of time, preaching at chapels, teaching personal evangelism, and/or preaching revivals at Southwest Baptist University,

Hannibal-La Grange University, Missouri Baptist University and William Jewell College, leading associational evangelism training events, leading one state evangelism conference for student pastors and their students, and leading one for pastors and church leadership each year provided me the unbelievable joyous privilege of making and building countless friendships with university and seminary presidents, professors, pastors, church staff and their people. During this time, I also enjoyed the privilege of leading Super Summer Evangelism Schools that grew to involve over two thousand participants annually, which included middle school, high school, college students, and adults.

It was truly a time, in listening to so many stories, for me to understand that regardless of how good anyone looks from "the outside," everyone has a story with more disappointments, hurts, heartaches, insecurities, struggles, challenges, temptations, frustrations, failures, fears, and sin than you could ever imagine. But the good news God taught me to tell everyone was:

"No matter how horrible your sin is," when I was preaching to death row inmates at the prison in Potosi, "Jesus is enough!"

"No matter how hopeless your situation seems to be," when I would be listening to a pastor who had been fired for being faithful in standing for righteousness and preaching God's Word as the authority for our lives, "Jesus is enough!"

"No matter how dark your situation seems to be," when I would be listening to a woman whose husband had just been unfaithful to her and had left her, "Jesus is enough!"

"No matter what your questions are," when I would be listening to a student whose parents had just divorced, "Jesus is enough!"

If I had lunch with you today and you were willing to trust me to tell me about your disappointments, hurts, heartaches, insecurities, struggles, challenges, temptations, frustrations, failures, fears, and sin—things maybe you have never been able to be honest about with anyone, could you say, "Jesus is enough?" Could you say, "Jesus has been enough in my life to forgive and cleanse every sin and I have no guilt, or shame from my past" (Romans 8:1; John 1:9)? Could you say, "Jesus has been enough to comfort every heartache in my life, and I have no resentments or bitterness over anything bad that has happened in my life because Jesus is my healer and restorer" (2 Corinthians 1:3-5)? Could you say, "Jesus has been enough to change my life completely, and I live every day to God's glory overflowing with thankfulness (Colossians 2:6–7) and anticipation of what God is going to do in and through my life" (Ephesians 3:20)?

Think how everyone's story would radically change if Thinking God, they humbly believed and lived that "Jesus is enough!" It is what the Bible promises from Matthew to Revelation. Do not live beneath your privileges in Christ any longer (Colossians 1:27). Whatever your reasons, if you have not experienced the all-surpassing power and sufficiency of Christ and do not believe that is really possible as a professing Christian (and the way you live tells what you believe), you will not have the joy of daily sharing Jesus with others.

This is the good news: God saved you to know that joy. The Holy Spirit gives everyone that joyous desire when he enters their lives. Just read the book of Acts. Remember the Lord's promise: "But you will receive power when the Holy Spirit has come upon you, and you will be my witnesses in

Jerusalem and in all Judea and Samaria, and to the end of the earth" (Acts 1:8).

God loves you more than you will ever be able to comprehend and wants you to experience and enjoy living in his all surpassing power (2 Corinthians 4:7) and sufficiency (2 Corinthians 12:9). God wants you to know the joy and peace of resting and rejoicing that "Jesus is enough" regardless of what you have in your past, present, or what you think you have in your future (Matthew 11:28–30; Philippians 4:6–7). The Apostle Paul wrote in the epistle to Ephesians:

> "For this reason I bow my knees before the Father, from whom every family in heaven and on earth is named, that according to the riches of his glory he may grant you to be strengthened with power through his Spirit in your inner being, so that Christ may dwell in your hearts through faith—that you, being rooted and grounded in love, may have strength that they would be able to comprehend with all the saints what is the breadth and length and height and depth, and to know the love of Christ that surpasses knowledge, that you may be filled with all the fullness of God. Now to him who is able to do far more abundantly than all that we ask or think, according to the power at work with us, to him be glory in the church and in Christ Jesus throughout all generations, forever and ever. Amen" (Ephesians 3:14–21).

Isn't it amazing how most Christians live so differently than how the Word of God says we should live? In 1983, I heard Vance Havner say at an evangelism conference in Portland, Oregon, "Most in the church have become so abnormal, when someone is just normal, they think he is abnormal." I encourage you with all my heart to share Jesus everyday and make appointments with others to take them through the Scriptures. Show them who God is, who Jesus is, who the Holy Spirit is, and how they can repent and receive Christ by the person of the Holy Spirit into their lives. Let this be the first day of the rest of your life to the glory of God.

"Jesus is enough" to cover every sin, comfort every heartache and change every life. That's what the New Testament is all about. That's why sharing Jesus with others everywhere you go all the time is just normal Christianity.

Thinking God—Think how normal it should be for each of us to daily share who is most important in our lives—Jesus Christ. (Romans 1:16).

Truth to Remember—Sharing Jesus will always take us out of our way to be on God's way because God's love always cares enough to go out of its way (Luke 19:10).

Thinking God in Reflecting—Imagine how everyone's story would radically change if Thinking God, they humbly believed and lived "Jesus is enough?" It is what the Bible promises from Matthew to Revelation. For whatever reasons, if you have not experienced the all-surpassing power and sufficiency of Christ, humble yourself before the Lord today and surrender your life to him. When your life has truly been changed by the Lord, you will be just like the Christians in the book of Acts regardless of your circumstances: "Now those who were scattered (because of persecution) went about preaching the word" (Acts 8:4).

PART III

BECAUSE GOD IS THE ONE LORD GOD

Thinking God: Humility

Memorize God's Word!

"If my people who are called by my name humble themselves, and pray and seek my face and turn from their wicked ways, then I will hear from heaven and will forgive their sin and heal their land" (2 Chronicles 7:14).

"He leads the humble in what is right, and teaches the humble his way" (Psalm 25:9).

"The fear of the Lord is hatred of evil. Pride and arrogance and the way of evil and perverted speech I hate" (Proverbs 8:13).

"When pride comes, then comes disgrace, but with the humble is wisdom" (Proverbs 11:2).

"Pride goes before destruction and a haughty spirit before a fall" (Proverbs 16:18).

"Come to me, all who labor and are heavy laden, and I will give you rest. Take my yoke upon you, and learn from me, for I am gentle and lowly in heart, and you will find rest for your souls" (Matthew 11:28–29).

"The greatest among you shall be your servant" (Matthew 23:11).

"I therefore, a prisoner for the Lord, urge you to walk in a manner worthy of the calling to which you have been called, with all humility and gentleness, with patience, bearing with one another in love, eager to maintain the unity of the Spirit in the bond of peace" (Ephesians 4:1–3).

"Do nothing from selfish ambition or conceit, but in humility count others more significant than yourselves. Let each of you look not only to his own interests, but also to the interests of others. Have this mind among yourselves, which is yours in Christ Jesus" (Philippians 2:3–5).

"And being found in human form, he humbled himself by becoming obedient to the point of death, even death on a cross" (Philippians 2:8).

"Put on then, as God's chosen ones, holy and beloved, compassionate hearts, kindness, humility, meekness, and patience bearing with one another and, if one has a complaint against another, forgiving each other; as the Lord has forgiven you, so you also must forgive" (Colossians 3:12–13).

"But he gives more grace. Therefore it says, 'God opposes the proud, but gives grace to the humble'" (James 4:6).

"Likewise, you who are younger, be subject to the elders. Clothe yourselves, all of you, with humility toward one another, for 'God opposes the proud but gives grace to the humble.' Humble yourselves, therefore, under the mighty hand of God so that at the proper time he may exalt you, casting all your anxieties on him, because he cares for you" (1 Peter 5:5–7).

๛Ꭷ

You are in a spiritual battle so understand fully and remember always: The devil does not want you to ever see what God has done for you in Jesus Christ or has purposed to do in you and through you by the power of the Holy Spirit (Luke 8:12; John 8:44;10:10; Ephesians 4:27; 1 Peter 5:8; Revelation 12:10). Furthermore, the devil will scheme against you in every way he can to divert, distract, discourage, deceive, and defeat you (Ephesians 6:10-13). And the devil will succeed in "outwitting you" (2 Corinthians 2:11) until you learn to think and live humbly before God and others. The devil does not want you to ever understand this foundational truth taught in the Old and New Testaments: "God opposes the proud, but gives grace to the humble" (Proverbs 3:34; James 4:6; 1 Peter 5:5–6).

It is impossible for anyone to experience what we have discussed in the first seven chapters of this book—the preeminence of Christ (Colossians 1:16–22), enjoy loving and lasting relationships (John 13:34–35), the power of being submitted to the authority of God's Word (2 Timothy 3:15–16), the peace of knowing God better than anything else (Philippians 4:6–7), the purpose of living out God's promises and commands to the glory of God (Colossians 1:27), the privilege of a loving and lasting relationship in a covenant marriage (Ephesians 5:17–33), the provision of raising righteous children (Proverbs 23:24–25), and the priority of sharing Jesus daily and often with others to trust Christ as their Lord and Savior (Philemon 6)—without God's grace.

God's grace is only given to experience each of these joys to those who are humble (Proverbs 3:34; James 4:6; 1 Peter 5:5–6).

Without thinking and living in the attitude of Christ, which is the attitude of humility, which is "becoming obedient to the point of death" (Philippians 2:5–8), we will never experience what God has promised us: abundant life (John 10:10), being more than a conqueror in the power of God's love (Romans 8:37), being filled with joy and peace in believing and abounding in hope (Romans 15:13), always being led in victory in Christ and spreading everywhere the fragrance of the knowledge of him (2 Corinthians 2:14), rejoicing in the Lord always (Philippians 4:4), and having his divine power to give us everything we need for life and godliness through our knowledge of him (2 Peter 1:3–4). That's because God opposes the proud (Proverbs 3:34; James 4:6; 1 Peter 5:5–6)!

I hope these statements make you think: "Having the attitude of being humble before God and others is more important than I have ever understood!" Pay attention! Listen! Focus! If you do not understand and apply the teaching of this chapter in your life, you will stay as most professing Christians do—in a crisis of pride which leads them to compromise in obeying God's Word, leaving them in a conflict of pride which leads them to have hurting and unforgiving relationships, and in a confusion of pride which leaves them victims of life.

The passage in 2 Chronicles 7:14 has been preached and taught by countless pastors, evangelists, and seminary professors as God's requirement for revival: "If my people who are called by my name humble themselves, and pray and seek my face and turn from their wicked ways, then I will hear from heaven and will forgive their sin and heal their land."

They have emphasized, "Before God asks his people to 'pray, seek his face, or turn from their wicked ways (repent), they are asked to humble themselves.'"

Yet, most pastors including this one have spent years preaching and teaching but not understanding and living what Andrew Murray so profoundly taught in his book, *Humility— The Journey toward Holiness:*

> "In our salvation, Jesus makes us partakers of humility. His salvation is to be our humility as he modeled and taught throughout his earthly ministry (John 13:15–17). An absence of humility is the explanation of every defect and failure in the Christian walk. Humility alone takes the right attitude before God and allows him as God to be all and do all in our lives. In every temptation of life, there is the lie: you do not need to be humble. Pride makes faith impossible. Pride and faith are irreconcilably at odds. We can never have more of true faith than we have of true humility. Is it any wonder that our faith is weak when pride still reigns and we have hardly learned to long or pray for humility as the most necessary and blessed art of salvation. We go to such lengths to believe, while the old self in its pride seeks to avail itself of God's blessings and riches. No wonder we can't believe. We need to change our course. We need to humble ourselves under the mighty hand of God; he will exalt us. Until then, pride makes a fool out of us!"
>
> (Andrew Murray 2001, 16–18)

Until we learn to think and live humbly before God and others, we fail to understand God always wants to do more in our lives than through our lives. Humbling ourselves is moving from our independent and rebellious minds of thinking: "whether right or wrong, no matter what anyone says, I am going to do it my way." Humble, I understand I was created by God and for God. God's Word is perfect, and it is not about me being first. It's all about God—his way and his will accomplished in my life according to his Word. Humbling ourselves is submitting our lives to the authority of God's Word and to godly authority regardless of the cost just as Christ "humbled himself by becoming obedient to the point of death" (Philippians 2:8). Humbling ourselves is obeying the Word of God "not as a burden but out of our love for God" (1 John 5:3–4).

If you ever want God to do anything in your life, you must understand the significance of 1 Peter 5:5–6. Humbling yourself before God is what opens the door of your life, not only to receive the grace of God to be saved (Ephesians 2:8–9) but also to grow in the grace and knowledge of the Lord (2 Peter 3:18). Pride and church attendance will not bring spiritual growth. Pride and church service will not bring spiritual growth. Pride and giving will not bring spiritual growth. Pride and Bible study will not bring spiritual growth. Pride and earning seminary degrees will not bring spiritual growth. Church attendance and service, giving, Bible study, and furthering one's education are all good, but we are instructed in God's Word to do them humbly before God and others. Doing these things or other good things without humility will not bring grace and spiritual growth into our lives. Attempting to live the Christian life without humility is why so many who have been in church for decades are still lost or are spiritually babies and still think and live out of the "flesh" (1 Corinthians 3:1–3).

If they do not get their way, they become upset and watch out!

You will not make any progress in your walk with God apart from being a participant of God's grace. Jesus really did mean what he said, "Apart from me you can do nothing (John 15:5). Until you make God's priority of humility your priority as an attitude in your life (Philippians 2:5), you will stay: with little or no hunger for God's Word and frustrated in obeying God's Word because pride fails in doing the things of God; wounded from the hurts of life because pride never can heal; worried over the needs of life because pride wants to control, manage, and fix everything; aggravated, angry, and /or anxious because pride is easily overwhelmed in the challenges of life; and in wilderness living forever grumbling because pride cannot enjoy trusting and resting in God's promises.

Humility is a transformed way of thinking and living. This new way of thinking and living "a living sacrifice, holy and acceptable to God, not conformed to this world, but transformed by the renewal of one's mind" (Romans 12:1–2) understands and intentionally chooses to live, "it's not about me anymore, it's all about God." In Christ, a humble person walks with godly conviction, confidence, and courage, knowing that he or she is simply an empty vessel totally dependent to be filled with the Holy Spirit to live an obedient and supernatural life to God's glory (Luke 24:49; Acts 1:8; Galatians 5:16–26; Ephesians 5:17–18).

Psalm 25:9 teaches us being led by the LORD is impossible unless we are humble: "He leads the humble in what is right, and teaches the humble his way." The more we see who we are in light of who God is, the more we will see as Job saw the necessity of being humble before God (Job 42:5–6). I encourage you right now to get on your knees (if physically possible) and praise God for being:

Almighty	Just
All-Sufficient	Kind
Awesome	King
Beautiful	Life
Comforter	Light
Compassionate	LORD
Creator	Love
Deliverer	Lovely
Eternal	Majestic
Faithful	Merciful
Forever Friend	Mighty
Forgiving	Most High God
Gentle	My God
Good	None like Him
Gracious	Omnipotent
Great	Omnipresent
Guide	Omniscient
Healer	One
Help	Patient
Holy	Perfect
Hope	Personal
I AM	Protector
Immutable	Provider
Infinite	Quick to Forgive
Invincible	Reconciler
Invisible	Redeemer
Jealous	Refuge
Judge	Reigning

Restorer	Steadfast
Righteous	Strong tower
Rock of our salvation	True
Savior	Trustworthy
Self-existent	Unchangeable
Shepherd	Understanding
Shield	Victorious
Sovereign	Wise
Sufficient	

In light of who God is, Proverbs 6:16–17 tells us of the "six things that the LORD hates, a proud look" is number one on his list. Proverbs 8:13 emphatically tells us God hates pride: "Pride and arrogance and the way of evil and perverted speech I hate." Understand how pride is the root of every sin because "it goes before destruction and a haughty spirit before a fall" (Proverbs 16:18). Whereas other sins turn us away from God, pride is a direct attack upon God. Pride lifts our hearts above God and against God. Pride makes a fool out of us (Proverbs 28:26). Pride, which is an absence of humility, is a great thief of thinking and experiencing God.

Pride steals, kills, and destroys God's abundance in our lives (John 10:10). Think how it has ripped you off. Isn't it amazing how pride can steal us blind of enjoying a loving and meaningful relationship with God, a family member, a good friend, or a brother or sister in Christ?

Are you tolerating any of these ten common destructive attitudes of pride to steal, kill, and destroy what should be a meaningful relationship in your life?

1) "I have to be in control and have it done my way."
2) "I am right and if there is a disagreement, I will prove that I am right."
3) "Because it's all about me, when I don't get my way, I quit on the relationship."
4) "If there is a problem, it's always someone else's fault."
5) "Since I don't need to change, you change."
6) "I don't want anyone to find out anything that is less than perfect in my life."
7) "It's hard for me to say, 'I was wrong, please forgive me.'"
8) "When there is a misunderstanding, I want the other person to come and ask for forgiveness."
9) "I enjoy focusing on the failures and faults of others."
10) "I have been hurt too deeply to ever trust again."

Philippians 2:3–5, if lived out by every marriage would end divorce; if lived out by every family would end unresolved resentments, bitterness, anger, and blame in families; if lived out by every church family would end church fights and splits. Even though I have taught this life-changing passage—"Do nothing from selfish ambition or conceit, but in humility count others more significant than yourselves. Let each of you look not only to his own interests, but also to the interests of others. Have this mind among yourselves, which is yours in Christ Jesus" (Philippians 2: 3–5)—to others for years, it amazes me what a daily challenge it is to live in my own life before the Lord, my wife, children, and all those I serve and lead in ministry. I am so grateful for God's "mercy and unlimited patience" (1 Timothy 1:16) in my life.

Because God opposes the proud, the work we all so desperately need God to do in each of our lives will never be accomplished until we think and live humbly before the Lord (Philippians 2:5). Isn't it unbelievable what it takes in all of our lives to learn to think and live humbly? It is so tragic that too many Christians live and die and never learn to think and live this transformational way. Only by God's grace, mercy, and patience (1 Timothy 1:2, 16) can we learn it. As God works in and through our lives to do mighty things we are amazed at and others are impressed about, we must daily remember to think and live humbly.

How about you? Do you daily think and live humbly before God and others? God has used a lifetime of temptations, trials, troubles, tests, failures, and many tears to lead me by his grace to practice this attitude in my life. In my discouragement and desperate cry for God to change so many different situations and circumstances, God has chosen the better of changing me and my perspective about the situation and given me "a new song to sing praise to my God" (Psalm 40:1–3). God graciously continues to open the eyes of my heart (Ephesians 1:18–20) and lets me see my bankruptcy and brokenness before him and the need to be meeked before him (Matthew 5:3–5).

God graciously and perseveringly has shown me throughout my life how even though he gives us gifts and mercifully uses us to be a means to accomplish great things in his redemptive work, it is never to be a substitute for what he has purposed to do in us the moment we were "born again" (John 3:3)—to be "conformed to the image of Christ" (Romans 8:29). This glorious work of learning to see every challenge (every temptation, trial, and test) in our lives as an opportunity to learn to "rely upon God more" (2 Corinthians 1:8–9) is only possible in the perspective of being humble before God and others.

I encourage you with all my heart to memorize the following ten Scriptures and guard your heart and mind daily from ever forgetting:

1. "He leads the humble in what is right, and teaches the humble his way" (Psalm 25:9).

2. "When pride comes, then comes disgrace, but with the humble is wisdom" (Proverbs 11:2).

3. "All these things my hand has made, and so all these things came to be, declares the Lord. But this is the one to whom I will look: he who is humble and contrite in spirit and trembles at my word" (Isaiah 66:2).

4. "Come to me, all who labor and are heavy laden, and I will give you rest. Take my yoke upon you, and learn from me, for I am gentle and lowly in heart, and you will find rest for your souls. For my yoke is easy, and my burden is light" (Matthew 11:28–30).

5. "The greatest among you shall be your servant" (Matthew 23:11).

6. "I therefore, a prisoner for the Lord, urge you to walk in a manner worthy of the calling to which you have been called, with all humility and gentleness, with patience, bearing with one another in love, eager to maintain the

unity of the Spirit in the bond of peace" (Ephesians 4:1–3).

7. "Do nothing from selfish ambition or conceit, but in humility count others more significant than yourselves. Let each of you look not only to his own interests, but also to the interests of others. Have this mind among yourselves, which is yours in Christ Jesus" (Philippians 2:3–5).

8. "Put on then, as God's chosen ones, holy and beloved, compassionate hearts, kindness, humility, meekness, and patience, bearing with one another and, if one has a complaint against another, forgiving each other; as the Lord has forgiven you, so you also must forgive. And above all these put on love, which binds everything together in perfect harmony. And let the peace of Christ rule in your hearts, to which indeed you were called in one body. And be thankful. Let the word of Christ dwell in you richly, teaching and admonishing one another in all wisdom, singing psalms and hymns and spiritual songs, with thankfulness in your hearts to God. And whatever you do, in word or deed, do everything in the name of the Lord Jesus, giving thanks to God the Father through him" (Colossians 3:12–17).

9. "But he gives more grace. Therefore it says, 'God opposes the proud, but gives grace to the humble'" (James 4:6).

10. "Likewise, you who are younger, be subject to the elders. Clothe yourselves, all of you, with humility toward one another, for 'God opposes the proud but gives grace to the humble.' Humble yourselves, therefore, under the

mighty hand of God so that at the proper time he may exalt you, casting all your anxieties on him, because he cares for you" (1 Peter 5:5–7).

In closing this chapter, here are twelve "always-remember insights" God has taught me, and uses daily to bring great conviction in my life and humility before him and others. I pray these truths will be a great encouragement for you to think and live humbly before God and others:

1. Humility was the only way Jesus could do the will of the Father (Philippians 2:6–8).

2. Humility allows us to be graced by God to learn of Jesus and find rest in him (Matthew 11:29).

3. Humility allows us to be graced by God to cast all our cares on him and leave them with him (1 Peter 5:5–7).

4. Humility allows us to be graced by God to live with the gift of God's perspective and not lose heart in staying faithful to God and to others (2 Corinthians 4:16–18).

5. Humility allows us to be graced by God with the privilege of living out God's purpose, becoming increasingly intentional in being a faithful, fruitful and fulfilled disciple of Christ instead of being continually tossed to and fro in pride (Ephesians 4:14–16).

6. Humility allows us to be graced by God to live the Spirit-filled life (Ephesians 5:17–18).

7. Humility allows us to be graced by God to see God's sufficiency is always greater than our suffering (2 Corinthians 12:8–9).

8. Humility allows us to be graced by God to think and live abounding in his perfect love that drives out all fear (Romans 8:35–39).

9. Humility allows us to be graced by God to think and live overflowing with hope by the power of the Holy Spirit (Romans 15:13).

10. Humility allows us to be graced by God to be and do what God saved us to be and to do—enjoy the significance of accomplishing his will in and through our lives being guarded by his peace (Philippians 4:4–7).

11. Humility allows us to be graced by God to learn how to be content in any and every circumstance in the strength of Christ (Philippians 4:11–13).

12. Humility allows us to be graced by God to live with his conviction, confidence and courage regardless of our circumstances or feelings knowing his divine power has granted to us all things that pertain to life and godliness, through the knowledge of him who called us to his own glory and excellence (2 Peter 1:3).

Thinking God—The devil never wants you to see what God has done for you in Jesus Christ or has purposed to do in you and through you by the power of the Holy Spirit (Luke 8:12; John 8:44; Ephesians 4:27; Revelation 12:10).

Truth to Remember—The devil never wants you to understand this foundational truth taught in the Old and New Testaments: "God opposes the proud, but gives grace to the humble" (Proverbs 3:34; James 4:6; 1 Peter 5:5–6).

Thinking God in Reflecting—Attempting to live the Christian life without humility is why so many who have been in church for decades are still lost or are spiritual babies and still think and live in the "flesh," a fruitless, faithless, and frustrated life (Galatians 5:16–26).

Thinking God: Obedience

Memorize God's Word!

"I am the LORD your God, who brought you out of the land of Egypt, out of the house of slavery. You shall have no other gods before me" (Exodus 20:2–3).

"Not one of these men of this evil generation shall see the good land that I swore to give to your fathers, except Caleb the son of Jephunneh. He shall see it, and to him and to his children I will give the land on which he has trodden, because he has wholly followed the LORD" (Deuteronomy 1:36)!

"And when Moses had finished speaking all these words to all Israel, he said to them, 'Take to heart all the words by which I am warning you today, that you may command them to your children, that they may be careful to do all the words of this law. For it is no empty word for you, but your very life, and by this word you shall live long in the land that you are going over the Jordan to possess'" (Deuteronomy 32:45–47).

"Only be strong and very courageous, being careful to do according to all the law that Moses my servant commanded you. Do not turn from it to the right hand or to the left, that you may have good success wherever you go. This Book of the Law shall not depart from your mouth, but you shall meditate on it day and night, so that you may be careful to do according to all that is written in it. For then you will make your way prosperous, and then you will have good success" (Joshua 1:7–8).

"And Samuel said, 'Has the LORD as great delight in burnt offerings and sacrifices, as in obeying the voice of the LORD? Behold, to obey is better than sacrifice, and to listen than the fat of rams'" (1 Samuel 15:22).

"The law of the LORD is perfect, reviving the soul; the testimony of the LORD is sure, making wise the simple; the precepts of the LORD are right, rejoicing the heart; the commandment of the LORD is pure, enlightening the eyes" (Psalm 19:7–8).

"With my whole heart I seek you; let me not wander from your commandments! I have stored up your word in my heart, that I might not sin against you. Blessed are you, O LORD; teach me your statutes! With my lips I declare all the rules of your mouth. In the way of your testimonies I delight as much as in all riches. I will meditate on your precepts and fix my eyes on your ways. I will delight in your statutes; I will not forget your word" (Psalm 119:10–16).

"Teach me, O LORD, the way of your statues; and I will keep it to the end. Give me understanding, that I may keep your law and observe it with my whole heart. Lead me in the path of your commandments, for I delight in it. Incline my heart to your testimonies, and not to selfish gain" (Psalm 119:33-36)!

"For I the LORD do not change; therefore you, O children of Jacob, are not consumed. From the days of your fathers you have turned aside from my statutes and have not kept them. Return to me, and I will return to you, says the LORD of hosts. But you say, 'How shall we return?' Will man rob God? Yet you are robbing me. But you say, 'How have we robbed you?' In your tithes and contributions" (Malachi 3:6–8).

"Not everyone who says to me, 'Lord, Lord,' will enter the kingdom of heaven, but the one who does the will of my Father who is in heaven" (Mathew 7:21).

"But the cares of the world and the deceitfulness of riches and the desires for other things enter in and choke the word, and it proves unfruitful" (Mark 4:19).

"For which of you, desiring to build a tower, does not first sit down and count the cost, whether he has enough to complete it? Otherwise, when he has laid a foundation and is not able to finish, all who see it begin to mock him" (Luke 14:28–29).

"When he has brought out all his own, he goes before them, and the sheep follow him, for they know his voice" (John 10:4).

"Do you not know that if you present yourselves to anyone as obedient slaves, you are slaves of the one whom you obey, either of sin, which leads to death, or of obedience, which leads to righteousness? But thanks be to God, that you who were once slaves of sin have become obedient from the heart to the standard of teaching to which you were committed, and, having been set free from sin, have become slaves of righteousness" (Romans 6:16–18).

"Do your best to present yourself to God as one approved, a worker who has no need to be ashamed, rightly handling the word of truth" (2 Timothy 2:15).

"All Scripture is breathed out by God and profitable for teaching, for reproof, for correction, and for training in righteousness, that the man of God may be complete, equipped for every good work" (2 Timothy 3:16–17).

"Whoever says he abides in him ought to walk in the same way in which he walked" (1 John 2:6).

"There is no fear in love, but perfect love casts out fear. For fear has to do with punishment, and whoever fears has not been perfected in love. We love because he first loved us" (1 John 4:18–19).

"For this is the love of God, that we keep his commandments. And his commandments are not burdensome. For everyone who has been born of God overcomes the world. And this is the victory that has overcome the world—our faith" (1 John 5:3–4).

ℰℭ

Since chapter three and this chapter both deal with the necessity of God's authority in our lives, some review would be helpful to distinguish the difference between the two chapters. Chapter three (Thinking God: What Were You Saved For?) was written to encourage and equip two groups of persons who make up a large part of many churches: First, it was for those who are doing the best they know how, but still are lost because they have never known the joy of godly sorrow leading them to repentance (2 Corinthians 7:10). They have asked God many times to forgive them but they have never understood the need to change their minds about their sinfulness. Looking back on the fruitlessness of their lives, hopefully from the study of chapter three, many would be convicted of what Jesus said, "You will recognize them by their fruits" (Matthew 7:16) and would have changed their minds about their sinfulness (repentance), and would have been reconciled by God to become a new creation in Christ (2 Corinthians 5:17–18). Praise the Lord for his "mercy and unlimited patience" (1 Timothy 1:16) to "have the eyes of our hearts enlightened" (Ephesians1:18), enabling us to repent and receive Jesus Christ by the person of the Holy Spirit to transform our lives from the inside out. Second, chapter three was for those who have by God's grace received Christ in their lives, repenting from their sinfulness, but still often find themselves discouraged and defeated because they have never learned the necessity of "being filled with the Spirit" (Ephesians 5:18). Hopefully, from the study in chapter three, many are now living, daily moment by moment, humbly in the victorious preeminence, power, purpose, passion, provision, perspective, and peace of a Spirit-filled walk (Galatians 5:16–26).

This chapter has been written to encourage and equip another group of very special persons in many churches. This group truly knows the Lord, loves the Lord, and is doing their best to faithfully serve in their church, but they are not experiencing the following: the Lord's abundance and victory in their marriage and family (John 10:10), the Lord's fruitfulness and joy in their life and ministry (John 15:1–11), the passion and power of leading others to Christ (Acts 1:8), and/or the Lord's peace and rest regardless of any tribulation in their lives (John 16:33). These persons are very frustrated because they know God's promises, and they secretly wonder, *Why am I so defeated and overwhelmed by the challenges of life and ministry?* Many of these persons even know about the Spirit-filled life and have taught the need for it, but feel "burned out" and blame it on their circumstances, past hurts, and/or disappointments.

It was during my seven years of working in the evangelism office of the Missouri Baptist Convention that I began to realize how many of our leaders know much in their heads but are living far beneath their privilege as God's children in their daily lives. They are precious brothers and sisters in Christ who love the Lord as much as they know how, but have become careless in living out a foundational truth found throughout the Bible—there is no substitute for obedience to God if you are going to know the power of his love, joy, and peace.

If this describes you, remember what Romans 15:4 teaches us, "For whatever was written in former days was written for our instruction, that through endurance and through the encouragement of the Scriptures we might have hope." Think about the abundance of the goodness and grace the one LORD God promised throughout the Old Testament that was not based on one's circumstances or one's past, but to those he chose to love, make his own, and would obey him:

> "So God created man in his own image, in the image of God he created him; male and female he created them. And God blessed them. And God said to them, 'Be fruitful and multiply and fill the earth and subdue it, and have dominion over the fish of the sea and over the birds of the heavens and over every living thing that moves on the earth.' And God said, 'Behold, I have given you every plant yielding seed that is on the face of all the earth, and every tree with seed in its fruit. You shall have them for food. And to every beast of the earth and to every bird of the heavens and to everything

that creeps on the earth, everything that has the breath of life, I have given every green plant for food.' And it was so. And God saw everything that he had made, and behold, it was very good. And there was evening and there was morning, the sixth day."

(Genesis 1:27–31)

"The LORD God took the man and put him in the garden of Eden to work it and keep it. And the LORD God commanded the man, saying, 'You may surely eat of every tree of the garden, but of the tree of the knowledge of good and evil you shall not eat, for in the day that you eat of it you shall surely die.'"

(Genesis 2:15–17)

"Now the LORD said to Abram, 'Go from your country and your kindred and your father's house to the land that I will show you. And I will make of you a great nation, and I will bless you and make your name great, so that you will be a blessing. I will bless those who bless you, and him who dishonors you I will curse, and in you all the families of the earth shall be blessed.'"

(Genesis 12:1–3)

"And the angel of the LORD called to Abraham a second time from heaven and said, 'By myself I have sworn, declares the LORD, because you have done this and have not withheld your son, your only son, I will surely bless you, and I will surely multiply your offspring as the stars of heaven and as the sand that is on the seashore. And your offspring shall possess the gate of his enemies, and in your offspring shall all the nations of the earth be blessed, because you have obeyed my voice.'"

(Genesis 22:15–18)

"Then he said, 'I am God, the God of your father. Do not be afraid to go down to Egypt, for there I will make you into a great nation. I myself will go down with you to Egypt, and I will also bring you up again, and Joseph's hand shall close your eyes.'"

(Genesis 46:3–4)

"Say therefore to the people of Israel, 'I am the Lord, and I will bring you out from under the burdens of the Egyptians, and I will deliver you from slavery to them, and I will redeem you with an outstretched arm and with great acts of judgment. I will take you to be my people, and I will be your God, and you shall know that I am the Lord your God, who has brought you out from under the burdens of the Egyptians. I will bring you into the land that I swore to give to Abraham, to Isaac, and to Jacob. I will give it to you for a possession. I am the Lord.'"

(Exodus 6:6–8)

"Thus the Lord saved Israel that day from the hand of the Egyptians, and Israel saw the Egyptians dead on the seashore. Israel saw the great power that the Lord used against the Egyptians, so the people feared the Lord, and they believed in the Lord and in his servant Moses."

(Exodus 14:30–31)

"I am the LORD your God, who brought you out of the land of Egypt, out of the house of slavery. 'You shall have no other gods before me.'"

(Exodus 20:2–3)

"Then the cloud covered the tent of meeting, and the glory of the LORD filled the tabernacle. And Moses was not able to enter the tent of meeting because the cloud settled on it, and the glory of the LORD filled the tabernacle. Throughout all their journeys, whenever the cloud was taken up from over the tabernacle, the people of Israel would set out. But if the cloud was not taken up, then they did not set out till the day that it was taken up. For the cloud of the LORD was on the tabernacle by day, and fire was in it by night, in the sight of all the house of Israel throughout all their journeys."

(Exodus 40:34–38)

"The LORD spoke to Moses, saying, 'Send men to spy out the land of Canaan, which I am giving to the people of Israel. From each tribe of their fathers you shall send a man, everyone a chief among them.'"

(Numbers 13:1–2)

"Now this is the commandment—the statutes and the rules—that the LORD your God commanded me to teach you, that you may do them in the land to which you are going over, to possess it, that you may fear the LORD your God, you and your son and your son's son, by keeping all his statutes and his commandments, which I command you, all the days of your life, and that your days may be long. Hear therefore, O Israel, and be careful to do them, that it may go well with you, and that you may multiply greatly, as the LORD, the God of your fathers, has promised you, in a land flowing with milk and honey. 'Hear, O Israel: The LORD our God, the LORD is one. You shall love the LORD your God with all your heart and with all your soul and with all your might.'"

(Deuteronomy 6:1–5)

"And when all these things come upon you, the blessing and the curse, which I have set before you, and you call them to mind among all the nations where the LORD your God has driven you, and return to the LORD your God, you and your children, and obey his voice in all that I command you today, with all your heart and with all your soul, then the LORD your God will restore your fortunes and have mercy on you, and he will gather you again from all the peoples where the LORD your God has scattered you."

(Deuteronomy 30:1–3)

"And when Moses had finished speaking all these words to all Israel, he said to them, 'Take to heart all the words by which I am warning you today, that you may command them to your children, that they may be careful to do all the words of this law. For it is no empty word for you, but your very life, and by this word you shall live long in the land that you are going over the Jordan to possess.'"

(Deuteronomy 32:45–47)

"Only be strong and very courageous, being careful to do according to all the law that Moses my servant commanded you. Do not turn from it to the right hand or to the left, that you may have good success wherever you go. This Book of the Law shall not depart from your mouth, but you shall meditate on it day and night, so that you may be careful to do according to all that is written in it. For then you will make your way prosperous, and then you will have good success."

(Joshua 1:7–8)

"And Samuel said, 'Has the LORD as great delight in burnt offerings and sacrifices, as in obeying the voice of the LORD? Behold, to obey is better than sacrifice, and to listen than the fat of rams. For rebellion is as the sin of divination, and presumption is as iniquity and idolatry. Because you have rejected the word of the LORD, he has also rejected you from being king.'"

(1 Samuel 15:22–23)

"Now the LORD has fulfilled his promise that he made. For I have risen in the place of David my father, and sit on the throne of Israel, as the LORD promised, and I have built the house for the name of the LORD, the God of Israel."

(1 Kings 8:20)

"And at the time of the offering of the oblation, Elijah the prophet came near and said, 'O LORD, God of Abraham, Isaac, and Israel, let it be known this day that you are God in Israel, and that I am your servant, and that I have done all these things at your word. Answer me, O

LORD, answer me, that this people may know that you, O LORD, are God, and that you have turned their hearts back.' Then the fire of the LORD fell and consumed the burnt offering and the wood and the stones and the dust, and licked up the water that was in the trench."

(1 Kings 18:36–38)

"And all the assembly of those who had returned from the captivity made booths and lived in the booths, for from the days of Jeshua the son of Nun to that day the people of Israel had not done so. And there was very great rejoicing. And day by day, from the first day to the last day, he read from the Book of the Law of God. They kept the feast seven days, and on the eighth day there was a solemn assembly, according to the rule."

(Nehemiah 8:17–18)

"And the LORD blessed the latter days of Job more than his beginning. And he had 14,000 sheep, 6,000 camels, 1,000 yoke of oxen, and 1,000 female donkeys. He had also seven sons and three daughters."

(Job 42:12–13)

"Blessed is the man who walks not in the counsel of the wicked, nor stands in the way of sinners, nor sits in the seat of scoffers; but his delight is in the law of the LORD, and on his law he meditates day and night. He is like a tree planted by streams of water that yields its fruit in its season, and its leaf does not wither. In all that he does, he prospers…for the LORD knows the way of the righteous, but the way of the wicked will perish."

(Psalm 1:1–3, 6)

"The law of the LORD is perfect, reviving the soul; the testimony of the LORD is sure, making wise the simple; the precepts of the LORD are right, rejoicing the heart; the commandment of the LORD is pure, enlightening the eyes; the fear of the LORD is clean, enduring forever; the rules of the LORD are true, and righteous altogether. More to be desired are they than gold, even much fine gold; sweeter also than honey and drippings of the honeycomb. Moreover, by them is your servant warned; in keeping them there is great reward."

(Psalm 19:7–11)

"The LORD is my shepherd; I shall not want. He makes me lie down in green pastures. He leads me beside still waters. He restores my soul. He leads me in paths of righteousness for his name's sake. Even though I walk through the valley of the shadow of death, I will fear no evil, for you are with me; your rod and your staff, they comfort me. You prepare a table before me in the presence of my enemies; you anoint my head with oil; my cup overflows. Surely goodness and mercy shall follow me all the days of my life, and I shall dwell in the house of the LORD forever."

(Psalm 23:1–6)

"The LORD is my light and my salvation; whom shall I fear? The LORD is the stronghold of my life; of whom shall I be afraid? When evildoers assail me to eat up my flesh, my adversaries and foes, it is they who stumble and fall. Though an army encamp against me, my heart shall not fear; though war arise against me, yet I will be confident."

(Psalm 27:1–3)

"Oh, taste and see that the LORD is good! Blessed is the man who takes refuge in him!"

(Psalm 34:8)

"I waited patiently for the LORD; he inclined to me and heard my cry. He drew me up from the pit of destruction, out of the miry bog, and set my feet upon a rock, making my steps secure. He put a new song in my mouth, a song of praise to our God. Many will see and fear, and put their trust in the LORD. Blessed is the man who makes the LORD his trust, who does not turn to the proud, to those who go astray after a lie."

(Psalm 40:1–4)

"Your kingdom is an everlasting kingdom, and your dominion endures throughout all generations. The LORD is faithful in all his words and kind in all his works."

(Psalm 145:13)

"Trust in the LORD with all your heart, and do not lean on your own understanding. In all your ways acknowledge him, and he will make straight your paths. Be not wise in your own eyes; fear the LORD, and turn away from evil. It will be healing to your flesh and refreshment to your bones. Honor the LORD with your wealth and with the first fruits of all your produce; then your barns will be filled with plenty, and your vats will be bursting with wine."

(Proverbs 3:5–10)

"For the LORD will be your confidence and will keep your foot from being caught."

(Proverbs 3:26)

"Every word of God proves true; he is a shield to those who take refuge in him."

(Proverbs 30:5)

"You keep him in perfect peace whose mind is stayed on you, because he trusts in you."

(Isaiah 26:3)

"But they who wait for the LORD shall renew their strength; they shall mount up with wings like eagles; they shall run and not be weary; they shall walk and not faint."

(Isaiah 40:31)

"For I know the plans I have for you, declares the LORD, plans for welfare and not for evil, to give you a future and a hope. Then you will call upon me and come and pray to me, and I will hear you. You will seek me and find me, when you seek me with all your heart."

(Jeremiah 29:11–13)

"The steadfast love of the LORD never ceases; his mercies never come to an end; they are new every morning; great is your faithfulness. 'The LORD is my portion,' says my soul, 'therefore I will hope in him.'"

(Lamentations 3:22–24)

"For I the LORD do not change; therefore you, O children of Jacob, are not consumed. From the days of your fathers you have turned aside from my statutes and have not kept them. Return to me, and I will return to you, says the LORD of hosts. But you say, 'How shall we return?' Will man rob God? Yet you are robbing me. But you say, 'How have we robbed you?' In your tithes and contributions. You are cursed with a curse, for you are robbing me, the whole nation of you. Bring the full tithe into the storehouse, that there may be food in my house. And thereby put me to the test, says the LORD of hosts, if I will not open the windows of heaven for you and pour down for you a blessing until there is no more need. I will rebuke the devourer for you, so that it will not destroy the fruits of your soil, and your vine in the field shall not fail to bear, says the LORD of hosts. Then all nations will call you blessed, for you will be a land of delight, says the LORD of hosts."

(Malachi 3:6–12)

God's instruction is so repetitively clear and consistent— we are to wholeheartedly obey him. Whoever God chooses, one or a nation to have a covenant relationship with, there must be complete obedience because "I, the LORD your God, am a jealous God visiting the iniquity of the fathers on the children to the third and the fourth generation of those who hate me, but showing steadfast love to thousands of those who love me and keep my commandments" (Exodus 20:5–6).

Remember what Romans 15:4 tells us about Old Testament teaching: "For whatever was written in former days was written for our instruction"—we have been instructed over and over that we might learn—in a relationship with the one LORD

God, there is only one kind of obedience—"wholehearted" obedience (Deuteronomy 1:36). There is no substitute for that obedience—nothing! "For this is the love of God, that we keep his commandments. And his commandments are not burdensome" (1 John 5:3).

So how do you think there can be abundance and victory in your life, marriage, family and/or ministry if you tolerate disobedience in your life toward a holy God who is omniscient and knows everything about you? Immediately following his promise of abundant life (John 10:10), Jesus taught about the good shepherd laying his life down for the sheep and his sheep knowing him and listening to his voice (John 10:11–18). No matter who you are, what your title is, or what you have done for God, you will not experience his abundance apart from wholehearted listening and obeying him as the one LORD God.

A word used often in the New Testament describing abundant life in Christ is *perisseuo* which is translated "abound" or "overflow." In Christ, we are to:

- Abound/overflow in thanksgiving (2 Corinthians 4:15);
- Abound/overflow in hope (Romans 15:13);
- Abound/overflow in love (1 Thessalonians 3:2; 4:1,10);
- Abound/overflow in our work done for the Lord (1 Corinthians 15:58);
- Abound/overflow in the comfort and help through Christ in our sufferings (2 Corinthians 1:5);
- Abound/overflow with glory in the ministry of righteousness (2 Corinthians 1:5); and

- Abound/overflow in the gracious work of God's grace and giving (2 Corinthians 8:7; 9:8,12–13).

I have three soul searching questions for you:

1. Why do so many who love the LORD and actively serve in their church, including pastors, church staff, and church leaders not abound/overflow in this abundance?

2. Why do most of us not know many church leaders who, regardless of their circumstances or feelings, "in season and out of season" (2 Timothy 4:2) abound/overflow in this abundance?

3. Why do many college and seminary professors, pastors, church staff and other church leaders not have a countenance of abundance on their face as they worship the one LORD God daily and each Sunday with their church family?

As we have already seen throughout God's Word, the answer to each of these questions is that "there is no substitute for obedience to God if you are going to experience his abundance in your life, marriage, family, and ministry."

From little churches to big churches, bi-vocational pastors to mega-church pastors, uneducated to highly educated, middle school students to seminary students, church staff to directors of missions, denominational leaders to college and seminary professors and/or administrators, the title, the position, the background, and/or the circumstances surrounding any person does not determine if he/she is living in the abundance of the Lord.

What makes the difference in everyone's life, marriage, family and/or ministry is this: Are we defined by the Word of God or just influenced by the Word of God? Have we resolved to daily, moment by moment "consider ourselves dead to sin and alive to God in Christ Jesus" (Romans 6:11)? Are we "trusting in the LORD with all our heart, and not leaning on our own understanding" (Proverbs 3:5)? Are we "in all our ways acknowledging the LORD" (Proverbs 3:6)? Are we "no longer trying to be wise in our own eyes, but fearing the LORD, and turning away from evil" (Proverbs 3:7)?

God has promised us when we do these things, "it will be healing to your flesh and refreshment to your bones" (Proverbs 3:8). This passage of Scripture goes on to promise when we "honor the LORD with our wealth and with the first fruits of all our produce then our barns will be filled with plenty, and our vats will be bursting with wine" (Proverbs 3:10).

If you are sick and tired of being sick and tired of knowing about God's promises but not experiencing them in the love, joy, peace, and power of the LORD, the glorious and good news is, "he restores my soul. He leads me in paths of righteousness for his name's sake" (Psalm 23:3).

Do not live any longer in the neighborhood of being discouraged and defeated as Jeremiah expressed in Lamentations 1:1-3:20. Rejoice in the provision and hope of Lamentations 3:21–24: "The steadfast love of the LORD never ceases; his mercies never come to an end; they are new every morning; great is your faithfulness. The LORD is my portion, says my soul, therefore I will hope in him."

Praise the LORD—he is the God of new beginnings. Take a bath in Philippians 3:10–16: "That I may know him and the power of his resurrection, and may share his sufferings, becoming like him in his death, that by any means possible I may attain the resurrection from the dead. Not that I have already obtained this or am already perfect, but I press on to make it my own, because Christ Jesus has made me his own. Brothers, I do not consider that I have made it my own. But one thing I do: forgetting what lies behind and straining forward to what lies ahead, I press on toward the goal for the prize of the upward call of God in Christ Jesus. Let those of us who are mature think this way, and if in anything you think otherwise, God will reveal that also to you. Only let us hold true to what we have attained."

Praise the LORD for the privilege of his grace to live out his purpose of salvation by being:

- Submitted to the authority of God's Word and godly authority (John 8:31–32);

- Surrendered to the Holy Spirit's presence (Ephesians 5:17–18);

- Settled to whose we are (1 Corinthians 6:19–20);

- Surrounded by Christians for encouragement and accountability (Hebrews 10:23–25); and

- Sharing Christ every day, everywhere, all the time (Acts 5:42).

Let this be the first day of the rest of your life to the glory of God. Never again live beneath your privilege in Jesus Christ. He paid far too much for you to live with anything other than his abundance and victory!

Thinking God—There is no substitute for obedience to God if you are going to know the power of his love, joy, and peace (James 2:22–25).

Truth to Remember—We have been instructed over and over from Genesis to Revelation in a relationship with the one LORD God, there is only one kind of obedience, "wholehearted" obedience (Deuteronomy 1:36), and that kind of obedience shows we love God (1 John 5:2–4).

Thinking God in Reflecting—How do you think there can be abundance in your life, marriage, family, and/or ministry if you tolerate disobedience toward a holy God who is omniscient and has called you to "be holy, for I am holy" (1 Peter 1:13–16)?

THINKING GOD: FAITHFUL STEWARDSHIP

Memorize God's Word!

"Do not lay up for yourselves treasures on earth, where moth and rust destroy and where thieves break in and steal, but lay up for yourselves treasures in heaven, where neither moth nor rust destroys and where thieves do not break in and steal. For where your treasure is, there your heart will be also" (Matthew 6:19–21).

"No one can serve two masters, for either he will hate the one and love the other, or he will be devoted to the one and despise the other. You cannot serve God and money" (Matthew 6:24).

"His master said to him, 'Well done, good and faithful servant. You have been faithful over a little; I will set you over much. Enter into the joy of your master'" (Matthew 25:21).

"And truly, I say to you, 'wherever the gospel is proclaimed in the whole world, what she has done will be told in memory of her'" (Mark 14:9).

"Why do you call me 'Lord, Lord,' and not do what I tell you" (Luke 6:46)?

"This is how one should regard us, as servants of Christ and stewards of the mysteries of God. Moreover, it is required of stewards that they be found faithful" (1 Corinthians 4:1–2).

"On the first day of every week, each of you is to put something aside and store it up, as he may prosper, so that there will be no collecting when I come" (1 Corinthians 16:2).

"And this, not as we expected, but they gave themselves first to the Lord and then by the will of God to us" (2 Corinthians 8:5).

"Each one must give as he has decided in his heart, not reluctantly or under compulsion, for God loves a cheerful giver. And God is able to make all grace abound to you, so that having all sufficiency in all things at all times, you may abound in every good work" (2 Corinthians 9:7–8).

"Only let your manner of life be worthy of the gospel of Christ, so that whether I come and see you or am absent, I may hear of you that you are standing firm in one spirit, with one mind striving side by side for the faith of the gospel" (Philippians 1:27).

"Brothers, I do not consider that I have made it my own. But one thing I do: forgetting what lies behind and straining forward to what lies ahead, I press on toward the goal for the prize of the upward call of God in Christ Jesus" (Philippians 3:13–14).

"And my God will supply every need of yours according to his riches in glory in Christ Jesus" (Philippians 4:19).

"Therefore, since we are surrounded by so great a cloud of witnesses, let us also lay aside every weight, and sin which clings so closely, and let us run with endurance the race that is set before us, looking to Jesus, the founder and perfecter of our faith, who for the joy that was set before him endured the cross, despising the shame, and is seated at the right hand of the throne of God" (Hebrews 12:1–2).

"As each has received a gift, use it to serve one another, as good stewards of God's varied grace" (1 Peter 4:10).

ℰℭℜ

I was born very nearsighted. For almost seven years, I did not know I had a problem. My parents did not know I had a problem. My doctor did not know I had a problem. I grew up thinking blindness was normal. I sure did miss out on a lot. Seeing really is a special thing. Because I had such poor vision, I didn't even know how to compare it with the indescribable privileges of sight.

The first time I heard someone telling my mom "You need to have Phillip's eyes checked" was my piano teacher after watching me continually press my face closer to the music to see the notes. If you have ever seen a beginning piano book for children, you know they print the notes extra large, so it was easy for my teacher to see I had poor eyesight. For reasons unknown to me, I was never taken to the eye doctor for almost two years from the time of that conversation between my piano teacher and my mom. I do not ever remember complaining about my blindness or even saying, "Mom, I need to go see a doctor. I need glasses." I was blind and didn't know what I was missing. I did not know good eyesight was even possible.

The next time I heard someone telling my mom, "You really need to have Phillip's eyes checked" was my first grade teacher. She told my mom, "Phillip is sitting in the first row, but any time he can, he goes to the blackboard to see what I have written down during the previous class."

I know my mom and dad loved me. They always took good care of me, but they did not take me to the eye doctor. Maybe it was because I appeared to be doing just fine even with poor eyesight. I made straight A's every six weeks on my report card in school. I was progressing rapidly in my piano lessons. I enjoyed playing in the backyard with my friends. I had a good appetite. I was healthy, happy, and sleeping good at night. Finally, something "serious enough" happened that caused my dad to realize I needed to see an eye doctor.

In southeast Arkansas in the fifties, one of the most important days in a six or seven year old boy's life was when he got his first shotgun and was able to go hunting with his dad. This was almost as important as getting your driver's license. Saturday after Saturday in the fall, my dad, older brother, and I would go out in the country to one of my dad's farmer friends, and we would go squirrel hunting. It was especially fun when the farmer had a "squirrel dog." This dog would run ahead of us smelling for a scent of some little squirrel. When the dog got a scent on a trail leading him to the tree he thought the squirrel was in, he would begin to bark like the world was coming to an end. We would all run through the woods as fast as we could with the hope the squirrel wouldn't get away. Once we arrived where the dog had "treed the squirrel," we would circle the tree and look for this terrified helpless creature with four shotguns ready to open fire on him. Often my dad or his farmer friend would yell out, "I see him. There he is." Because

I was the younger brother, my dad or the farmer would often say to me, "Shoot him, Phillip." I would have to reply, "I can't see him." They would point in the squirrel's direction, describe which branch he was on, and finally with me still not able to see where the squirrel was, they would point the barrel of my gun in the vicinity of the squirrel and tell me to shoot, which I would do. Several times I heard different men ask my dad as we were walking through the woods, waiting for the dog to tree another squirrel, "Have you ever had Phillip's eyes checked?" My dad would reply, "We probably need to do that."

What if my parents would never have taken me to a doctor to have my eyes checked? How old would I have become before I would have figured out for myself, "I don't have to stay blind." Or would I have just stayed blind and done the best I could throughout my life? Isn't it amazing at times how long we can be blind about real important things in life and what it takes to bring a dramatic change for the good in our lives?

Fifty-six years ago, my mom took me to an optometrist for an eye exam and my glasses were ordered. I was in the second grade. I can remember the moment when the doctor put those glasses on me like it was yesterday. Even though they were ugly horn-rimmed black glasses, I didn't care because I could finally see. I yelled excitedly, "Wow, I can see!" I began to tell my mom about all the things I could see for the first time in my life. I could see faces in the pictures on the wall across the room. I could see the colors red, blue, yellow, and green in the paintings on the walls of the doctor's office. When my mom and I walked out of the doctor's office, I could not believe everything I could see. I exclaimed with great joy, "Mom, I can see the people's faces across the street. I can see the people's faces in the cars. I can see the birds flying in the sky. I can see the letters on the street signs. I can see the colors red, yellow, and green on the stoplight a block away." It was unbelievable and incredible. It was indescribable. I could see! It was one of the greatest moments of my life. *I could see!* My life has never been the same. In my blindness, I didn't even know what I was missing—the joy of seeing and all the blessings that come with sight.

When it comes to being faithful stewards or managers (oikonomos) of everything God has entrusted to us, it is heartbreaking how many in our churches are blind to God's vision for them (1 Corinthians 4:1–2). They have never known the joy of being faithful, fruitful, and fulfilled in the Lord. Sadly, they do not even know what they are missing—the joyous privilege of being faithful stewards of everything God has entrusted to them to his honor and glory. As the Lord did in his earthly ministry, he invites each of us to: "Come to him, all who labor and are heavy laden, and I will give you rest. Take my yoke upon you, and learn from me, for I am gentle and lowly in heart, and you will find rest for your souls. For my yoke is easy, and my burden is light" (Matthew 11:28–30).

Faithful stewardship is learned from the Lord. The only way to learn from the Lord is by being "yoked" by the Lord (Matthew 11:28–30). We must come to Jesus, just like I had to go to an optometrist and be examined. The Lord has already examined us (Isaiah 53:6; Jeremiah 17:9; Romans 3:10–12; Ephesians 2:1–3), and he knows if we are not "yoked"—put ourselves under the authority of his Word and surrendered to the Spirit's control—we will not learn the joy of faithful stewardship from him.

This is one of many reasons there is such a need to start new churches—many established churches are filled with spiritually nearsighted persons, like I was physically nearsighted, and they do not even know it. According to recent surveys taken by Christian organizations, less than five percent of the Christian community knows the joy of being a faithful steward in bringing their tithes and offerings to their church. Tragically in their blindness, they will not go to Doctor Jesus and be yoked so they can see. Even after others have suggested they are blind and need to have their "eyes (hearts) checked," nothing happens to change their blindness.

On October 17, 1993, I was asked to start a new church in the west part of St. Louis County of the state of Missouri. Our goal was to love God more than anything else (Matthew 22:37), and to make God known to others more than anything else (Acts 1:8) in being faithful stewards to his glory (1 Corinthians 4:1–2).

West County Community Church had its first Sunday service on October 24, 1993 with the vision: "We are committed to be a dynamic community of faith endeavoring to impact the world by experiencing, living, modeling, and communicating authentic faith in the Lord Jesus Christ. Increasingly, our intention is to become fully:

- A worshipping, caring, and sharing community— Exalting the Savior;
- A learning community—Equipping the saints;
- An influential community—Evangelizing the world."

A few months after we began, we were convicted by God to change the word *committed* to *surrendered*, understanding apart from the Spirit's power to "walk by the Spirit" (Galatians 5:16), this vision was impossible for us to live out. Realizing many of our members did not know the freedom, joy, and peace of Thinking God in being faithful stewards in their giving of tithes and offerings, we began and have continued through the years to equip our people with the truth of God's Word, trusting the Holy Spirit to set the captives free (John 8:32). Little by little, many have been set free to trust the Lord "in giving themselves first to the Lord" (2 Corinthians 8:5) and in their giving of their time, talents, and tithes and offerings. The following insights are truths we have shared with our people continuously:

What is the Tithe?

I. Tithe–dekatoo from dekatos–tenth.

II. Giving of tithes was a recognition of *belonging* to the Lord God.

  A. Old Testament

    1. Abraham gave "Melchizedek, a priest of God Most High, a *tenth* of everything" (Genesis 14:18–20).

    2. From Mt. Sinai, among the commands the Lord gave Moses for the Israelites was: "A tithe of everything from the land *belongs* to the Lord; it is *holy* to the Lord" (Leviticus 27:30).

    3. God told Moses to tell the Levites, "*Tithe* the tithes you receive from the Israelites" (Numbers 18:25–26).

    4. Throughout the Old Testament, Israel's worship and revivals were always accompanied by the *celebration* of tithing, *acknowledging* their belonging

to God (Deuteronomy 12:4–14; 2 Chronicles 31:1–12; Nehemiah 10:37–38).

5. Severe warning was given to Israel to *return* to God by giving their tithes and offerings to the Lord (Malachi 3:8–10).

B. Jesus's Teachings

1. Jesus taught we are to *invest* eternally (Matthew 6:19–20).
2. Jesus taught our giving reveals our *heart* (Matthew 6:21).
3. Jesus taught our giving declares who or what is our *master* (Matthew 6:24).
4. Jesus taught not to worry about our needs, but to put him first and *know* he will meet our every need (Matthew 6:33).
5. Jesus taught it is *hard* for a rich man to enter the kingdom of heaven (Matthew 19:23–26).
6. Jesus taught to give to Caesar what is Caesar's, and to God *what* is God's (Matthew 22:21).
7. Jesus taught the *tithe* is God's (Matthew 23:23).
8. Jesus taught "give and it will be *given* to you" (Luke 6:38).
9. Jesus taught *sacrificial* giving is significant to him (Mark 14:3–9).
10. Jesus warned about hearing his teaching and not *obeying* (Luke 6:46–49).

C. New Testament Churches' Examples and Teachings

1. *Sacrificial* giving resulted from "giving themselves first to the Lord" (2 Corinthians 8:1–5).
2. *Lying* to God about our giving brings God's judgment (Acts 5:1–10).
3. The Apostle Paul's teaching to the churches:

    a. Each Sunday, bring your *tithe* and no collections will have to be made (1 Corinthians 16:2).
    b. Each Sunday, give obediently to the Lord *out* of gratefulness, love and joy (2 Corinthians 9:7).
    c. Each Sunday, give obediently to the Lord, *confident* that he has promised to provide from his abundance all your need (2 Corinthians 9:8; Philippians 4:19).

God Expects Those in Relationship with Him to Be Gracious Givers

Genesis 14:18–20, NIV–"Then Melchizedek king of Salem brought out bread and wine. He was priest of God Most High, and he blessed Abram, saying, 'Blessed be Abram by God Most High, Creator of heaven and earth. And blessed be God Most High, who delivered your enemies into your hand.' Then Abram gave him a tenth of everything."

Leviticus 27:30, NIV–"A tithe of everything from the land, whether grain from the soil or fruit from the trees, belongs to the Lord; it is holy to the Lord."

Numbers 18:25–26, NIV–"The Lord said to Moses, 'Speak to the Levites and say to them: When you receive from the

Israelites the tithe I give you as your inheritance, you must present a tenth of that tithe as the Lord's offering.'"

Deuteronomy 12:4–14, NIV–"You must not worship the Lord your God in their way. But you are to seek the place the Lord your God will choose from among all your tribes to put his Name there for his dwelling. To that place you must go; there bring your burnt offerings and sacrifices, your tithes and special gifts, what you have vowed to give and your freewill offerings, and the firstborn of your herds and flocks. There, in the presence of the Lord your God, you and your families shall eat and shall rejoice in everything you have put your hand to, because the Lord your God has blessed you. You are not to do as we do here today, everyone as he sees fit, since you have not yet reached the resting place and the inheritance the Lord your God is giving you. But you will cross the Jordan and settle in the land the Lord your God is giving you as an inheritance, and he will give you rest from all your enemies around you so that you will live in safety. Then to the place the LORD your God will choose as a dwelling for his Name—there you are to bring everything I command you: your burnt offerings and sacrifices, your tithes and special gifts, and all the choice possessions you have vowed to the Lord. And there rejoice before the Lord your God, you, your sons and daughters, your menservants and maidservants, and the Levites from your towns, who have no allotment or inheritance of their own. Be careful not to sacrifice your burnt offerings anywhere you please. Offer them only at the place the Lord will choose in one of your tribes, and there observe everything I command you."

2 Chronicles 31:1–12, NIV–"When all this had ended, the Israelites who were there went out to the towns of Judah,

smashed the sacred stones and cut down the Asherah poles.
They destroyed the high places and the altars throughout Judah
and Benjamin and in Ephraim and Manasseh. After they had
destroyed all of them, the Israelites returned to their own towns
and to their own property. Hezekiah assigned the priests and
Levites to divisions—each of them according to their duties
as priests or Levites—to offer burnt offerings and fellowship
offerings, to minister, to give thanks and to sing praises at the
gates of the Lord's dwelling. The king contributed from his
own possessions for the morning and evening burnt offerings
and for the burnt offerings on the Sabbaths, New Moons
and appointed feasts as written in the Law of the Lord. He
ordered the people living in Jerusalem to give the portion due
the priests and Levites so they could devote themselves to the
Law of the Lord. As soon as the order went out, the Israelites
generously gave the firstfruits of their grain, new wine, oil and
honey and all that the fields produced. They brought a great
amount, a tithe of everything. The men of Israel and Judah
who lived in the towns of Judah also brought a tithe of their
herds and flocks and a tithe of the holy things dedicated to
the Lord their God, and they piled them in heaps. They began
doing this in the third month and finished in the seventh
month. When Hezekiah and his officials came and saw the
heaps, they praised the Lord and blessed his people Israel.
Hezekiah asked the priests and Levites about the heaps; and
Azariah the chief priest, from the family of Zadok, answered,
'Since the people began to bring their contributions to the
temple of the Lord, we have had enough to eat and plenty
to spare, because the Lord has blessed his people, and this
great amount is left over.' Hezekiah gave orders to prepare
storerooms in the temple of the Lord, and this was done.

Then they faithfully brought in the contributions, tithes and dedicated gifts. Conaniah, a Levite, was in charge of these things, and his brother Shimei was next in rank."

Nehemiah 10:37–38, NIV–"Moreover, we will bring to the storerooms of the house of our God, to the priests, the first of our ground meal, of our offerings, of the fruit of all our trees and of our new wine and oil. And we will bring a tithe of our crops to the Levites, for it is the Levites who collect the tithes in all the towns where we work. A priest descended from Aaron is to accompany the Levites when they receive the tithes, and the Levites are to bring a tenth of the tithes up to the house of our God, to the storerooms of the treasury."

Malachi 3:8–10, NIV–"Will a man rob God? Yet you rob me. But you ask, 'How do we rob you?' In tithes and offerings. You are under a curse—the whole nation of you—because you are robbing me. Bring the whole tithe into the storehouse, that there may be food in my house. Test me in this, says the Lord Almighty, and see if I will not throw open the floodgates of heaven and pour out so much blessing that you will not have room enough for it."

Matthew 6:19–21, 24, 33, NIV–"Do not store up for yourselves treasures on earth, where moth and rust destroy, and where thieves break in and steal. But store up for yourselves treasures in heaven, where moth and rust do not destroy, and where thieves do not break in and steal. For where your treasure is, there your heart will be also. No one can serve two masters. Either he will hate the one and love the other, or he will be devoted to the one and despise the other. You cannot serve both God and Money. But seek first his kingdom and his righteousness, and all these things will be given to you as well."

Matthew 19:23–26, NIV–"Then Jesus said to his disciples, 'I tell you the truth, it is hard for a rich man to enter the kingdom of heaven. Again I tell you, it is easier for a camel to go through the eye of a needle than for a rich man to enter the kingdom of God.' When the disciples heard this, they were greatly astonished and asked, 'Who then can be saved?' Jesus looked at them and said, 'With man this is impossible, but with God all things are possible.'"

Matthew 22:21b, NIV–"Then he said to them, 'Give to Caesar what is Caesar's, and to God what is God's.'"

Matthew 23:23, NIV–"Woe to you, teachers of the law and Pharisees, you hypocrites! You give a tenth of your spices— mint, dill and cummin. But you have neglected the more important matters of the law—justice, mercy, and faithfulness. You should have practiced the latter, without neglecting the former."

Luke 6:38, NIV–"Give, and it will be given to you. A good measure, pressed down, shaken together, and running over will be poured into your lap. For with the measure you use, it will be measured to you."

Mark 14:3–9, NIV–"While he was in Bethany, reclining at the table in the home of a man known as Simon the Leper, a woman came with an alabaster jar of very expensive perfume, made of pure nard. She broke the jar and poured the perfume on his head. Some of those present were saying indignantly to one another, 'Why this waste of perfume? It could have been sold for more than a year's wages and the money given to the poor.' And they rebuked her harshly. 'Leave her alone,' said Jesus. 'Why are you bothering her? She has done a beautiful thing to me. The poor you will always have with you, and you can help them any time you want. But you will not always have me. She did what she could. She poured perfume on my body beforehand to prepare for my burial. I tell you the truth, wherever the gospel is preached throughout the world, what she has done will also be told, in memory of her.'"

Luke 6:46–49, NIV–"Why do you call me, 'Lord, Lord,' and do not do what I say? I will show you what he is like who comes to me and hears my words and puts them into practice. He is like a man building a house, who dug down deep and laid the foundation on rock. When a flood came, the torrent struck that house but could not shake it, because it was well built. But the one who hears my words and does not put them into practice is like a man who built a house on the ground without a foundation. The moment the torrent struck that house, it collapsed and its destruction was complete."

Acts 5:1–10, NIV–"Now a man named Ananias, together with his wife Sapphira, also sold a piece of property. With his wife's full knowledge he kept back part of the money for himself but brought the rest and put it at the apostles' feet. Then Peter said, 'Ananias, how is it that Satan has so filled your heart that you have lied to the Holy Spirit and have kept for yourself some of the money you received for the land? Didn't it belong to you before it was sold? And after it was sold, wasn't the money at your disposal? What made you think of doing such a thing? You have not lied to men but to God.' When Ananias heard this, he fell down and died. And great fear seized all who heard what had happened. Then the young men came forward, wrapped up his body, carried him out, and buried him. About three hours later his wife came in, not knowing what had happened. Peter asked her, 'Tell me, is this the price you and Ananias got for the land?' 'Yes,' she said, 'that is the price.' Peter said to her, 'How could you agree to test the Spirit of the Lord? Look! The feet of the men who buried your husband are at the door, and they will carry you out also.' At that moment she fell down at his feet and died. Then the young men came in and, finding her dead, carried her out, and buried her beside her husband."

1 Corinthians 16:2, NIV–"On the first day of every week, each one of you should set aside a sum of money in keeping with his income, saving it up, so that when I come no collections will have to be made."

2 Corinthians 8:1–5, NIV–"And now, brothers, we want you to know about the grace that God has given the Macedonian churches. Out of the most severe trial, their overflowing joy and their extreme poverty welled up in rich generosity. For I testify that they gave as much as they were able, and even beyond their ability. Entirely on their own, they urgently pleaded with us for the privilege of sharing in this service to the saints. And they did not do as we expected, but they gave themselves first to the Lord and then to us in keeping with God's will."

2 Corinthians 9:7–8, NIV–"Each man should give what he has decided in his heart to give, not reluctantly or under compulsion, for God loves a cheerful giver. And God is able to make all grace abound to you, so that in all things at all times, having all that you need, you will abound in every good work."

Philippians 4:19, NIV–"And my God will meet all your needs according to his glorious riches in Christ Jesus."

For the last twenty-one years, by the LORD's greatness, goodness, grace, mercy, patience, and faithfulness, we have continued to increasingly learn and experience the joy of living out this vision of surrender to walk by faith and know the inexpressible joy and peace of learning to be faithful stewards of everything the Lord has entrusted to us.

As faithful stewards of God's goodness and grace, we have been called by God to be Christ-like by being defined by God's Word, not just influenced by God's Word. We have been called by God to be faithful (Matthew 25:21), fruitful (John 15:5), and fulfilled (Colossians 1:27) as faithful stewards in living out God's purpose of salvation in us by living with the following values because whatever we value determines what we do.

1. Holiness–Our first value is personal holiness. God empowers and we obey in experiencing practical holiness. We agree corporately this is God's standard and our intention. *"For it is written, 'Be holy, because I am holy'"* (1 Peter 1:16, NIV).

2. Stewardship–We believe all we are and have is a gift from God and in truth belongs to him. Therefore, we are continuously making a concerted effort to manage our lives and resources wisely for the glory of God, and let all we do be done with godly excellence. *"Moreover, it is required of stewards, that a man be found faithful"* (1 Corinthians 4:2, NIV*).*

3. Biblical–Our standard for faith and practice is God's Word rightly interpreted and honestly applied. *"All Scripture is God-breathed and is useful for teaching, rebuking, correcting and training in righteousness, so that the man of God may be thoroughly equipped for every good work"* (2 Timothy 3:16–17, NIV).

4. Compassion–Knowing that compassion for people marked our Lord's earthly ministry, we choose to see worth in every individual and commit ourselves to minister to and encourage those within our sphere of influence. *"Therefore, as God's chosen people, holy and dearly loved, clothe yourselves with compassion, kindness, humility, gentleness, and patience. Bear with each other and forgive whatever grievances you may have against one another. Forgive as the Lord forgave you. And over all these virtues put on love, which binds them all together in perfect unity"* (Colossians 3:12–14, NIV).

5. Servant-hearted–Knowing that Jesus came, not to be served but to serve, we choose to model servant-heartedness as God's method for touching the world, and God's will for each believer. The servant's primary task is to accomplish the will of the Master. *"Your attitude should be the same as that of Christ Jesus: Who, being in very nature God, did not consider equality with God something to be grasped, but made himself nothing, taking the very nature of a servant, being made in human likeness"* (Philippians 2:5–7, NIV).

6. Humility–Knowing we can be rebellious to God or we can submit our lives to God, we are increasingly choosing to not waste our lives and walk by the Spirit and obey the Word of God just as the Lord Jesus did even unto death. *"And being found in human form, he humbled himself by becoming obedient to the point of death, even death on a cross"* (Philippians 2:8, NIV).

7. Development–Knowing that growing in spiritual maturity and ministry effectiveness is a continual

process, we choose to set upon a course of lifelong development ever striving to be conformed to the image of Christ. We choose to be seeking constantly new and relevant ways to improve our ministry and impact our world for Christ. *"Not that I have already obtained all this, or have already been made perfect, but I press on to take hold of that for which Christ Jesus took hold of me. Brothers, I do not consider myself yet to have taken hold of it. But one thing I do: Forgetting what is behind and straining toward what is ahead, I press on toward the goal to win the prize for which God has called me heavenward in Christ Jesus"* (Philippians 3:12–14, NIV).

8. Integrity–Knowing that Jesus Christ always lived out a strict alignment between what he knew and believed and what he did, we also choose to insist on absolute integrity of character as God's standard for our lives. *"Do not merely listen to the word, and so deceive yourselves. Do what it says"* (James 1:22, NIV).

9. Leadership by Example–Our model for leadership is Jesus Christ who led by example. We desire to impact our world through Christ-like leadership. *"But if anyone obeys His word, God's love is truly made complete in him. This is how we know we are in Him: Whoever claims to live in Him must walk as Jesus did"* (I John 2:5–6, NIV).

10. Reproduction–Just as Jesus Christ reproduced himself in the ministry of the Apostles, we believe it is our responsibility as individual believers and as a church to win and disciple every person possible within our corporate sphere of influence. *"Then Jesus came to them and said, 'All authority in heaven and on earth has been*

given to me. Therefore go and make disciples of all nations, baptizing them in the name of the Father and of the Son and of the Holy Spirit, and teaching them to obey everything I have commanded you. And surely I am with you always, to the very end of the age"' (Matthew 28:18–20, NIV).

Living with such values is all a part of being faithful stewards to God of everything he has entrusted to us. Understanding our salvation, how could we ever be or do less (1 Corinthians 6:19–20)?

Understanding that God is a covenant God, the Bible is a covenant book, in Christ we are a covenant people, and covenant is the foundational concept throughout the Old and New Testaments, we made a covenant to God and to each other to be faithful stewards in the following:

I Will Protect the Unity of My Church

"Therefore, as God's chosen people, holy and dearly loved, clothe yourselves with compassion, kindness, humility, gentleness and patience. Bear with each other and forgive whatever grievances you may have against one another. Forgive as the Lord forgave you. And over all these virtues put on love which binds them all together in perfect unity" (Colossians 3:12–14, NIV).

"Do not let any unwholesome talk come out of your mouths, but only what is helpful for building others up according to their needs, that it may benefit those who listen" (Ephesians 4:29, NIV).

"Obey your leaders and submit to their authority. They keep watch over you as men who must give an account. Obey them so that their work will be a joy, not a burden, for that would be of no advantage to you" (Hebrews 13:17, NIV).

This calls us to live as faithful stewards the discipline of being humble (Philippians 2:8–13), which is obeying God's Word as a joy, not a burden (1 John 5:3).

I Will Share the Responsibility of My Church

"We always thank God for all of you, mentioning you in our prayers. We continually remember before our God and Father your work produced by faith, your labor prompted by love, and your endurance inspired by hope in our Lord Jesus Christ" (1 Thessalonians 1:2–3, NIV).

"But you will receive power when the Holy Spirit comes on you; and you will be my witnesses in Jerusalem, and in all Judea and Samaria, and to the ends of the earth" (Acts 1:8, NIV).

"Accept one another, then, just as Christ accepted you, in order to bring praise to God" (Romans 15:7, NIV).

This calls us to live as faithful stewards the discipline of the way of the cross (Galatians 2:20), which is denying ourselves to serve the will of the Father (Luke 9:23–24).

I Will Serve the Ministry of My Church

"Each one should use whatever gift he has received to serve others, faithfully administering God's grace in its various forms" (1 Peter 4:10, NIV).

"It was he who gave some to be apostles, some to be prophets, some to be evangelists, and some to be pastors and teachers, to prepare God's people for works of service, so that the body of Christ may be built up" (Ephesians 4:11–12, NIV).

"Each of you should look not only to your own interests, but also to the interests of others. Your attitude should be the same as that of Christ Jesus" (Philippians 2:4–5, NIV).

This calls us to live as faithful stewards the discipline of perseverance (Hebrews 12:1) which is staying faithful and fruitful under pressure to be fulfilled in staying fixed on pleasing God (John 15:5–11).

I Will Support the Ministry of My Church

"Let us not give up meeting together, as some are in the habit of doing, but let us encourage one another–and all the more as you see the Day approaching" (Hebrews 10:25, NIV).

"Whatever happens, conduct yourselves in a manner worthy of the gospel of Christ. Then, whether I come and see you or only hear about you in my absence, I will know that you stand firm in one spirit, contending as one man for the faith of the gospel" (Philippians 1:27, NIV).

"On the first day of every week, each one of you should set aside a sum of money in keeping with his income, saving it up, so that when I come no collections will have to be made" (1 Corinthians 16:2, NIV).

This calls us to live as faithful stewards the discipline of being single-minded (Philippians 3:13–16)—and staying fixed on pleasing God (1 Corinthians 4:1–2).

Burdened over the growing number in our fellowship who were not living out the joy and peace of being faithful stewards of God as reflected in our vision, values, and covenant they had agreed to when they became members of West County Community Church (WCCC), we began several years ago each January reviewing our vision, values, and covenant during four Sunday morning worship services. Each year we encourage the members of WCCC to reaffirm their commitment to be a covenant member of WCCC. It's all a part of understanding faithful stewardship as a church member is much more than a one-time exciting decision. It is the active participation of fulfilling that decision as a faithful steward God led us to make when we became a part of WCCC.

Has this been easy? No. Have we been criticized by many? Yes. Have many left WCCC because they did not want to pay the cost of discipleship and be a faithful steward? Yes. Have some of our original members refused to reaffirm their commitment to be a covenant member? Yes. So why do we continue to persevere in teaching our people the joy of discipleship (Matthew 28:19–20) lived out in faithful stewardship (1 Corinthians 4:1–2)?

The authority for our lives and teaching is God's Word. As teachers of God's Word, we are accountable to be faithful to God (James 3:1), not man. The Bible tells us there are two ways to live our lives: 1) "Walk by the Spirit, and you will not gratify the desires of the flesh," or 2) "Walk by the flesh, for the desires of the flesh are against the Spirit, and the desires of the Spirit are against the flesh, for these are opposed to each other to keep you from doing the things you want to do" (Galatians 5:16–17). Walking by the Spirit and being a faithful manager of everything God has entrusted to you is like seeing. It is wonderful. It is living out God's created and reconciled purpose for us to live (Colossians 1:16; 3:1–4). Walking by the flesh and being an unfaithful manager of everything God has entrusted to you is like living in blindness. You may think you are doing just fine even though you are missing the abundance of God's faithfulness, fruitfulness, and fulfillment in your life by not being a faithful steward of God's grace (2 Corinthians 9:6–8).

We have resolved at WCCC that whatever comes in our lives—disappointments, disagreements, and/or difficulties—by God's grace we will live out our vision, values, and covenant in being faithful, fruitful, and fulfilled stewards of God as we are commanded to be throughout God's Word to the glory of God.

In every church I have ever served or know anything about, until there was much prayer, loving, encouraging, modeling, and teaching of God's Word on the joy of faithful stewardship, not more than fifteen percent of the fellowship had the vision and joy of being faithful stewards. If you are presently one who is spiritually blind of seeing God's claim and call upon your life of being a faithful, fruitful, and fulfilled steward of God, understand who and what is against you:

1. *We are all born spiritually blind.* The Bible tells us: "The god of this world has blinded the minds of the unbelievers, to keep them from seeing the light of the gospel of the glory of Christ, who is the image of God" (2 Corinthians 4:4). Part of that blindness is we are all born "getters and takers." We were born self-absorbed, selfish, and thinking: "it's all about me." Until we truly become "new creations in Christ and are reconciled to God" (2 Corinthians 5:17–18) and have our thinking changed from being a "getter and a taker" to being a giver and a servant, we remain blind to the joys of being faithful stewards.

2. *The world in which we live.* The Bible instructs us: "Do not love the world or the things in the world. If anyone loves the world, the love of the Father is not in him. For all that is in the world—the desires of the flesh and the

desires of the eyes and pride of life—is not from the Father but is from the world" (1 John 2:15–16). Each of us have grown up listening to thousands of radio commercials and watching thousands of television commercials persuading us the only way to be happy and satisfied is to be individualistic and consume as much as we can with the attitude of: "Get all you can and can all you get;" "Be your own person and get yours;" and "Go for the gusto. You only go around once." Believing the lie that contentment is found only by "getting more things" rather than by Thinking God and learning contentment in the Lord (Philippians 4:11–13), we continually fall to the temptation of buying things we do not need with money we do not have to impress people who really don't care. Instead of finding contentment, we discover the bondage of indebtedness and find that all those new things we thought would make us happy and satisfied become old and outdated quickly.

3. *We are in a spiritual war with the devil.* The Bible warns us to: "Be strong in the Lord and in the strength of his might. Put on the whole armor of God that you may be able to stand against the schemes of the devil. For we do not wrestle against flesh and blood, but against the rulers, against the authorities, against the cosmic powers over this present darkness, against the spiritual forces of evil in the heavenly places. Therefore take up the whole armor of God, that you may be able to withstand in the evil day, and having done all, to stand firm" (Ephesians 6:10–13). Until we are "transformed by the renewal of our minds" by Thinking God (Romans12:2), we will

keep falling to the temptations of staying conformed to this world and will be deceived by the devil's schemes and live in the futility of being a "getter and a taker."

If you are a "getter and a taker," do not remain blind another day of seeing the blessedness Jesus promised of being a faithful, gracious, and joyous giver (Acts 20:35). Do not remain blind another day of being able to anticipate the joy of receiving the rewards of living as a faithful steward to God. Enjoy looking forward to hearing the Lord say to you at the end of your life: "Well done, good and faithful servant. You have been faithful over a little; I will set you over much. Enter into the joy of your master" (Matthew 25:21). Do not remain blind another day of knowing the joy of a fruitful life the Lord intended for you to have (John 15:5–11). Do not remain blind another day of experiencing faithfulness, fruitfulness, and fulfillment in the Lord of living out the purpose God saved you to have (Colossians 1:27).

Do not remain blind another day of living like those without God in their lives. No matter how many things they are able to have and keep on getting, they live frustrated and empty in their striving to have more things. Without being transformed by Christ, they will likely raise children who will follow their path of emptiness and never know the indescribable joy of being gracious givers and faithful stewards of the Lord.

Here's the good and glorious news: Because of God's grace demonstrated in giving us Jesus (Romans 5:8), none of us have to remain blind if we would just go to the doctor. Go to Doctor Jesus. This could be the day you see! See you were created by God and for God (Colossians 1:16). See the transforming truth of the privileges from Thinking God of living in the freedom of being a faithful steward of everything God has entrusted to you (Galatians 5:1).

In closing this chapter, I want to encourage every pastor to be a faithful steward by not being silent about teaching God's people God's Word concerning biblical stewardship. I know you know such teaching can often cause many to become uncomfortable and even quite upset, since the majority of people, even many of your leadership, probably do not know the joy and peace of this obedience in their lives. Some pastors have discovered they can even be fired for asking their leadership to be obedient to God's Word and to tithe and give offerings to the Lord (Malachi 3:6–12). Out of their fearfulness of man and what man can do to them, many pastors live their lives in compromise and teach very little on the abundance and victory God has saved us to experience in being faithful, fruitful, and fulfilled stewards of everything God has entrusted to us and commanded us to be (1 Corinthians 4:2).

I know some of the cost that can come when you do as Paul admonished Timothy to do, "Preach the word; be ready in season and out of season; reprove, rebuke, and exhort, with complete patience and teaching. For the time is coming when people will not endure sound teaching, but having itching ears they will accumulate for themselves teachers to suit their own passions, and will turn away from listening to the truth and wander off into myths. As for you, always be sober-minded, endure suffering, do the work of an evangelist, fulfill your ministry" (2 Timothy 4:2–5).

Pastors, I encourage you with all my heart to not be intimidated by the threats of sinful man, remembering the courage of Peter when he prayed, "And now, Lord, look upon their threats and grant to your servants to continue to speak your word with all boldness (Acts 4:29). Being a faithful steward as God commands us to be (1 Corinthians 4:2) is really a special privilege of God's claim and call in our lives. Be faithful (2 Timothy 3:7–8)!

Thinking God—If you have not yet known the joy of being a faithful steward of everything God has entrusted to you, the Lord invites you to "come to him, all who labor and are heavy laden, and he will give you rest. Take his yoke upon you and learn from him, for he is meek and humble in heart, and you will find rest for your soul. For his yoke is easy, and his burden is light" (Matthew 11:28–30).

Truth to Remember—Seeing who the one LORD God is, you will increasingly learn to trust him with everything you are and have (1 Corinthians 4:1–2).

Thinking God in Reflecting—Is it not amazing at times how long we can stay blind about real important things in life and what it takes to do those things that will bring a dramatic change for the good in our lives? Read Malachi 3:6–12 and test the LORD and see like everyone else who has trusted the LORD—he is faithful!

Thinking God: Forgiveness

Memorize God's Word!

"As for you, you meant evil against me, but God meant it for good, to bring it about that many people should be kept alive as they are today. So do not fear; I will provide for you and your little ones. Thus he comforted them and spoke kindly to them" (Genesis 50:20–21).

"He does not deal with us according to our sins, nor repay us according to our iniquities. For as high as the heavens are above the earth, so great is his steadfast love toward those who fear him; as far as the east is from the west, so far does he remove our transgressions from us" (Psalm 103:10–12).

"Give us this day our daily bread, and forgive us our debts, as we also have forgiven our debtors" (Matthew 6:12).

"For if you forgive others their trespasses, your heavenly Father will also forgive you, but if you do not forgive others their trespasses, neither will your Father forgive your trespasses" (Matthew 6:14–15).

"Then Peter came up and said to him, 'Lord, how often will my brother sin against me, and I forgive him? As many as seven times?' Jesus said to him, 'I do not say to you seven times, but seventy-seven times'" (Matthew 18:21–22).

"Then his master summoned him and said to him, 'You wicked servant! I forgave you all that debt because you pleaded with me. And should not you have had mercy on your fellow servant, as I had mercy on you'" (Matthew 18:32–33)?

"And Jesus said, 'Father, forgive them, for they know not what they do.' And they cast lots to divide his garments" (Luke 23:34).

"So then each of us will give an account of himself to God" (Romans 14:12).

"All this is from God, who through Christ reconciled us to himself and gave us the ministry of reconciliation; that is in Christ God was reconciling the world to himself, not counting their trespasses against them, and entrusting to us the message of reconciliation" (2 Corinthians 5:18–19).

"When I was a child, I spoke like a child, I thought like a child, I reasoned like a child. When I became a man, I gave up childish ways" (1 Corinthians 13:11).

"Do not be deceived: God is not mocked, for whatever one sows, that will he also reap. For the one who sows to his own flesh will from the flesh reap corruption, but the one who sows to the Spirit will from the Spirit reap eternal life" (Galatians 6:7–8).

"Let no corrupting talk come out of your mouths, but only such as is good for building up, as fits the occasion, that it may give grace to those who hear. And do not grieve the Holy Spirit of God, by whom you were sealed for the day of redemption. Let all bitterness and wrath and anger and clamor and slander be put away from you, along with all malice. Be kind to one another, tenderhearted, forgiving one another, as God in Christ forgave you" (Ephesians 4:29–32).

"We love because he first loved us" (1 John 4:19).

❧

For the first thirty-four years of my life, based on my circumstances and/or feelings, I would sometimes find myself where I did not want to be, following an unexpected deep hurt and wound from someone who I loved and trusted. I would be holding on to things and walking in the bondage of resentment, bitterness, blame, stewing and spewing to the Lord or my wife about the wounds in my life. I hated living with this unstableness from being double-minded in my life as described in James 1:6–7. I knew I was living beneath my privilege as God's child. It was especially a horrible existence, knowing I was supposed to be living and modeling what I believed with all my heart and taught with great passion— "in Christ, we always have his abundance (John 10:10), his victory (2 Corinthians 2:14), and his sufficiency in all things (2 Corinthians 12:9–10)." Praise God for his unlimited patience, mercy, and teaching in my life (1 Timothy 1:16–17).

God used the following series of events to open my eyes to see the foolishness of holding on to things God tells me to release. In the winter of 1985, I was invited by Knox Talbert to preach in the adult school for one week at "Super Summer Texas" at Baylor University that coming June. A few weeks before the event, Knox called me and asked if I could also preach at the weekend retreat for the leadership and preach for the joy explosion each night during that week because the pastor scheduled to do that had cancelled because of health concerns for his pregnant wife. All together, the request was for "twelve messages in seven days." I was young and excited about the opportunity, and said, "Of course, I can do that."

My flight from St. Louis to Dallas was delayed and my drive from Dallas to Waco took longer than I expected. I was frustrated, hot, sweaty, and somewhat "out of sorts" from how the day had gone. I had planned to get settled in my room, take a shower, eat, and be refreshed from the day's travel, so I could be at my best to preach that evening. However, after finding and parking in a "Super Summer" parking lot on the Baylor campus, a representative of Super Summer told me, "I had better go straight to the place where they were meeting because their planning time had already begun. Take all your baggage with you so you will not have to return to your car after the meeting." That was not what I wanted to hear, but being new on campus, I did what I was told.

Shortly after entering the room where we were meeting and hearing some announcements, the worship time in singing to the LORD began. As excited as I was to be there, I was also struggling with my attitude over how the day had gone. The theme for the week was "Free Indeed" taken from John 8:36, "So if the Son sets you free, you will be free indeed." As I said earlier, it is a horrible existence to believe and teach God's truth that you are not experiencing in your own life.

It is also an indescribable challenge to attempt to teach and lead others to do what you are not experiencing, but it is the task far too many pastors, student pastors, and worship pastors find themselves attempting to do every Sunday. I believe it is one of the primary reasons so many of our leaders say they have "burned out" and no longer can do ministry.

Following a Spirit-led time of praising the Lord, a young man, as a mime, gave a powerful visual of the struggle of our faithful and loving God attempting to enter the heart of a stubborn man who is exhaustingly fighting and resisting God to enter his heart with the music in the background playing "Jesus Loves Me."

As I watched this very physical and emotional struggle, I sensed the Holy Spirit's conviction, "Carry all of your bags tonight when you preach." I thought, *I can't do that. They're heavy. Besides, no one knows me here except Knox. I don't want them to think I'm crazy. I only have this first time to make a good impression. I don't want to start the week in a bad way.* The conviction continued with intensity, "Carry your bags. Do not expect me to bless what you are about to say if you are not going to obey me. Carry all your bags with you and hold them as you preach." The conviction was amazingly strong. The mime ended. Knox introduced me as: "Dr. Phil Hunter is a man who knows how to trust and obey God no matter what others do or think."

I picked up my four bags with straps and put two on each shoulder. I then picked up my bag of carry-on clothes, which had eight shirts, several pairs of pants, and a sport coat with one hand and my tennis racket and Bible in the other hand, walked up to the stage and began to speak not saying anything about my baggage.

When I said, "Open your Bible to John 8," it was quite a challenge to open my Bible to John 8. I had to reposition my tennis racket in one hand, holding the carry-on clothes bag in the same hand and then turn to John 8 with the other hand. It was a pathetic sight to watch this struggle when all I had to do was "let it all go" and be free to do what I had been asked to do—"come and lead us in seeing from God's Word the freedom we have in Christ" (Galatians 5:1).

I had only been holding my bags for a few minutes when I realized, "these things are heavier than I thought. I have got to speed up." After ten minutes, my neck and back began to get tense because my neck and back had still not fully recovered from the car accident I had been in a year earlier. But the Lord convicted me, "You keep holding those bags." I felt awkward, but I kept holding them. After twenty minutes, my body was aching, and I was getting a terrible headache, but I kept on preaching with passion the message God had given me on how we could be free in Christ no matter what our sin was, no matter what our hurts were, no matter what our past, present, or future was.

As I was preaching with an urgency to finish because I thought I was physically going to drop from holding the weight of those bags, it finally hit me why I was holding all that baggage. God was letting me see the foolishness of what I had been doing in my own life—learning, teaching, and preaching the great truths of Scripture that are intended to set us free (John 8:31–32) but holding on to some great secret hurts. Wounded and bitter, I was not free. I began to tell my fellow leaders with "godly sorrow" (2 Corinthians 7:10) of what God was doing in my life. I encouraged them to likewise, not live a double-minded life of learning and teaching the truth of God's Word intended to set them free but refusing to "let those things, whatever they are, go." I pleaded with them, "Stop holding on—holding on to your past sin, guilt, and shame; holding on to your past hurts and wounds; holding on to your disagreements and disappointments; holding on to your resentments, bitterness, anger and blame; holding on to your fears, frustrations, and the lies of the devil."

I shouted, "LET IT GO!" And I let go! I stopped holding on to my baggage, and it all hit the floor with an amazingly loud noise as the weight of it hit the floor. I cannot describe to you the relief my body felt and my mind and spirit experienced. I had let it go—the baggage in my hands and the bondage in my heart. I was free indeed of the weight and pain of that baggage and bondage. I began to shout to those three hundred pastors, student pastors, and worship pastors. "Be freed, let it go! Be freed, let it go! Be freed, let it go!"

As only God can do, the Holy Spirit mightily moved that night in many who were just like me: loving God with everything they knew; serving God and people with everything they had; and teaching God's Word with conviction, confidence, and courage, but still holding on to baggage and being in bondage, they needed to "let it go." I returned to Missouri with a new resolve in my heart for the rest of my life to live a disciplined life of "letting it go" instead of being defeated by my hurts, feelings, and circumstances.

That's what forgiveness (*aphiemi*) is:

It is the discipline of submitting to the authority of God's Word and "leaving, abandoning, releasing"—"So if you are offering your gift at the altar and there remember that your brother has something against you, leave your gift there before the altar and go. First be reconciled to your brother, and then come and offer your gift" (Matthew 5:23–24). "Let it go!"

It is the discipline of surrendering to the presence of the Holy Spirit and "leaving, abandoning, releasing"—"For if you forgive others their trespasses, your heavenly Father will also forgive you, but if you do not forgive others their trespasses, neither will your Father forgive your trespasses" (Matthew 6:14–15). "Let it go!"

It is the discipline of settling the issue of whose you are and "leaving, abandoning, releasing"—"And do not grieve the Holy Spirit of God, by whom you were sealed for the day of redemption. Let all bitterness and wrath and anger and clamor and slander be put away from you, along with all malice. Be kind to one another, tenderhearted, forgiving one another, as God in Christ forgave you" (Ephesians 4:30–32). "Let it go!"

It is the discipline of surrounding yourself with other Christians from whom you receive great encouragement and accountability with and "leaving, abandoning, releasing." "Therefore, confess your sins to one another and pray for one another, that you may be healed" (James 5:16a). "Let it go!"

Are you one of many who love and serve the Lord, but are not Thinking God and are still holding on to baggage and living in bondage from your past hurts and refusing to forgive? Do you not understand that bitterness is like drinking poison and hoping the other person will become sick?

If you're thinking, I understand what you are saying, but I just cannot forgive because:

- "The loss and pain is too great and the wounds are too deep."

- "The person who hurt me deeply and cost me more than I could ever say doesn't deserve forgiveness."

- "If I forgive, he/she gets off free as if they never did anything."

- "I could never forget what that person did to me."

- "The person has never said, he/she was sorry and would like to make things right."

- "The person in all his/her wrongdoing toward me feels justified in his/her actions even blaming me for his/her wrongdoing."

I know all of those feelings. I have been there. I have felt all of those thoughts and held on to the baggage of bitterness and blame even though it was wearing me out. It grieves the Holy Spirit. It is a miserable existence of living without God's abundance, joy, and peace. It is living far beneath your privilege as God's child.

God did not save you by your feelings or to live by your feelings. God saved you by grace through faith (Ephesians 2:8–9) to walk in his grace by faith (Romans 1:16–17). Stop walking by your feelings. Stop allowing your feelings to run over you like a train. Stop walking by your past. Stop walking by your circumstances and continuing to be a victim. Instead walk in God's abundance, victory, and sufficiency that you were saved to live out. Thinking God, "let it go!"

"Letting it go" (forgiveness) understands, the ones who have hurt and wounded you need your mercy and kindness just as you desperately need God's mercy and kindness in your life (Ephesians 2:7–9; 4:30–32).

You are not saying they did not do something wrong, even terrible, against you. Rather, under the authority of God, you are simply turning them over to the justice of God, knowing "each of us will give an account of himself to God" (Romans 14:12) and "vengeance is mine, I will repay, says the Lord," not you (Romans 12:19).

You are not forgetting everything painful and hurtful that has happened to you, but in light of God's grace in your life and your grateful desire to submit your life to the authority of

God's Word to "obey him which is not burdensome" (1 John 5:3), you are choosing not to hold the bad memories against the person. You are choosing not to bring up the offense before the offender or others ever again. You are choosing to live as if the offense is forgotten, just as God has done with your sins against him (Psalm 103:10–12; 1 John 1:9).

"Letting it go" is a disciplined humble act of your will because of your love and gratefulness unto the Lord (Philippians 2:5–8), and in that humility, it is denying your feelings and living by faith, "not as you will, but as your Father wills" (Matthew 26:39).

Your willingness to obey God does not depend on someone's confession of wrongdoing, but rather is an overflow of your walking in the presence and power of the Holy Spirit (Galatians 5:16–17).

God has not called you to change others or figure out why everything has happened to you, but God wants you to "grow in his grace and knowledge," trusting and obeying his perfect Word in your life (2 Peter 3:18; 1 Corinthians 13:11).

There are two ways of responding to your hurts and wounds: You can become a debt collector and live on the road of resentment, bitterness, unresolved anger, blame, stewing, spewing, and wanting vengeance which is a miserable existence, or you can choose to be a humble and grateful participant of God's grace and forgive (Philippians 2:5–8; 1 Thessalonians 5:16–18; Ephesians 4:31–32).

It is all about your conviction that God is greater in your life than any hurt, pain, loss, and/or wound in your life (Romans 8:28–29).

It is all about your focus. Since forgiveness is God's will for your life and your fellowship with God requires it, forgiving is more important than holding on to anything (Matthew 6:14–15; 1 John 5:3).

It is all about Thinking God instead of thinking me (Galatians 2:20).

The outcome of your life is not determined by what happens to you, but how you respond to what happens to you (James 1:2–4) as you "trust in the LORD with all your heart and do not lean on your own understanding" (Proverbs 3:5).

God is sovereign and is greater than everyone else and their sin against you, and God can take what others meant for evil and use it for good in your life (Genesis 50:20-21).

It is not a one-time act. Since we all have trouble remembering what we should forget and forgetting what we should remember—whenever your mind brings up a past hurt and you feel intense pain, you must choose to renew your forgiveness and choose to not mention it again just as you have trusted God to fully forgive the sins you have committed against him and not bring them up again against you (Psalm 103:12; Romans 8:1).

It is being kind to oneself. Refusing to forgive is like drinking poison and thinking it hurts the other person (Ephesians 4:31–32; Colossians 3:12–17).

The hurts and wounds of life, horrendous as they may be, do not have the power to control the outcome of your life when you choose "walking by faith" (Hebrews 11:6) to "let it go!"

Walking by faith is living by God's disciplines of grace. It is the only way we can do what God tells us to do and "work out our own salvation with fear and trembling, for it is God who works in you, both to will and to work for his good pleasure" (Philippians 2:12–13).

God has used the following four disciplines of grace in my life to teach me how to "let it go" and be graced with his abundance, victory, and sufficiency in the midst of all of my hurts and wounds. If you are struggling in "letting it go," I encourage you with all my heart to let God use these four disciplines modeled by our Lord throughout his ministry to move you from being "double minded and unstable" (James 1:6–8) to becoming "more than a conqueror through him who loves you" (Romans 8:37):

1. The discipline of humility as seen in Jesus as he "humbled himself by becoming obedient to the point of death, even death on a cross" (Philippians 2:8). I finally realized how I had allowed the blindness of my pride to lead me to live by my wounded feelings instead of Thinking God and exercising the same discipline I do when I must get up at 5:00 a.m. to do something I want to do. Even though my feelings are having a battle with the blankets and are screaming at me to stay in bed, I say, "Shut up feelings, I am getting up." And I'm up. You must understand how your feelings will bully you and run over you and ruin your life as long as you let them. God continues to teach me if I am going to know the fruit of the Spirit, I must "walk in the Spirit, not in the flesh" (Galatians 5:16–25). Therefore, feelings, circumstances, sinful nature, devil, and world—I will no longer listen to you and be run over by you! I am going to humbly obey God's Word, moment by moment, day by day, and "let it go" to those things the Lord has told me to release!

Until you apply this discipline of humbling yourself before the Lord and obeying his Word as the authority of your life, you will be robbed of the joy, peace, and freedom of forgiveness in your life!

2. The discipline of the way of the cross as seen in Jesus and in his teaching. In the garden before going to the cross, Jesus prayed: "My Father, if it be possible, let this cup pass from me; nevertheless, not as I will, but as you will" (Matthew 26:39). "Again, for the second time, he went away and prayed, 'My Father, if this cannot pass unless I drink it, your will be done'" (Matthew 26:42). "The third time, saying the same word again" (Matthew 26:44). That is the way of the cross—it is not about my feelings or circumstances, it is about Thinking God and obeying the authority of the Father's will—and Jesus went to the cross. As Jesus lived, so he said to all who would follow him: "If anyone would come after me, let him deny himself and take up his cross daily and follow me. For whoever would save his life will lose it, but whoever loses his life for my sake will save it" (Luke 9:23–24). You will never know the abundance, victory, and sufficiency of Christ promised throughout the New Testament until you know the discipline of denying yourself and telling your feelings, circumstances, sinful nature, the devil, the world, and often a compromising church, "I have been crucified with Christ. It is no longer I who live, but Christ who lives in me. And the life I now live in the flesh I live by faith in the Son of God, who loved me and gave himself for me" (Galatians 2:20).

Until you apply this discipline of denying yourself in the way of the cross, you will be robbed of the joy, peace, and freedom of forgiveness in your life!

3. The discipline of perseverance as seen in Jesus who stayed faithful under the pressure of temptation (Hebrews 4:15); who stayed faithful under the pressure, persecution, and suffering in every challenge of his earthly life and ministry (Hebrew 12:2–5); and could say, "It is finished" (John 19:30)—it is completed—everything has been accomplished! Therefore, Jesus could say, "Father, into your hands I commit my spirit" (Luke 23:46). Until you discipline your life to "run with endurance, looking to Jesus" (Hebrews 12:1–2), you will let your feelings, your past, your wounds, the devil's and the world's lies run over you and defeat you into constantly quitting on the will of God in your life. Do not allow it anymore. Persevere in God, knowing there is no rest in quitting but only in finishing when God calls.

Until you apply this discipline of persevering in the Lord, you will be robbed of the joy, peace, and freedom of forgiveness in your life!

4. The discipline of single-mindedness as seen in Jesus who modeled this discipline every moment recorded in Matthew, Mark, Luke, and John's accounts of the gospel. Jesus knew who he was (John 5:19), who his Father was (John 5:20), what his Father's mission was (John 5:21-29), when his hour had come (John 16:25-33), and

where he was going (John 14:3). Nothing could divert him, distract him, or could defeat him from being faithful to his Father—not the rejection of his own people (John 1:14), not the rejection of his own family (Mark 3:21), not the continual failures of his disciples (John 6:66), not the hard heartedness of the religious leaders (Mark 3:22), not the threats of Caiaphas and the council (Matthew 26:57-68), not the beating and sufferings of the cross (John 19), and not the Father's will of "becoming sin who knew no sin" (2 Corinthians 5:21). Jesus "let it go," saying, "Father, forgive them for they do not know what they are doing" (Luke 23:34). Thinking God, you resolve to be single-minded and be like the apostle Paul who wrote: "One thing I do: forgetting what lies behind and straining forward to what lies ahead, I press on toward the goal for the prize of the upward call of God in Christ Jesus. Let those of us who are mature think this way, and if in anything you think otherwise, God will reveal that also to you" (Philippians 3:13–15).

Until you apply this discipline of being single-minded in knowing and pleasing the Lord, you will be robbed of the joy, peace, and freedom of forgiveness in your life!

Thinking God—Forgiveness is a matter of Jesus Christ being the Lord of your life. Therefore, under the authority of God's Word and in the power of the Holy Spirit, "let it go" to the glory of God (Ephesians 4:30–32).

Truth to Remember—Forgiveness is being kind to oneself. Refusing to forgive does not understand the foolishness of thinking that bitterness is like drinking poison and hoping the other person will become sick (Philippians 2:3–5).

Thinking God in Reflecting—You can choose to be a debt collector and live on the road of resentment, bitterness, unresolved anger, blame, stewing, spewing, and wanting vengeance which is a miserable existence. For your joy and to the glory of God, choose to be a humble and grateful participant of God's mercy and grace and forgive knowing: God is greater in my life than any hurt, pain, loss, and/or wound in my life (1 Thessalonians 5:16–18; Genesis 50:20; Romans 8:28–29).

Thinking God: Suffering

Memorize God's Word!

"Trust in the LORD with all your heart, and do not lean on your own understanding. In all your ways acknowledge him, and he will make straight your paths. Be not wise in your own eyes; fear the LORD, and turn away from evil. It will be healing to your flesh and refreshment to your bones" (Proverbs 3:5–8).

"For the LORD will be your confidence and will keep your foot from being caught" (Proverbs 3:26).

"Keep your heart with all vigilance, for from it flow the springs of life" (Proverbs 4:23).

"But they who wait for the LORD shall renew their strength; they shall mount up with wings like eagles; they shall run and not be weary; they shall walk and not faint" (Isaiah 40:31).

"I have said these things to you, that in me you may have peace. In the world you will have tribulation. But take heart; I have overcome the world" (John 16:33).

"Not only that, but we rejoice in our sufferings, knowing that suffering produces endurance, and endurance produces character, and character produces hope, and hope does not put us to shame, because God's love has been poured into our hearts through the Holy Spirit who has been given to us" (Romans 5:3–5).

"For this light momentary affliction is preparing for us an eternal weight of glory beyond all comparison, as we look not to the things that are seen but to the things that are unseen. For the things that are seen are transient, but the things that are unseen are eternal" (2 Corinthians 4:17–18).

"But he said to me, 'My grace is sufficient for you, for my power is made perfect in weakness.' Therefore I will boast all the more gladly of my weaknesses, so that the power of Christ may rest upon me. For the sake of Christ, then, I am content with weaknesses, insults, hardships, persecutions, and calamities. For when I am weak, then I am strong" (2 Corinthians 12:9–10).

"Do not be anxious about anything, but in everything by prayer and supplication with thanksgiving let your requests be made known to God. And the peace of God, which surpasses all understanding, will guard your hearts and your minds in Christ Jesus" (Philippians 4:6–7).

"Not that I am speaking of being in need, for I have learned in whatever situation I am to be content. I know how to be brought low, and I know how to abound. In any and every circumstance, I have learned the secret of facing plenty and hunger, abundance and need. I can do all things through him who strengthens me" (Philippians 4:11–13).

"Jesus Christ is the same yesterday and today and forever" (Hebrews 13:8).

"Count it all joy, my brothers, when you meet trials of various kinds, for you know that the testing of your faith produces steadfastness. And let steadfastness have its full effect, that you may be perfect and complete, lacking in nothing" (James 1:2–4).

"In this you rejoice, though now for a little while, if necessary, you have been grieved by various trials, so that the tested genuineness of your faith—more precious than gold that perishes though it is tested by fire—may be found to result in praise and glory and honor at the revelation of Jesus Christ" (1 Peter 1:6–7).

"Casting all your anxieties on him, because he cares for you" (1 Peter 5:7).

"Worthy are you, our Lord and God, to receive glory and honor and power, for you created all things, and by your will they existed and were created" (Revelation 4:11).

☙❧

It is a fact of life. Everyone has more suffering, struggle, and sorrow in their lives than anyone could ever imagine. Until we learn to humbly surrender our lives to the authority of God's Word and surrender our lives to the presence of the Holy Spirit, we will miserably waste our lives suffering in resentment, bitterness, unresolved anger, blame, discouragement, stewing, spewing, vengeance, defeat, depression, addictions, hopelessness, and/or fits of rage. This is a horrible existence compared to the abundance (John 10:10), the victory (2 Corinthians 2:14), the sufficiency (2 Corinthians 12:9-10), the contentment (Philippians 4:11-13), and the joy, peace, and hope (Romans 15:13), God has promised to those who learn the discipline of keeping their minds stayed on him (Isaiah 26:3) in all their suffering.

If you have not yet learned how to live in God's abundance, victory, sufficiency, contentment, joy, peace, and hope promised throughout the Old and New Testament regardless of your suffering, I pray these three life-changing lessons and breakthroughs God is continually teaching me by Thinking God instead of thinking me can be a great encouragement and equipping in your life (Ephesians 4:11-16).

First Life-Changing Lesson and Breakthrough

"A wonderful life in Christ" is not a life free of suffering *(John 16:33; Romans 5:3–5; 8:31–39; Philippians 4:6–7; James 1:2–4; 1 Peter 1:6–7).*

Immediately after I trusted Jesus Christ to be my Lord and Savior, my pastor, parents, and other church leaders told me," Phillip you just love Jesus with all your heart, and you will have a wonderful life." I liked that because in my seven-year-old mind, I defined wonderful as "life without any problems." And sure enough, that's how my life was for the next six years. Just like they told me, it was wonderful. I had loving parents and brothers. We were all healthy. We enjoyed many loving and caring friendships. We were a part of a great church family where we were loved, encouraged, and equipped in the Word of God. My mom and I were constantly sharing Jesus with others and rejoicing in seeing many transformed by the saving power of the Lord. We lived on a small farm where we worked hard, enjoyed riding horses, milking cows, and taking care of our chickens, ducks, goats, and pigs. We had our own pond to fish and swim. We had a big backyard to play football, baseball, and basketball. We were surrounded with miles of woods to hunt and to trap squirrels and rabbits. A neighbor allowed us to fish throughout the year at his thirty-acre lake. My dad took us on several camping trips each summer to a state park and lake where we caught hundreds of fish and enjoyed the greatest of times together. We were able to play organized football, basketball, and baseball through the YMCA programs. The first thirteen years of my life were so unbelievably wonderful I would not trade them for any experience I have ever heard of. Life was unbelievably "wonderful" just as they had said it would be if I loved Jesus.

Then the first real big thing happened in my life that brought significant emotional suffering. My family moved from Warren, Arkansas to Ephrata, Washington during the summer before my eighth grade. Leaving my friends and everything I was so familiar with and enjoyed, I was miserably homesick for a year following our move. At different times during that year when my new classmates would make fun of me because of my southern accent, or when sitting by myself during the lunch hour and missing my friends, or when walking home from school alone, I would think, *God, this is not wonderful,* and I began to suffer greatly because of the unrealistic expectation (and unbiblical expectation) of thinking God gave me a "wonderful life that would be without any problems and any suffering."

When I was sixteen, a good friend, Bill, was killed in an automobile accident thirty minutes after we had played football together for several hours. I still remember saying, "I'll see you tomorrow" as we departed that day. In my shock and grief upon hearing of Bill's death that evening, I thought, *Why God? How could this happen? This is not wonderful.* Feeling increasingly like God was failing me, I began to question secretly in my heart if everything I had been taught about God was true and could be trusted.

When I was eighteen, I watched my dad and my pastor engage in a power struggle with other men in our church that led to our family and, eventually, the pastor leaving the church. I thought, *God, this is not wonderful.* Seeing this kind of bickering and fighting between church leadership and church members repeatedly through my college and seminary years as I was serving as a part-time staff member, I would think, *God, I love you and am serving you as much as I know how, but this sure is not wonderful.*

After graduating from seminary and serving in my first full-time church as a minister of music and youth, I was increasingly grieved at the lack of accountability expected of persons serving in church leadership. When I would visit with my senior pastor about providing needed leadership in giving biblical accountability to church leaders, I would be told, "Phil, you need to be quiet and not stir up anything. You have no idea of what we are dealing with."

In my ongoing disappointment and disagreement of what was taking place—ungodly church leaders and a fearful pastor of getting in trouble or possibly losing his job if he asked men to be godly men or have the integrity to resign their position of leadership according to 1 Timothy 3:1-12 and 2 Timothy 2:22-26, I would think, *God, this sure is not the way you intended the church to be. This sure is not wonderful.* My discouragement only increased during the next couple of years after visiting with several other youth pastors and music ministers who were serving in similar staff positions, and I discovered the same lack of Christ-like character among their leaders and a fearfulness of their pastor to do anything about it.

Increasingly discouraged in my perceptions of little change in this kind of church, I decided I would resign from the ministry of serving in that church or any other church. Having my eyes on people instead of the Lord, I began to write a letter of resignation to my church and did my best to make it sound very convincing that it was God's will for me to leave them and do music evangelism and teach piano/music at a Christian college or university. Each time I would finish my resignation letter "claiming it was God's leading in my life," I would read my resignation letter back to myself and think, *This is not true and they will not believe this.* Isn't it amazing what we try to blame on God?

Finally, I had a breakthrough. It amazes me how I struggled with this misunderstanding about suffering for twenty years as a Christian. Mercifully, the Lord opened my eyes to see he had not promised me a life without problems or heartaches. It was just the opposite—Jesus had promised me a life of tribulation, but with him in my suffering, I could have his peace and overcome in him. "I have said these things to you that in me you may have peace. In the world you will have tribulation. But take heart; I have overcome the world" (John 16:33).

The Apostle Paul understood this truth during his four years of prison and house arrest when he wrote, "Do not be anxious about anything, but in everything by prayer and supplication with thanksgiving let your requests be made known to God. And the peace of God, which surpasses all understanding, will guard your hearts and your minds in Christ Jesus" (Philippians 4:6–7).

"Do not be anxious about anything" covers everything. Understanding a wonderful life in Christ included suffering, gave me a whole new definition for "wonderful" and a breakthrough in being more than a conqueror in Christ as the Apostle Paul wrote:

> "What then shall we say to these things? If God is for us, who can be against us? He who did not spare his own Son but gave him up for us all, how will he not also with him graciously give us all things? Who shall bring any charge against God's elect? It is God who justifies. Who is to condemn? Christ Jesus is the one who died—more than that, who was raised—who is at the right hand of God, who indeed is interceding for us. Who shall separate us from the love of Christ? Shall tribulation, or distress, or persecution, or famine, or nakedness, or danger or sword? As it is written 'For your sake we are being killed all the day long; we are regarded as sheep to be slaughtered.' No, in all these things we are more than conquerors through him who loved us. For I am sure that neither death nor life, nor angels nor rulers, nor things present nor things to come, nor powers, nor height nor depth, nor anything else in all creation, will be able to separate us from the love of God in Christ Jesus our Lord."

> (Romans 8:31–39)

With this breakthrough came the Lord's conviction to see much clearer why he had called me into ministry—not to escape heartache, difficulty, pain, loss, or opposition in my life but to be "steadfast, immovable, always abounding in the work of the Lord, knowing that in the Lord your labor is not in vain" (1 Corinthians 15:58). Rather than resign in difficulty, God had called me to be faithful to those who were sinful, struggling, and suffering. God convicted me deeply to never again think about resigning to what "Christ loved and gave himself up for—the church" (Ephesians 5:25).

Sharing this breakthrough shortly after I had experienced it with some dear, older, and much wiser Christian leaders, they replied, "Phil, God has used all kinds of things and persons we have not enjoyed or liked to help us see how much we need him and how much we need to be changed by him. God is going to give you difficult things and persons all your life to help you be more like Jesus. That's what the Apostle Paul was thinking about when he wrote: 'We rejoice in our sufferings, knowing that suffering produces endurance, and endurance produces character, and character produces hope, and hope does not put us to shame, because God's love has been poured into our hearts through the Holy Spirit who has been given to us' (Romans 5:3–5). That's what James was speaking of when he wrote: 'Count it all joy, my brothers, when you meet trials of various kinds, for you know that the testing of your faith produces steadfastness. And let steadfastness have its full effect, that you may be perfect and complete, lacking in nothing' (James 1: 2–4). And that's what Peter was speaking about when he wrote: 'In this you rejoice, though now for a little while, if necessary, you have been grieved by various trials, so that the tested genuineness of your faith—more precious than gold that perishes though it is tested by fire—may be found to result in praise and glory and honor at the revelation of Jesus Christ' (1 Peter 1:6–7). Isn't that what you want—to be more like Jesus lacking in nothing, bringing praise, glory and honor to him?" With a smile, I said, "Yes, that's what I want."

In this breakthrough, God taught me to stop asking "Why, God?" when I went through heartache, opposition, darkness, pain, and loss. I began to ask, "God, what or how are you going to use this in my life for your praise, glory, honor, and to make me more like Jesus?"

Do you need this breakthrough in your life? Whatever you have gone through that has broken your heart and brought you more pain and loss than you could ever verbalize, I encourage you to stop asking, "Why, God?" Humble yourself before God and ask, "God, what or how can you use this in my life, as horrible as it is, for your praise, glory, honor, and to make me more like Jesus, lacking in nothing?" Trust God to give you a new breakthrough in your life.

Second Life-Changing Lesson and Breakthrough

Until God truly becomes my confidence instead of his blessings, I will fall apart in my sufferings (Psalm 100:1–5; Proverbs 3:26; Psalm 40:1–3; Matthew 11:28–30; 1 Thessalonians 5:16–18; Hebrews 13:8).

Even though I wrote about this in the beginning of the book, I want to repeat a story enough to tell of the life-changing lesson and breakthrough God gave me through this experience that is so needed in each of our lives. As with each of these lesson and breakthrough, this working of God in me gave me a new level of Thinking God and walking in his abundance, victory, sufficiency, contentment, joy, peace, and hope regardless of my circumstances.

In the spring of 1984, I resigned as pastor of Forest Avenue Baptist Church in Redmond, Oregon to become the associate director of evangelism of the Missouri Baptist Convention. A month after arriving in Jefferson City, Missouri, I was rear-ended in a car accident and was in bed for several weeks with back injuries and a whiplash to my neck. Struggling with migraine headaches and an upset stomach from the medication I was taking for my pain, I suffered physically and emotionally because my condition was not improving after several weeks.

Frustrated and increasingly discouraged over my situation, I forgot the wonderful lesson and breakthrough I just told you about and found myself asking "Why, God?" instead of asking "What or how are you going to use this in my life, as horrible as it is, to your praise, honor, and glory?" Isn't it amazing how we can so easily forget what God wants us to remember, and we remember what God wants us to forget. I am exceedingly grateful God does not give up on me, and "displays his perfect patience" (1 Timothy 1:16) in the slowness of my spiritual progress in learning to trust him with all my heart in the process of becoming more like Jesus.

I needed a new breakthrough, and God used my precious wife, Roni, to speak words of truth I desperately needed to hear. After saying to her about a month after the accident, "I wish we would have never come to Missouri. This is the worst decision I have ever made to move us here." She replied, "Why don't you go back to bed and listen to some of those great messages you have preached on how we always have victory in Jesus Christ? You sure are not acting like you have much victory." I responded, "I'll do just that."

I went back to bed, pulled the covers over my head and cried like a baby—hurting, frustrated, defeated, and desperate for God to deliver me out of my pit of being so defeated in the midst of my circumstances. Praise God for his greatness, goodness, and grace in always meeting us at the level of our desire and need and leading us where we need to be and to go.

God took me back to Thinking God by leading me to read through the Proverbs. When I got to Proverbs 3:26 (KJV): "For the LORD shall be thy confidence, and shall keep thy foot from being taken," the LORD spoke to me and said, "You do not know me as your confidence. You have made my blessings your confidence. I, the LORD your God, must be your confidence or you will always fall apart when things are not going as you would like." What a lesson I needed to learn and a breakthrough I needed to have. Unconsciously, in all of God's blessings I had received throughout my life, I had unknowingly become a grumbler like Israel was throughout the Old Testament when things were not as they would like (1 Corinthians 10:9–11).

With this breakthrough came a new desire to spend much more time daily during my prayer time and throughout the day praising God according to his attributes instead of spending so much of my time asking him for more of his blessings. Living in this new power of praise and confidence in the Lord is transforming because regardless of our changing circumstances, "Jesus Christ is the same yesterday and today and forever" (Hebrews 13:8). I discovered a new rest and rejoicing in the Lord regardless of my problems and pressures just as he promised: "Come to me, all who labor and are heavy laden, and I will give you rest. Take my yoke upon you, and learn from me, for I am gentle and lowly in heart, and you will find rest for your souls. For my yoke is easy, and my burden is light" (Matthew 11:28–30).

Only a few weeks after this fresh work of the Lord had begun in my life, Dr. Larry Lewis, then the president of Hannibal-LaGrange College, called me and said, "Phil, I figure you can preach since you are in the evangelism office. We have a revival each fall at Hannibal. Our evangelist we had scheduled had to cancel. We need a preacher to do a morning and evening service Monday through Wednesday (on such and such a date.) Can you do that for us?" I said, "I would love to." (I had not preached for almost two months since my accident, and I was thrilled for the opportunity to not only preach but also lead my first college revival since arriving in Missouri.)

Even as God was doing a greater work in my life, God was doing a great work in a group of students at Hannibal-LaGrange. One of those students was Tim Deatrick. Tim and another sixty to seventy students fasted and prayed throughout the weekend for God to move mightily in the coming week of services. As soon as I arrived on campus, Tim met me and when he told me what had been happening over the weekend, my anticipation and excitement of what God was about to do soared.

The first service was on a Monday morning at 9:00 a.m. When I gave the invitation to respond to the message of being "Willing to Pay Any Price to Know God's Will," over a hundred students responded publicly. Sensing this was not business as usual, Dr. Lewis, said, "Phil, let's do a noontime service." I responded, "Let me go to my room and put some ice on my neck, pray, and prepare, and I will be back in an hour."

Between classes, students began to share Christ with their lost friends all over campus. Several were coming to trust Christ as their Lord and Savior. Following the Monday evening service and more responses to the gospel, Dr. Lewis said, "Phil, how would you like to do another service tonight at 9:30 in one of the dorms?" With a big smile, "I said, "Let me go to my room and put some ice on my neck, pray, and prepare and I will be back at 9:20." We continued that schedule of four services a day the next two days.

Wednesday afternoon, Dr. Lewis and I discussed the specialness of what God was doing and if I could stay and continue to lead the services as we had been doing. Because of the prior commitments I already had, Dr. Lewis called a special chapel the next morning to share with the students, professors, and administrative staff: "Convinced this was truly a mighty move of God that was going to continue, they did not need me to stay. They would pray for me as I ministered across the state, and they would continue to let God work in and through their lives to accomplish his will and work." Even as Dr. Lewis was speaking, another student walked forward saying, "I need Christ to be my Lord and Savior." Dr. Lewis led her to Christ with everyone rejoicing in everything God was doing. The revival continued. For the next several months, fifty to a hundred students went out each week in the community sharing the gospel. Throughout that school year, there was a fervency to share Christ, to pray together, and to seek God deeply among students, professors, and administrative staff.

This past year, I unexpectedly ran into Dr. Woody Burt at the funeral of our dear friend, Gary Taylor. I had not seen Woody since he had retired as president of (now) Hannibal-LaGrange University after serving as president for the past eighteen years. Dr. Burt also was serving in Dr. Lewis's administrative staff during this revival which was almost thirty years ago. After I thanked Woody for his faithful service at Hannibal-LaGrange and the privilege of ministering with him for many weeks of preaching and teaching at Hannibal-LaGrange during all these years, he responded, "Phil, I want you to know, that first week of revival you led us in was one of the highlights of my entire career at Hannibal." I replied, "It was a very special time in my life as well—praise the Lord! We truly witnessed a special move of God."

During those three days I was overwhelmed by what I saw God do. In light of the recent discouragement, defeat, and depression I had been struggling with and my breakthrough to praise God regardless of my feelings and circumstances, I had experienced what the psalmist declared: "I waited patiently for the LORD; he inclined to me and heard my cry. He drew me up from the pit of destruction, out of the miry bog, and set my feet upon a rock, making my steps secure. He put a new song in my mouth, a song of praise to our God. Many will see and fear, and put their trust in the LORD. Blessed is the man who makes the LORD his trust, who does not turn to the proud, to those who go astray after a lie! You have multiplied, O LORD my God, your wondrous deeds and your thoughts toward us; none can compare with you! I will proclaim and tell of them, yet they are more than can be told" (Psalm 40:1–5).

Throughout that week God continually convicted me as I was watching him move in a mighty way with this thought— "If you will stay humble before me and trust me with all of your heart in the good times and the hard times, I will do exceedingly, abundantly more in and through your life than you could ever imagine." And God did. The word began to spread throughout Missouri and to other states about the revival at Hannibal-LaGrange and this new young man in the evangelism office in Missouri. From being unknown, depressed, and thinking I was in the worst place of my life, God began to grace me with the privilege of preaching and ministering at several college and university campuses and some of the largest churches and youth camps in Missouri and across the country.

Do you need this breakthrough in your life? Like me, have you unknowingly made what God has done for you more important than who God is in your life? "Guard your heart" (Proverbs 4:23) against making what God does for you as the reason you live with thanksgiving and praise instead of "being joyful always; praying continually; and giving thanks in all circumstances" (1 Thessalonians 5:16–18) because of who God is in your life. Practice what the psalmist declared: "Make a joyful noise to the LORD, all the earth! Serve the LORD with gladness! Come into his presence with singing! Know that the LORD, he is God! It is he who made us, and we are his; we are his people, and the sheep of his pasture. Enter his gates with thanksgiving, and his courts with praise! Give thanks to him; bless his name! For the LORD is good; his steadfast love endures forever and his faithfulness to all generations" (Psalm 100:1–5). God alone is due all of your thanksgiving and praise!

Third Life-Changing Lesson and Breakthrough

When I struggle with suffering, I always need God to teach me a deeper surrender to him (Proverbs 3:5–8), so I can enjoy a greater satisfaction (Matthew 5:6), sufficiency (2 Corinthians 12:8–10), and strength (Philippians 4:11–13), in him.

I cannot remember how young I was when I memorized: "Trust in the LORD with all your heart, and do not lean on your own understanding. In all your ways acknowledge him, and he will make straight your paths. Be not wise in your own eyes; fear the LORD, and turn away from evil" (Proverbs 3:5–7), but I do know this: Continuing to learn what those words mean has continued to lead me to a deeper surrender to God which has continued to lead to every breakthrough I have ever needed in experiencing God's abundance, victory, sufficiency, contentment, peace, joy, and hope in any and every suffering God has led me through.

Have you figured it out yet? When you do not trust the Lord with all your heart; when you try to lean on your own understanding; when you do not acknowledge the LORD in all your ways; when you try to be wise in your own eyes and call the shots; when you do not fear the LORD and are careless in doing what your flesh wants to do, you will not enjoy the LORD's satisfaction, sufficiency and strength.

As God began to launch me into incredible opportunities to minister following the revival at Hannibal-LaGrange College, the suffering in my life certainly did not end because it was not the end of God teaching me:

1. A deeper surrender to God so I could enjoy a greater satisfaction in him as Jesus taught: "Blessed are those who hunger and thirst for righteousness, for they shall be satisfied" (Matthew 5:6);

2. A deeper surrender to God, so I could enjoy a greater sufficiency in him as the Apostle Paul discovered and wrote: "Three times I pleaded with the Lord about this, that it should leave me. But he said to me, 'My grace

is sufficient for you, for my power is made perfect in weakness.'Therefore I will boast all the more gladly of my weaknesses, so that the power of Christ may rest upon me. For the sake of Christ, then, I am content with weaknesses, insults, hardships, persecutions, and calamities. For when I am weak, then I am strong" (2 Corinthians 12:8–10);

3. A deeper surrender to God so I could enjoy a greater strength in him as the Apostle Paul discovered in the hardships of life: "I can do all things through him who strengthens me" (Philippians 4:13).

For the next seven years while I was serving in the evangelism office of Missouri Baptist Convention, depending on the amount of travel I was doing, I continued to struggle with neck and back pain, often needing chiropractic care. Sleeping on so many different beds, I would often wake up in the middle of the night with a migraine headache.

A few months after the Hannibal-LaGrange revival, the doctors thought our eight-year-old son, Phillip, had cancer. If you have been through that experience as a parent, you worry yourself sick, question God, get angry, do some of all of them, or Thinking God, you choose to trust the LORD with all your heart one moment at a time. God graced us to daily choose to trust him with all our hearts.

It never ceases to amaze me what God does in and through our suffering when we are willing to surrender and trust him in everything as his Word always calls us to do. God kept reminding us: "What I have shown you in the light does not change in the dark." We rested in a deep conviction that nothing could touch our lives without our perfect, all-knowing, all-powerful, all-loving, kind, merciful, faithful, and good Father's sovereign permission. We learned to use our needs as a means to minister instead of an excuse to minister. I would often leave a doctor's office with questions and uncertainties about Phillip's condition to travel to preach in a revival meeting, trusting and surrendering everything I was and had to my heavenly Father. Over and over, I would experience God's satisfaction, sufficiency, and strength in my life and his mighty working in bringing many to Christ in the service where I was preaching. The weaker I was, the stronger God was in my life and in making himself known in the lives of others.

After several months of waiting for test results from the University of Missouri and the University of Houston and living one day at a time, trusting "His divine power has given us everything we need for life and godliness through our knowledge of him who called us by his own glory and goodness" (2 Peter 1:3), the condition our son had suddenly disappeared. After taking more blood tests, our doctor told us with a smile, "We may never know what Phillip had, but he doesn't have it now." Praise the Lord for answered prayer and this miracle of healing in our son's life!

At the same time God had healed our son, my older brother, Doug, continued to suffer with a heart condition. This heart condition took him on a journey of suffering he endured for seventeen years, which included five open heart surgeries where they had to replace his aorta valve each time. One year after his first surgery, he and his wife, Shirley, were in an automobile accident where Shirley severed her spinal cord and was paralyzed from her chin down. During the last three years of Doug's life, both he and Shirley battled cancer.

When Doug died at the age of forty-six, Shirley said to me with many tears and great anguish, "Why didn't you tell God to heal Doug?" After hugging her and crying with her, I said, "Shirley, I can only ask God to heal, and then I must trust him. In everything I do not understand about Doug and your suffering, I do know this: Just as God has been sufficient for you all these years in your paralysis, God will be sufficient for you without Doug. Suffering is a mystery, and I do not understand why God heals some when we pray and some die when we pray. But I know we can trust God." Even though I said, "I know we can trust God," I have had to relearn that life-transforming truth over and over through the many different seasons of suffering in my life.

After preaching "Super Summer Texas" at Baylor University in 1986, I returned to Missouri with a terrible sore throat and a severe condition of laryngitis. I rushed to my doctor because I was planning to lead and teach at "Super Summer Missouri" for the next three weeks beginning the next day. After looking at my throat, my doctor said with great concern, "Phil, you need to see someone else. You may have nodules on your vocal cords." After the specialist looked at my vocal cords, he said those dreaded words: "You have nodules on each of your vocal cords. You should not talk for the next two to three weeks. I will check you in two weeks, and we will see how you are doing." I responded, "You don't understand. I am leading three weeks of Super Summer schools with two thousand students and adults and then a state-wide youth conference. I have been planning and promoting this for a year. I have to speak." The doctor, somewhat frustrated at my response, replied, "Then let's schedule your surgery at the end of those three weeks." That abrupt statement got my attention.

I thought, *Silence or surgery?* I responded, "I don't know how, but I choose silence. So what do I need to do?"

After the initial shock of the announcement at Super Summer, I had nodules on my vocal cords and could not speak for the next three weeks, God began to move powerfully in our weekend planning staff and leadership retreat. During our last worship time of the retreat on a Monday morning before all the students and adults came to the Southwest Baptist University campus for the first of three Super Summer weeks, I began to have a pity party. I struggled greatly as I thought about everything I was not going to be able to do the next three weeks—all the things I had planned and prepared for and had anticipated with great expectations during the past year—preaching in the joy explosions, teaching in the adult schools, encouraging, singing, witnessing, and just having fun and fellowship with countless friends, students, and co-laborers in the Lord.

Do you know one of the overwhelming things about the pit of pity? It can be bottomless. As I was going deeper in the darkness of that pit, the worship leader, Tracy, began to sing a song I had never heard. He introduced the song by saying, "The Lord has put this song on my heart this morning because I feel like someone really needs to hear it as we prepare for the coming week." The song was "Make Me A Servant" by Kelly Willard. As Tracy and a hundred other leaders sang about the Lord making us servants, humble and meek, I knew that someone Tracy was speaking of was me.

Listening to the words of that song, God spoke to me powerfully this message, "My little boy, I don't need a preacher. I need a servant. You are struggling greatly because you have not surrendered everything to me. You are feeling sorry for yourself because you are not being my servant." Weeping in brokenness over my pride and stinking thinking of "it's all about me," I prayed, "Father, make me a servant."

Whenever we think we have rights and we suffer loss of those rights, we suffer greatly with our suffering. Remember whose you are if you are in Christ: "Or do you not know that your body is a temple of the Holy Spirit within you, whom you have from God? You are not your own, for you were bought with a price. So glorify God in your body" (1 Corinthians 6:19–20).

As I daily prayed and lived those three weeks one moment at a time, "Lord, make me a servant today," it was amazing to everyone attending the schools how God moved mightily during the three weeks in the schools, and then, in the conference. It was also amazing to everyone how God graced me with contentment, rejoicing, and peace as I served him and others. Many who served in leadership with me for several years at Super Summer have commented through the years how that year was the most special year of experiencing God we ever had. God really does make his strength perfect in our weakness (2 Corinthians 12:9).

I spoke only once during those three weeks when I was awakened from taking an afternoon nap to answer a phone call. I then only spoke a few words before I realized I should not be talking. Returning to my doctor and following his examination, he said, "You can talk. Your vocal cords look good." I said, "Praise the Lord!" During those three weeks of silence, I had realized like never before what a precious gift it is to be able to talk, preach, and teach God's Word. However, my season of learning to be a servant, having no rights, and trusting the Lord with the privilege of speaking his Word had just begun.

During the next few years, almost every time I would preach, I would become hoarse and sometimes totally lose my voice after preaching. No one knew for sure when they invited me to preach a revival if I would be able to complete what we were praying and preparing to do. After several years of suffering with this uncertainty, constant sickness, and apologies to pastor friends when I would have to cancel a preaching commitment because I had lost my voice, my struggle with discouragement intensified over the uncertainty of my future. Once when I had been struggling with laryngitis for weeks and during a quiet time with the Father, he asked me, "If you lose your voice completely and are not able to ever preach or teach my Word again, will you still love me, praise me, obey me, and serve me with all your heart, all your mind, all your soul, and all your strength?" With that question came the Lord's conviction to me, "I am always more concerned about your love for me than your love for what you can do for me."

As I thought about that, the Lord brought to my mind (Thinking God), the eternal perspective the Apostle Paul had written concerning the sufferings of his life: "For this light momentary affliction is preparing for us an eternal weight of glory beyond all comparison, as we look not to the things that are seen but to the things that are unseen. For the things that are seen are transient, but the things that are unseen are eternal" (2 Corinthians 4:17–18). Graced and empowered by the Holy Spirit, I was able to say, "Yes Father, with a voice or without a voice, I am yours and I will praise you and serve you all of my life and throughout eternity because you alone are worthy of praise" (Revelation 4:11).

Because I have struggled almost annually with laryngitis to this present time, God has used this weakness in my body to continually teach me how resting in him is never a one-time surrender, but a never ending surrender to him. Each suffering we walk through is either going to cause us to suffer fearfulness and anxiousness or open the door because of God's satisfaction, sufficiency, and strength to enjoy a greater life of faithfulness in bringing glory to him because of his greatness, grace, and goodness in our lives. It all depends if we are able to humbly surrender everything to God regardless of what we are going through. Because of who God is—sovereign and in charge of everything, we can rest and rejoice in him "casting all our anxieties on him, because he cares for us" (1 Peter 5:7).

God has used the Lord's teaching recorded in Matthew 5:3-10 to increasingly accomplish a deeper surrender in my life to him so I can enjoy a life of faithfulness rather than a life of fearfulness and anxiousness. In all our sufferings, we need a deeper level of understanding and the practice of humility because "God opposes the proud but gives grace to the humble" (James 4:6). Therefore, we need a deeper level of understanding and practicing of spiritual bankruptcy because "Blessed are the poor in spirit, for theirs is the kingdom of heaven" (Matthew 5:3). We need a deeper level of understanding and practicing of spiritual brokenness because "Blessed are those who mourn (over their spiritual poverty, not what has happened to them), for they shall be comforted" (Matthew 5:4). We need a deeper level of understanding and the practice of meekness because "Blessed are the meek, for they shall inherit the earth" (Matthew 5:5). We need a deeper level of understanding and the practice of hungering and thirsting for the Lord because "Blessed are those who hunger and thirst for righteousness, for they shall be satisfied" (Matthew 5:6). We need a deeper level of understanding and the practice of mercy because "Blessed are the merciful, for they shall receive mercy" (Matthew 5:7). We need a deeper level of understanding and the practice of purity in our hearts because "Blessed are the pure in heart, for they shall see God" (Mathew 5:8). We need a deeper level of understanding and the practice of being a peacemaker because "Blessed are the peacemakers for they shall be called sons of God" (Matthew 5:9). We need a deeper level of understanding and the practice of rejoicing and being glad in the midst of being persecuted for righteousness' sake because "Blessed are those who are persecuted for righteousness' sake, for theirs is the kingdom of heaven" (Matthew 5:10).

Because the LORD our God is all-powerful, all-present, and all-knowing, he knows everything you have ever done and everything done to you. Nothing in your past—your sin, your suffering, or your sorrow—can stop God from giving you the breakthrough of experiencing his greatness, grace, and goodness except you and your pride. God wants to use even your greatest failures, sufferings, and sorrows to lead you to experience the very best times in your life—being conformed to the image of Jesus Christ (Romans 8:28–29).

Because of our pride though, we are often like Job (Job 42:5–6). Sadly, it is most often only after great failure, suffering, and/or sorrow are we able to see how spiritually broken and bankrupt we are before the Lord. Until we have such vision, we will not have a longing to be meeked unto the Lord which he has told us is the only way we can have rest in him

(Matthew 11:28–30). Until we are meeked unto the Lord, we will not have a hunger and thirst for God's Word (Psalm 23:2). Not daily feeding on God's Word and carefully obeying God's Word (Joshua 1:8), we cannot be satisfied. Until we are satisfied in the Lord, we will live with stinking thinking—that is, thinking "it's all about me" concerning our own neediness, and find it impossible to be merciful when someone hurts us deeply. Until we are forgiving (Matthew 6:14–15), we cannot have a pure heart and see God in the midst of all our suffering. Until we see God above and greater than everything else in our lives, we will not be guarded by his peace as we are promised, and we will continue to be miserable in our anxiousness in the midst of our suffering (Philippians 4:6–7). Not walking in the peace of God, we cannot be peacemakers because we cannot give what we do not have—the peace of God which is the wholeness of God. Until we know the daily power of the wholeness of God, when persecution comes our way for righteousness' sake, we will shrink in fearfulness and will not rejoice in it.

Do you need this breakthrough in your life of learning a deeper surrender to him so you can enjoy a greater satisfaction, sufficiency and strength in Christ? Almost daily, persons call or come to me stuck in destructive and negative attitudes like resentment, bitterness, discouragement, grumbling, hopelessness and/or depression because of what they are suffering or have suffered in the past. They have not yet understood God is more concerned about changing their character and their perspective than he is about changing their problems. That's why it is so important to live our lives Thinking God. Until we do, we struggle needlessly, not understanding this life on earth is a battleground, not a playground. God's purpose for our lives is to be "conformed to the image of his Son" (Romans 8:29) in bringing honor and glory to God (1 Corinthians 10:31).

So do what the Apostle Peter wrote, "Clothe yourselves, all of you with humility toward one another, for 'God opposes the proud but gives grace to the humble.' Humble yourselves, therefore, under the mighty hand of God so that at the proper time he may exalt you casting all your anxieties on him, because he cares for you" (1 Peter 5:5–7).

Do not let the devil waste your suffering and spend your life discouraged and complaining about your suffering. Surrender your life to God and experience his satisfaction, sufficiency, and strength. Be patient with the Lord's patience in your suffering. Rest in knowing God wants you to walk through every kind of suffering with his conviction, confidence, courage, and peace because of who he is—the one LORD God. God does not want you to waste any suffering in your life.

Thinking God—What or who is your confidence? Is it the LORD's blessings or is it the LORD? Until the one LORD God becomes your confidence, you will always fall apart when things are not going as you would like (Proverbs 3:26). When you think you have rights and you suffer loss of those rights, you will suffer greatly with your suffering so remember whose you are in Christ. 1 Corinthians 6:19–20

Truth to Remember—The inability to see God is "for you" and "with you" in every challenge of your life causes you to suffer a life of fearfulness instead of enjoying a life of faithfulness to God. Surrender everything to God's sovereign rule in your life. Genesis 50:20; Romans 8:28

Thinking God in Reflecting—Think what would happen in your life if you would humble yourself before God and trust him with all of your heart in the good times and the hard times. Proverbs 3:5–7; Ephesians 3:20–21

Epilogue
Thinking God: Under God's Authority

Memorize God's Word!

"And that all this assembly may know that the LORD saves not with sword and spear. For the battle is the LORD's, and he will give you into our hand" (1 Samuel 17:47).

"Fret not yourself because of evildoers; be not envious of wrongdoers! For they will soon fade like the grass and wither like the green herb. Trust in the LORD, and do good; dwell in the land and befriend faithfulness. Delight yourself in the LORD, and he will give you the desires of your heart. Commit your way to the LORD; trust in him, and he will act. He will bring forth your righteousness as the light, and your justice as the noonday. Be still before the LORD and wait patiently for him; fret not yourself over the one who prospers in his way, over the man who carries out evil devices!

Refrain from anger, and forsake wrath! Fret not yourself; it tends only to evil. For the evildoers shall be cut off, but those who wait for the LORD shall inherit the land" (Psalm 37:1–9).

"Then he said to me, 'This is the word of the LORD to Zerubbabel: Not by might, nor by power, but by my Spirit says the LORD of hosts'" (Zechariah 4:6).

"But the centurion replied, 'Lord, I am not worthy to have you come under my roof, but only say the word, and my servant will be healed. For I too am a man under authority, with soldiers under me. And I say to one, 'Go,' and he goes, and to another, 'Come,' and he comes, and to my servant, 'Do this,' and he does it.' When Jesus heard this, he marveled and said to those who followed him, 'Truly, I tell you, with no one in Israel have I found such faith'" (Matthew 8:8–10).

"And Simon answered, 'Master, we toiled all night and took nothing! But at your word I will let down the nets'" (Luke 5:5).

"And when they had brought their boats to land, they left everything and followed him" (Luke 5:11).

"Then Jesus, calling out with a loud voice, said, 'Father, into your hands I commit my spirit!' And having said this he breathed his last" (Luke 23:46).

"And when they had inflicted many blows upon them, they threw them into prison, ordering the jailer to keep them safely. Having received this order, he put them into the inner prison and fastened their feet in the stocks. About midnight Paul and Silas were praying and singing hymns to God, and the prisoners were listening to them" (Acts 16:23–25).

"For you did not receive the spirit of slavery to fall back into fear, but you have received the Spirit of adoption as sons, by whom we cry, 'Abba! Father'" (Roman 8:15)!

"For this reason I bow my knees before the Father, from whom every family in heaven and on earth is named, that according to the riches of his glory he may grant you to be strengthened with power through his Spirit in your inner being, so that Christ may dwell in your hearts through faith—that you, being rooted and grounded in love, may have strength to comprehend with all the saints what is the breadth and length and height and depth, and to know the love of Christ that surpasses knowledge, that you may be filled with all the fullness of God. Now to him who is able to do far more abundantly than all that we ask or think, according to the power at work within us, to him be glory in the church and in Christ Jesus throughout all generations, forever and ever. Amen" (Ephesians 3:14–21).

"Finally, be strong in the Lord and in the strength of his might. Put on the whole armor of God, that you may be able to stand against the schemes of the devil. For we do not wrestle against flesh and blood, but against the rulers, against the authorities, against the cosmic powers over this present darkness, against the spiritual forces of evil in the heavenly places. Therefore take up the whole armor of God, that you may be able to withstand in the evil day, and having done all, to stand firm. Stand therefore, having fastened on the belt of truth, and having put on the breastplate of righteousness, and, as shoes for your feet, having put on the readiness given by the gospel of peace. In all circumstances take up the shield of faith, with which you can extinguish all the flaming darts of the evil one; and take the helmet of salvation, and the sword of the Spirit, which is the word of God, praying at all times in the Spirit, with all prayer and supplication. To that end keep alert with all perseverance, making supplication for all the saints, and also for me, that words may be given to me in opening my mouth boldly to proclaim the mystery of the gospel" (Ephesians 6:10–19).

"Do nothing from selfish ambition or conceit, but in humility count others more significant than yourselves. Let each of you look not only to his own interests, but also to the interests of others. Have this mind among yourselves, which is yours in Christ Jesus, who, though he was in the form of God, did not count equality with God a thing to be grasped, but emptied himself, by taking the form of a servant, being born in the likeness of men. And being found in human form, he humbled himself by becoming obedient to the point of death, even death on a cross. Therefore God has highly exalted him and bestowed on him the name that is above every name, so that at the name of Jesus every knee should bow, in heaven and on earth and under the earth, and every tongue confess that Jesus Christ is Lord, to the glory of God the Father" (Philippians 2:3–11).

"For God gave us a spirit not of fear but of power and love and self-control" (2 Timothy 1:7).

"And without faith it is impossible to please him, for whoever would draw near to God must believe that he exists and that he rewards those who seek him" (Hebrews 11:6).

"To the only God, our Savior, through Jesus Christ our Lord, be glory, majesty, dominion, and authority, before all time and now and forever. Amen" (Jude 25).

§ⅅⳘ

God has continually challenged me before writing each chapter to "Be still, and know that I am God"

(Psalm 46:10a). In that stillness, God has taken me back in my "memory bank" to events in my life which I have shared with you and how God has in all things worked for the good to teach me in my journey of Thinking God. Preparing to write this last chapter, God reminded me of how I first began to learn the significance of Thinking God when I started hearing Bible stories. From the time I was a toddler until I was six or seven, every night before we went to bed, my mom would say to my older brother and me, "Let's read our Bible story." We would excitedly climb up on our dad and mom's big bed with the "big red book" of Bible stories and listen to her read a new story, or often reread one of our requested favorites, and then we would pray.

Under the authority of God's Word: 1) They knew where to look—to the one LORD God who was all-powerful, all-knowing, and all-present to bring good in their lives (Genesis 50:20–21; Romans 8:28–29); and 2) They knew how to act by faith, humbly trusting and obeying the Word of the LORD wholeheartedly because "without faith it is impossible to please God" (Hebrews 11:6). The opposite of course was always true when anyone chose to not be under the authority of God's Word—they did not know where to look and how to act. Overwhelmed by their challenge, need, or problem, they reacted in fearfulness and anxiousness, and it never turned out good for anyone.

As we finish this journey together of Thinking God, wherever you are in the process of learning to submit every area of your life to the authority of God's Word, I pray that reviewing these examples of some of my requested favorites from the "big red book" might further encourage and equip you in Christ who wants to "always lead you in triumphal procession, and through you spread the fragrance of the knowledge of him everywhere" (2 Corinthians 2:14).

The story of Noah (Genesis 6–9)—Noah is described as a "man who found favor in the eyes of the Lord" (Genesis 6:8) and "a righteous man, blameless in his generation who walked with God" (Genesis 6:9). "And God said to Noah, 'I have determined to make an end of all flesh, for the earth is filled with violence through them. Behold, I will destroy them with the earth. Make yourself an ark of gopher wood. Make rooms in the ark, and cover it inside and out with pitch. This is how you are to make it: the length of the ark three hundred cubits, its breadth fifty cubits, and its height thirty cubits. Make a roof for the ark, and finish it to a cubit above, and set the door of the ark in its side. Make it with lower, second, and third decks. For behold, I will bring a flood of waters upon the earth to destroy all flesh in which is the breath of life under heaven. Everything that is on the earth shall die. But I will establish my covenant with you, and you shall come into the ark, you, your sons, your wife, and your sons' wives with you. And of every living thing of all flesh, you shall bring two of every sort into the ark to keep them alive with you. They shall be male and female. Of the birds according to their kinds, of every creeping thing of the ground, according to its kind, two of every sort shall come in to you to keep them alive. Also take with you every sort of food that is eaten, and store it up. It shall serve as food for you and for them'" (Genesis 6:13–21).

When you consider everything God was telling Noah to do—build an ark that could hold two of all the animals and protect them from a flood they had never had before—didn't that seem impossible to accomplish? Yet, because Noah was under the authority of God's Word and trusted and obeyed

God no matter how impossible the instruction seemed to be, "Noah did all that God commanded him" (Genesis 6:22). It turned out good for Noah and his family.

My mom would ask us questions after reading this story. Questions like "What would have happened to Noah and his family if he had not learned to be under the authority of God and keep his focus on God in all of his challenges?" or "What would have happened to Noah and his family if he had not trusted and obeyed God when everyone was talking about him as this crazy old man who was doing something that had never been done before?"

It did not take long for my brother and me to learn that whatever my mom asked us, if the person was not trusting and obeying God, we knew the answer was, "Not good!" Noah and his family would have drowned in the flood. Noah and his family would have missed out on experiencing God's protection, provision, power, and purpose for their lives.

The story of Abraham and Isaac (Genesis 12–22)—After Abraham and Sarah had struggled for twenty-five years at different times to live under the authority of God and to keep their focus on God when their timetable didn't agree with God's timetable concerning God's promise to give them a son, "Sarah conceived and bore Abraham a son in his old age at the time of which God had spoken to him" (Genesis 21:2). Then God tested Abraham after Isaac was a boy to see if he had learned to live under his authority no matter what the command was and said to him: "Abraham, take your son, your only son Isaac, whom you love, and go to the land of Moriah, and offer him there as a burnt offering on one of the mountains of which I shall tell you" (Genesis 22:1–2). Abraham had finally learned to submit his life to God's authority even when God's instructions did not make sense to him. Abraham kept his focus on God and trusted and obeyed God: "So Abraham rose early in the morning, saddled his donkey, and took two of his young men with him, and his son Isaac" (Genesis 22:3). Resting in the character of God and knowing the covenant he had with God, he told his servants, "Stay here with the donkey; I and the boy will go over there and worship and come again to you" (Genesis 22:5). It turned out good for Abraham and Isaac: The LORD provided a ram and "he offered it up as a burnt offering instead of his son" (Genesis 22:13).

My mom would ask us questions after reading this story. Questions like "What would have happened to Abraham if he had not learned under the authority of God to trust and obey God even when he could not understand why God would ask him to sacrifice his son?" or "What would have happened to Abraham if he had refused to trust and obey God because he did not think this command made any sense?"

We knew the answer was "Not good!" Abraham would not have pleased God (Hebrews 11:6). Abraham would have been disciplined by God. Abraham would not have seen the miracle of God providing the ram for the sacrifice. Abraham would have missed out on experiencing God's purpose and provision for his life.

The story of Joseph (Genesis 37–50)—Think about how many times when Joseph was doing right, he suffered wrong from someone. First, when he obeyed his father and went to see how his brothers were doing with the flocks (Genesis 37:12–14), his brothers sold him to the Midianites (Genesis 37:28). Second, when he was faithful to God and his new slave owner, Potiphar, and he refused day after day Potiphar's wife's request to "go to bed with her." Not getting what she wanted, she lied and said Joseph wanted to sleep with her (Genesis 39:6–18). Enraged, Potiphar put Joseph in prison (Genesis 39:19–20). Third, when he was faithful to the captain of the guard in the prison and was put in charge of the cupbearer and the baker of the king of Egypt (Genesis 40:1–15), and after Joseph's kindness to them, the chief cupbearer was released and forgot about Joseph (Genesis 40:23). And fourth, after his brothers had been reunited with Joseph for seventeen years and Jacob died, because their deceitful character had not changed, they lied to Joseph about their father's request to forgive them. But Joseph, knowing behind every wrong is the sovereign God of right who uses the wrong for good, said to them, "Do not fear, for am I in the place of God? As for you, you meant evil against me, but God meant it for good, to bring it about that many people should be kept alive, as they are today. So do not fear; I will provide for you and your little ones. Thus, he comforted them and spoke kindly to them" (Genesis 50:19–21).

My mom would ask us questions after reading this story. Questions like "What would have happened to Joseph if he had not been under the authority of God and trusted God to take care of him?" or "How would this story be different if Joseph would have become bitter at his brothers?" or "What would have happened to Joseph if he would have become so discouraged he stopped trusting God because everything was so unfair for him?"

We knew the answer was "Not good!" Joseph would have lived with broken dreams, a broken heart, and broken relationships. Joseph would have missed out on living God's incredible plan of blessing and provision for his life and family.

The story of Moses (Exodus 2–40)—Because Moses learned to be under the authority of God and know where to look and how to act, the writer of Hebrews summarized this about him: "When he was grown up, he refused to be called the son of Pharaoh's daughter, choosing rather to be mistreated with the people of God than to enjoy the fleeting pleasures of sin. He considered the reproach of Christ greater wealth than the treasures of Egypt, for he was looking to the reward. By faith he left Egypt, not being afraid of the anger of the king, for he endured as seeing him who is invisible. By faith he kept the Passover and sprinkled the blood, so that the Destroyer of the firstborn might not touch them. By faith the people crossed the Red Sea as on dry land, but the Egyptians, when they attempted to do the same, were drowned" (Hebrews 11:24–29).

My mom would ask us questions after reading this story. Questions like "What would have happened to Moses if he had allowed Israel's grumbling to get him down?" or "What would have happened to Moses if he had not learned to be under the authority of God and keep his focus on God?" or "What would have happened to Moses if he had not trusted and obeyed God in all the challenges he had in leading Israel out of Egypt and in the wilderness?"

We knew the answer was "Not good!" Moses would have lived and died only knowing the power of man instead of the power of God. Moses, in fact, did not get to go into the Promised Land because he did not trust and obey one of God's commands (Numbers 20:10–12).

The story of the twelve spies (Numbers 13–14)—After God spoke to Moses, saying, "Send men to spy out the land of Canaan, which I am giving to the people of Israel"

(Numbers 13:2), the twelve went up and spied out the land. After forty days, they returned and brought back the report: "We came to the land to which you sent us. It flows with milk and honey, and this is its fruit" (Numbers 13:27). But they did not go in the land and enjoy what God had given them because Israel believed ten of the spies who gave a bad report. They saw the people as giants and said: "We are not able to go up against the people, for they are stronger than we are" (Numbers 13:31). However, Joshua and Caleb, the two other spies, under God's authority, gave a far different report based on what they saw: "The land, which we passed through to spy it out, is an exceedingly good land. If the LORD delights in us, he will bring us into this land and give it to us, a land that flows with milk and honey. Only do not rebel against the LORD. And do not fear the people of the land, for they are bread for us. Their protection is removed from them, and the LORD is with us; do not fear them" (Numbers 13:7–9).

My mom would ask us questions after reading this story. Questions like "What would have happened to Joshua and Caleb if they had not been under God's authority and trusted him to protect them and give them the land he had promised them?" or "What would have happened to Joshua and Caleb if they would have stopped trusting God during those forty years of wandering in the wilderness?" or "What would have happened to Joshua and Caleb if they would not have stayed focused on God and started grumbling like everyone else?"

We knew the answer was "Not good!" Joshua and Caleb would have died in the wilderness with the other ten spies and all the others who did not trust the LORD was greater than the giants. They would have never enjoyed everything God promised to give them.

The story of David and Goliath (1 Samuel 17)—Since Israel had not learned to live under God's authority, they often grumbled and lived fearful when facing a great challenge, need, or problem. Even though The Lord had won many battles for them, when Goliath said, "I defy the ranks of Israel this day. Give me a man, that we may fight together" (1 Samuel 17:10), "they were dismayed and greatly afraid" (1 Samuel 17:11). Yet David, under the authority of God's Word and seeing the Lord and having learned to trust the Lord in his battles of protecting his father's sheep (1 Samuel 17:34–36), told Saul, "The Lord who delivered me from the paw of the lion and from the paw of the bear will deliver me from the hand of this Philistine" (1 Samuel 17:37). Facing Goliath, David, declared: "That all this assembly may know that the Lord saves not with sword and spear. For the battle is the Lord's, and he will give you into our hand" (1 Samuel 17:47). "So David prevailed over the Philistine with a sling and with a stone, and struck the Philistine and killed him" (1 Samuel 17:50).

My mom would ask us questions after reading this story. Questions like "What would have happened to David, if not under God's authority, he had not learned to see God and trust him in his battles?" or "What would have happened to David if he had thought Goliath was too big of a challenge for his God?"

We knew the answer was "Not good!" David would have been afraid just like his big brothers and the army of Israel. David would not have known the thrill of victory in this battle. David would not have experienced everything God had prepared to do in and through his life.

The story of Joseph betrothed to Mary (Matthew 1:18–25)— "When Mary had been betrothed to Joseph, before they came together she was found to be with child from the Holy Spirit. And her husband Joseph, being a just man and unwilling to put her to shame, resolved to divorce her quietly. But as he considered these things, behold, an angel of the Lord appeared to him in a dream, saying, 'Joseph, son of David, do not fear to take Mary as your wife, for that which is conceived in her is from the Holy Spirit. She will bear a son, and you shall call his name Jesus, for he will save his people from their sins'" (Matthew 1:18–21). Joseph could have naturally thought, "But this is impossible. This has never happened before. What will my parents say? What will the rest of my family say? What will everyone who knows I am a righteous man say?" Yet, because Joseph was under God's authority, he knew where to look and how to act. "Joseph woke from sleep and did as the angel of the Lord commanded him: he took his wife, but knew her not until she had given birth to a son. And he called his name Jesus" (Matthew 1:24–25).

My mom would ask us questions after reading this story. Questions like "What would have happened to Joseph if he would not have been under the authority of God and had the same conviction, confidence, and courage Mary had when the angel told her: 'Nothing will be impossible with God (Luke 1:37)?'" or "What would have happened to Joseph if it had been more important to him what others thought than what God thought?"

We knew the answer was "Not good!" Joseph would have missed out on one of the greatest privileges ever—being the husband of Mary, seeing Jesus born, and watching Jesus grow up.

The story of Simon Peter (Luke 5:1–11)—Peter had worked hard all night fishing and had not caught anything. He was tired and disappointed. He was washing his nets and looking forward to going home and sleeping. Then Jesus came by and was doing what he often did. Jesus was teaching the Word of God, and there was a crowd listening to him. Seeing Peter's boat at the water's edge, Jesus got into it and asked Peter to push it out a little from shore. Jesus then sat down and taught the people from the boat. When Jesus had finished speaking, he told Peter, "Put out into the deep and let down your nets for a catch" (Luke 5:4). If Peter had not understood the importance of being under the Lord's authority and knowing where to look—to see Jesus as the "Master," he would have looked at his circumstances and listened to his feelings and said, "Lord, I need to go home and rest. Besides, I have already fished all night. There are no fish to catch." But Peter answered Jesus, "Master, we toiled all night and took nothing! But at your word I will let down the nets" (Luke 5:5). Look at the result of being under the Lord's authority: "And when they had done this, they enclosed a large number of fish, and their nets were breaking. They signaled to their partners in the other boat to come and help them. And they came and filled both the boats, so that they began to sink" (Luke 5:6–7). Realizing the miracle of such a catch, and understanding he was in the presence of holiness, Peter fell down at Jesus's knees, saying, "Depart from me, for I am a sinful man, O Lord" (Luke 5:8). Then Jesus told Simon Peter and his fishing partners, James and John, "Do not be afraid; from now on you will be catching men" (Luke 5:10). "And when they had brought their boats to land, they left everything and followed him" (Luke 5:11).

My mom would ask us questions after reading this story. Questions like "What would have happened to Peter if he would had let his circumstances and feelings rule him instead of the Lord's authority in trusting and obeying the Lord's command?" or "What would have happened to Peter if he would have thought he knew more about fishing than the Lord?"

We knew the answer was "Not good!" Peter would have missed out on seeing the greatest catch of fish in his life. Peter would also have missed out on the greatest privilege of life— following the Lord Jesus and catching thousands of men for Christ (Acts 2:41-47) and writing two epistles in the New Testament (1 Peter; 2 Peter).

The story of the centurion and Jesus (Matthew 8:3–13)—Of all the stories in the New Testament where persons saw the privilege of being under the Lord's authority, this is the only one where it is recorded Jesus "marveled" (astonished, amazed) and said to those who followed him, "Truly, I tell you, with no one in Israel have I found such faith" (Matthew 8:10). Think about that incredible statement Jesus made about the centurion's faith. How could that Roman soldier have greater faith than Mary, Joseph, Elizabeth, and Zechariah (Matthew 1:18–24; Luke 1:5–56)? How could that Roman soldier have greater faith than all of the disciples who Jesus called to be "apostles" (Mark 3:13–19)? How could that Roman soldier have greater faith than Martha, Mary, and Lazarus following Lazarus's resurrection (John 11:1–44)? It was only because the centurion so completely understood the life-changing dynamic of being under authority which is necessary to practice Thinking God in season and out of season. In his humility and being under the complete authority of the Lord Jesus, the centurion replied to him after he had offered to come and heal his servant (Matthew 8:7), "Lord, I am not worthy to have you come under my roof, but only say the word, and my servant will be healed. For I too am a man under authority, with soldiers under me. And I say to one, 'Go,' and he goes, and to another, 'Come,' and he comes, and to my servant, 'Do this,' and he does it" (Matthew 8:8–9). "And to the centurion Jesus said, 'Go, let it be done for you as you have believed.' And the servant was healed at that very moment" (Matthew 8:13).

My mom would ask us questions after reading this story. Questions like "What would have happened if the centurion would not have had faith as a Roman soldier that Jesus would listen to him and meet his servant's needs?" or "What would have happened to the centurion's servant if the centurion had not understood the power of Jesus's authority and being under that authority?"

We knew the answer was "Not good!" Without the centurion's faith of submitting his life to Jesus's authority, the servant would not have been healed. The centurion would have missed out on the abundance and victory of trusting Jesus as his Lord and Savior.

The story of the Apostle Paul and Silas (Acts 16:16–34)— After Paul had delivered a slave girl from an evil spirit, her owners, realizing their hope of making money was gone, "seized Paul and Silas and dragged them into the marketplace before the rulers. And when they had brought them to the magistrates, they said, 'These men are Jews, and they are disturbing our city. They advocate customs that are not lawful for us as Romans to accept,' and they began to beat them with rods. And when they had inflicted many blows upon them, they threw them into prison, ordering the jailer to keep them safely. Having received this order, he put them into the inner prison and fastened their feet in the stocks" (Acts 16:19–24).

Amazingly, under the authority of the Lord, they knew where to look and how to act. Paul and Silas did not complain. They did not have a pity party or a panic attack. They did not lose heart. They did not quit on God. They did the opposite. They had a praise party and stayed on mission, reaching and teaching new converts the Word of God. "About midnight Paul and Silas were praying and singing hymns to God, and the prisoners were listening to them and (God was listening to them) suddenly there was a great earthquake so that the foundations of the prison were shaken. And immediately all the doors were opened, and everyone's bonds were unfastened. When the jailer woke and saw that the prison doors were open, he drew his sword and was about to kill himself, supposing that the prisoners had escaped. But Paul cried with a loud voice, 'Do not harm yourself, for we are all here.' And the jailer called for lights and rushed in and trembling with fear he fell down before Paul and Silas. Then he brought them out and said, 'Sirs, what must I do to be saved?' And they said, 'Believe in the Lord Jesus, and you will be saved, you and your household.' And they spoke the word of the Lord to him and to all who were in his house" (Acts 16:25–32). Always remember God always takes notice and so do others when we know where to look and how to act in trusting and obeying him in all our troubles.

My mom would ask us questions after reading this story. Questions like "What would have happened to Paul and Silas if they would have had a pity party instead of a praise party?" or "What would have happened to the jailor if Paul and Silas would have run away rather than staying and sharing Christ with him?"

We knew the answer was "Not good!" Without praising the Lord, they would have become greatly discouraged. They could have even thought: "This living for Christ and sharing Christ just gets us in trouble. We quit!" And if they had run away, the jailor would have killed himself. And he did not know the Lord.

The story of Jesus on the cross (Matthew 26:47–27:56; Mark 14:43–15:41; Luke 22:47–23:49; John 18:12–19:37)— Remember what they did to Jesus: In a court with Caiaphas, the high priest, false witnesses spoke against Jesus, so they might put him to death (Matthew 26:57–66). They spit in Jesus's face and struck him. And some slapped him, saying, "Prophesy to us, you Christ! Who is it that struck you" (Matthew 26:66–67)? After having Jesus scourged, Pilate delivered him to be crucified (Matthew 27:26). The soldiers stripped Jesus and put a scarlet robe on him and twisting together a crown of thorns, they put it on his head and put a reed in his right hand. And kneeling before him, they mocked him, saying, "Hail, King of the Jews!" And they spit on him and took the reed and struck him on the head. And when they had mocked him, they stripped him of the robe and put his own clothes on him and led him away to crucify him (Matthew 27:28–31). On the cross, there were those who passed by who mockingly said to Jesus, "'You who would destroy the temple and rebuild it in three days, save yourself! If you are the Son of God, come down from the cross.' So also the chief priests, with the scribes and elders, mocked him, saying, 'He saved others; he cannot save himself. He is the King of Israel; let him come down now from the cross, and we will believe in him'" (Matthew 27:40–42).

And yet, on the cross under the authority of the Father, Jesus prayed, "Father, forgive them, for they do not know what they are doing" (Luke 23:34). Under the authority of the Father, in the midst of everything Jesus was suffering, he ministered to the thief and in grace and truth said, "I tell you the truth, today you will be with me in paradise" (Luke 23:43). Under the authority of the Father, Jesus did not forget the need to care for his mother and said, "Dear woman, here is your son," and to the disciple, "Here is your mother" (John 19:26–27). Under the authority of the Father, even when "for our sake he made him to be sin who knew no sin, so that in him we might become the righteousness of God" (2 Corinthians 5:21), Jesus cried, "*Eloi, Eloi, lama sabachthani?*" which means "My God, my God, why have you forsaken me" (Matthew 27:46)? Yet, Jesus remained faithful. Under the authority of the Father, Jesus, "for the joy that was set before him endured the cross, despising the shame" (Hebrews 12:2), cried, "It is finished" (John 19:30). Under the authority of the Father, when "there was darkness over the whole land until the ninth hour, while the sun's light failed and the curtain of the temple was torn in two, (Luke 23:44–45), Jesus called out with a loud voice and said, "Father, into your hands I commit my spirit!" (Luke 23:46).

My mom would ask us questions after reading this story. Questions like "What would have happened to us if Jesus had not stayed under the authority of the Father and died to pay for our sins?" or "What would have happened to us if Jesus would have become so discouraged at what others said about him and did to him, that he refused to do what the Father asked him to do?"

We knew the answer was "Not good!" Without Jesus's death on the cross which led to his resurrection, we would not have any hope of salvation, a changed life, or eternal life. Furthermore, we could not experience all of the promises given to us in the New Testament. We would have no hope of living in the abundance and victory of the preeminence, perspective, purpose, power, passion, provision and peace of Jesus Christ!

If little boys could learn and know the answer over and over about every story in the Bible, it is "not good" for anyone not to be under the authority of God and trust and obey God's Word wholeheartedly, do you see how important it is to answer and settle the question (if you have not already settled it) I asked you at the beginning of this book: "*What is trustworthy to be your authority?*" Until you do, it will "not be good" for you.

You only have one life. I encourage you with all my heart to live every day Thinking God in the abundance and victory of Jesus Christ:

- Submitted to the authority of God's Word and godly authority because enjoying the fellowship of your relationship with the Father comes from trusting and obeying his authority in your life (John 8:31–32);

- Surrendered to God's presence because you were saved to live in the preeminence, perspective, purpose, power, passion, provision, and peace of the Spirit's control in your life (Ephesians 5:17–18);

- Settled to whose you are because until you know whose you are, you will not know what you are for (1 Corinthians 6:19–20);

- Surrounded by Christians for encouragement and accountability because you need tons of encouragement and lots of accountability (Hebrews 10:23–25); and

- Sharing Jesus Christ every day, everywhere, all the time, because you need to do what the Lord told you to do (Acts 5:42).

In closing, I pray for you this prayer the Apostle Paul prayed in his epistle to the Ephesians: "For this reason I bow my knees before the Father, from whom every family in heaven and on earth is named, that according to the riches of his glory he may grant you to be strengthened with power through his Spirit in your inner being, so that Christ may dwell in your hearts through faith—that you, being rooted and grounded in love, may have strength to comprehend with all the saints what is the breadth and length and height and depth, and to know the love of Christ that surpasses knowledge, that you may be filled with all the fullness of God" (Ephesians 3:14–19). That is Thinking God!

"Now to him who is able to do far more abundantly than all that we ask or think, according to the power at work within us, to him be glory in the church and in Christ Jesus throughout all generations, forever and ever. Amen" (Ephesians 3:20–21).

Thinking God—My mom, if she could, would ask you after reading this book, "What will happen to you if you let your past, others, circumstances, feelings and/or fears rule you instead of submitting your life under the authority of God's Word? Surely, you know the answer is "Not good!" You will miss out on living the changed life (2 Corinthians 5:17-18) and the exchanged life (Colossians 3:1–4) God wants you to have (Colossians 1:27)!

Truth to Remember—God wants you to always be led in triumphal procession and spread the fragrance of the knowledge of him in and through your life, marriage, family and ministry (2 Corinthians 2:14)!

Thinking God in Reflecting—Think what your life would be like if you humbly started every day with a resolve to live Thinking God as his child—victoriously submitted to the authority of his Word, thankfully walking by the Spirit, joyfully winning your battles with divine weapons, and abundantly staying surrounded with Christians to encourage you and give you loving accountability. You would be overflowing with a joyous passion of sharing Jesus daily with others. You would know every "impossibility" in your life can be reconciled by God's grace and truth regardless of your personality, your past, your sin, or your sorrow, because "nothing is impossible with God" (Luke 1:37). You would enjoy living the will of God "rejoicing always, praying without ceasing, and giving thanks in all circumstances in Christ Jesus" (1 Thessalonians 5:16–18). You only have one life. Just do it "that your joy may be full" (John 15:11). Just do it so your children and grandchildren will want to repeat your life (Proverbs 22:6). Just do it "to the honor and glory of God forever and ever. Amen" (1 Timothy 1:17)!